Elizabeth McCullough

1/3/09
North Berwick

Late Developer

In memory of my husband Fergus, who often bemoaned the fact that I had not written a diary during our days in Ghana

All colour photographs by the author

Copyright © E. McCullough 2006

First published in 2006 by
Serendipity
First Floor
37/39 Victoria Road
Darlington

British Library Cataloguing-in-Publication data
A catalogue record for this book is available from the British Library
ISBN 1-84394-169-4
Printed and bound by The Alden Press

Dedication

This volume is dedicated to my late husband Fergus, and to many of his colleagues and field assistants who worked within the Ghana Medical Field Units during the years 1960–65. I should like also to thank cousin Dorothy whose first experience of life in Africa was traumatic: her support during the first few months after the birth of our second daughter was invaluable. Towards the end of her life, my mother gave the letters on which this book is based to Dorothy for safe-keeping; now, at the age of 80, she is a much-loved Irish aunt. Mousa Moshi and Abdulai linger in memory as cheerful characters who made life at Wa much more tolerable.

Thanks are due to Vivien Gotto who wrote the Foreward, and did proof reading at short notice. My uncle Arthur, who spent some months in Accra while serving in the RAF, was also co-opted as a proof-reader.

The help of Bob Jones with computer problems, and Brian Ross in getting the colour transparencies reproduced, has been much appreciated.

North Berwick, East Lothian
July 2005

Foreword

By Dr Vivian Gotto, former Reader in Zoology, Queen's University, Belfast, now Honorary Senior Research Fellow of the School of Biology and Biochemistry, Queen's University, Belfast.

To a junior member of academic staff, one's early students are rather like those extra-terrestrial bodies which at intervals enter Earth's orbit. Be they comets, asteroids or whatever, they circulate with us for a while and become familiar before drifting off and vanishing, with no guarantee of future sightings: a rare Christmas card, the occasional letter or the chance gossip of a relative are often the only clues we have as to their continued existence, especially when careers are pursued in far off places.

Fergus McCullough and his future wife Elizabeth fit neatly into this genre. From the farming countryside near Comber at the head of Strangford Lough, Fergus came to Queen's University to read Zoology in the early 1940s. About this time, having already graduated, I left Belfast to join the Royal Air Force as a meteorologist. When I was demobilized some three years later, Fergus was writing up his M.Sc. thesis. Tall, fair, softly spoken and with an agreeable sense of humour, he had proved to be an excellent student and had revealed a fine talent for drawing. Post-graduate studies at the Veterinary Research Laboratory in Weybridge followed before he took a post as field research officer with the Gold Coast (now Ghana) Ministry of Health. By this time his interest had become focused in the parasitological world; and, in particular, the ecology, distribution and control of the serious tropical disease *schistosomiasis* – commonly known as bilharzia. The worm causing this condition develops in the human bloodstream, but its early stages are parasitic in many fresh-water snails. The presence of these snail hosts in water utilized by humans may lead to massive infestation by this sinister parasite. Much of Fergus's work with the World Health Organization in tropical Africa therefore centred on these snails, though later he also made notable contribution to the biology and control of *dracunculiasis* – better known as guinea-worm, another parasitic disease which causes excruciating suffering.

Elizabeth came to Queen's in 1955, the same year in which Fergus began preparing his Ph.D. dissertation: a competent professional photographer, with a strong creative bent, she was engaged by the University Library to reorganize its photographic department which was used by many departments, but principally Anatomy, Archaeology, Biochemistry, Botany, Geography and Zoology. Experience of a broken marriage had probably contributed to an alert and wary personality – this, enhanced by a tendency to shoot from the hip, greatly enlivened the Department. She recalls that it was I who introduced her to Fergus, but at the time I never dreamed that I was to become the Fairy Godmother. At all events they became an 'item', though it was only after Fergus left these shores to return to Africa that they were able to marry.

This, then, is their story of that time, as told by Elizabeth in letters to her mother. She evokes brilliantly the surreal atmosphere of post-war tropical Africa with all its frustrations, interminable red tape, jealousies and often considerable hardships. Here are the barely passable laterite roads, the broken fridges, the bizarre food items, the unreliable transport, the assault of innumerable biting insects, the uncertainty about future contracts with WHO. Throughout it all, their sense of the ridiculous sustains their perspective on life in that unreal setting. Having known them both well, I find their story true to type, fascinating in its delineation of curious details and, in many ways, profoundly touching. I believe other readers are likely to experience the same reactions.

Contents

Illustrations

Author's Note

WHEN I HAD FINISHED *A Square Peg* several people remarked that
they supposed I would shortly be starting on Africa. My immediate reaction was that Africa had been done *ad nauseam*, but on
reflection I realized that each person's experience is unique.
Recently all the letters I wrote to my mother during the years
1960–73 were unearthed, and on reading them it was apparent
they were, in effect, a diary of those years. I am surprised how dili-
gently I kept this lonely woman, with whom I had a guarded
relationship, based more on respect than love, informed of what
was going on in my life, almost every aspect of which must have
disturbed her.

Only now, when my own children have embarked on a variety
of relationships about which I have had reservations, do I realize
how apprehensive she must have felt about my future. My mother
took an eminently civilized attitude to my first marriage, always
maintaining courteous contacts with my husband, in contrast to
the ostracism imposed by her younger sister who, many years later,
apologized for her behaviour with the explanation: 'I just couldn't
stand him.'

My mother's first comment, when Fergus came on the scene,
was, 'What is *that* exotic specimen you have collected now?' He
had a beard, wore suede shoes and a Liberty silk scarf; his hair
was long, and his tweeds a strident shade of green. Not the most
promising of beginnings, but over the years they grew to like and
respect each other. One memorably hurtful remark my mother
made was: 'He's far too good for you' – in a number of respects
true. Yesterday would have been her 105th birthday.

30 November 2001

Introduction

IN MANY WAYS the less said about the decade 1950–60 the better: I made a marriage doomed to failure from its inception, from which release was legalized ten years later. It was not a miserable marriage, just totally misconceived, soon deteriorating to apathetic detachment as the uncompromising participants indulged their polarized interests. One of the benefits of my unconventional upbringing was that I never questioned the equality of the sexes, so the concept of deference to the male was alien to my philosophy. During that decade I suffered quite a number of what in Northern Ireland are colloquially known as 'gunks'.

I fought individuals and systems, including the NI Hospitals Authority who employed me on a temporary basis at a lower pay rate than that of permanent employees – a status barred to me because I was married – but who were not above using my above average competence when it suited them. I took on the National Union of Small Shopkeepers, for whom I had worked temporarily after hours, and whose representative had failed to pay me. Finally I took on the University, employing the assistance of the Association of Scientific Workers (heavily Communist infiltrated at the time) to fight my case for equal pay and elevation to the status of Chief Technician, which was the rank of the previous male incumbent who had been neither competent nor, if rumour were to be believed, honest. The only case I won was against the small shopkeepers, who eventually paid up, grudgingly remarking that 'your attitude has not commended itself to us.'

The days of tennis and evenings of ice-skating rapidly declined into a dreary routine of work, returning to a flat empty except for the cat, to await the late home-coming of my husband. Now something of an embarrassment to my contemporaries, existence became almost void of social contacts within my own age-group, or of any sporting activities: I had effectively sacrificed my twenties. I learned secretarial skills, and dabbled in architectural studies

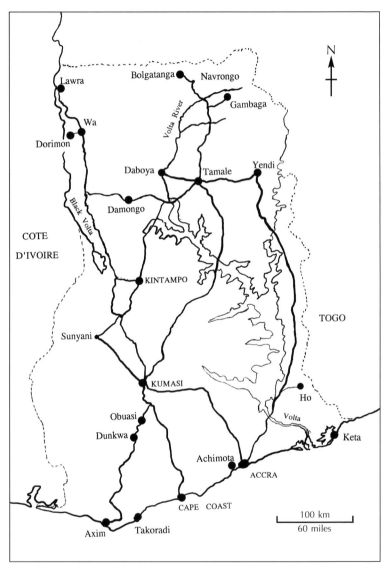

Map of Ghana showing places mentioned in the text. At the time the letters were written the Volta Dam had not been completed, and the huge lake shown was not formed till many years later.

Weighing Anchor

THERE CAN'T OF necessity yet be a great deal to relate, but I'll do my best. Transference of baggage was simple, and they even took care of the twelve red roses. Liverpool is not the most stimulating place to spend a loose-end morning, but I managed to kill the time hunting for camera accessories. It got oppressively hot as the day wore on and my foot swelled up hugely. [*I had been walking around for some weeks wearing a crêpe bandage to deal with what was basically a very serious condition following a thrombosis which had been dealt with dismissively by the University medical officer.*] This was the last time I have felt hot since leaving UK. The ship has been riddled with Arctic blasts and all stewards seem determined we shall have the maximum of fresh air. Curtains billow out in corridors, and where doors out to deck are opposite one makes a quick dash to the other side to avoid being swept out! I have been wearing woollen slacks, a shirt, sweater *and* my thick blue mohair, in which today for the first time I'm just about warm enough. We are by now I imagine level with Gib., though they don't keep passengers *au fait* with our position. The Bay of Biscay didn't live up to its reputation though many have been sick. Must be a good sailor after all. Nothing but sea, sea, sea. If another vessel is seen everyone springs to his feet and becomes wildly excited. Only events of the morning were the arrival of a rather tired house martin and a bee: the former went to refuge in one of the lifeboats, and is probably going the wrong way – back to Africa. Passengers still to a large extent eyeing each other suspiciously and place hiving with small children: they have their meals at different times mercifully. I wouldn't for anything do the trip with children as the mothers never have time to relax. They are afraid their offspring will fall overboard, which would be fairly easily achieved, and have to get the children ready for 7.30 breakfast, sit in the hot dining room watching the brats consume it, then appear with somewhat diminished appetites for their own meal at 8.30 or so. This pattern is repeated throughout the day.

The food is good, and there is plenty of fruit and veg. available. I have not been lucky in allocation of table companions, being stuck with a middle-aged north countryman who has been out for fifteen years in Nigeria. He was not unbearable on his own, and even became quite interesting, though necessitating constant 'feeding' which I found a strain. We were then joined by a middle-aged accountant and wife – also north country. They and No. 1 spent the entire meal saying, 'You must 'ave known so-and-so – decent chap, 'ad a little son last year – John. John they called 'im – ay that's right, John.' The awful thing is they are all going the whole way and there appears no means of escape. All are still terrified of anything 'odd' in the way of food and are happy to eat a British bacon, egg and sausage fry, followed by vanilla ice-cream. They regard my plate with horror when I try 'African National Dish' (which must have contained at least six chillies). Even frankfurters and sauerkraut are suspect. Will write from either Bathurst or Freetown.

m.v. Apapa, 6 June 1960

This should be a more interesting letter than the last when experience was confined to the ship. Since then we have called for roughly six hours in both Bathurst and Freetown. If you want to do any reading I can recommend *Four Guineas* by Elspeth Huxley and *Sierra Leone* by Roy Lewis – the former is probably better for general information. [*I wonder why* The Heart of the Matter *is not mentioned – maybe I had not yet read it.*] Shortly before we reached Bathurst the temperature and humidity soared, but it has not become appreciably worse even though we are now about 1,000 miles further round the bulge. One certainly does not do anything at a spanking pace, and I don't wonder the African population at Bathurst looked listless. It is a haphazard settlement rather than town, built on what appears to be an extensive sandspit at the wide mouth of the Gambia river. Decaying Portugese style houses with patios and balconies were the most prevalent buildings; there were a few fine new office blocks and many shacks constructed from corrugated iron, palm trunk and woven fencing. Nobody seems to repair or paint anything, they appear to prefer building a new one on the adjacent site (rather like Ireland). Everywhere there were mosaic patterns of mango and other fruits laid out on the dusty verges for sale: I got the impression that they didn't really expect to sell any, and indeed didn't greatly care. Mangoes are small and yellowish whereas I had always thought they were large, and everywhere there were decaying, spat-out hairy stones; the children eat them rather as ours chew gum. [*Seven years later, when I went to East Africa I encountered the proper mango, which neither tastes nor smells of turpentine. I am surprised that no mention is made of the tall, dignified Wolof women who traded at the quayside, most of whom wore massive solid gold earrings. Nor do I mention what will always remain with me as the first symbol of Africa – the ubiquitous pied-kingfisher.*] I can now recognise that indescribable smell, to which you must have seen references, which is Africa – a mixture of sweat, heat, dust, rotting vegetation, roasting plantain and murky roadside drain. It is not really unpleasant in an open space, but overpowering when the deck passengers crowd on board with their pathetic bundles of belongings. There was a sizeable exodus of these people going from Bathurst to Freetown. On enquiry I'm told by an African with whom I have had long discussions – name of Joe Appiah – that they go, much as people from Donegal used to go for seasonal labour to Scotland, to the mines of Freetown or to become itinerant traders. [*This was the husband of Sir Stafford Cripps's daughter Peggy. At that time the family lived in Kumasi and I often saw Peggy shopping in the Kingsway Stores. Both of us became pregnant at roughly the same time, and by strange coincidence our daughters ended up many years later in the same class of a Quaker boarding school in south-west England.*] Many were women and children who had been sent for to join their husbands. Some of their clothes were beautiful and dignified, but others wore dreadful shoddy Western stuff with giant medallion patterns of the Queen's head or Dr Nkrumah on their rumps. It is difficult to get photographs without appearing impertinent, and I missed an opportunity at Bathurst thinking it would be repeated at Freetown; it wasn't, as our gangway was in shadow when we got there.

Everything has to be sealed when we go into port because the ship is suddenly overrun with traders, porters and deck passengers, so all cabins are locked and windows jammed up. Last night a thief was discovered by a man who awoke at a slight noise and found this character extracting something silently; a knee was used with great effect where it hurts most, and the figure fled to its own part of the ship! Since then we have been locking the cabin doors – normally it is so hot that one just has a curtain across the door. My cabin steward is charming (Afro-Indian I should say), and takes care to warn me about 'they outside', and not to leave the window unscreened or 'they come take them shoes with long stick'.

Freetown was a most pleasant surprise to me; some bone-heads had said glumly that there was nothing to see there, and it was just like Bathurst. Nothing could be less similar. On the port side in the morning there was an endless horizon of mangrove swamp, but when I went to the other side I saw 2,000 ft. hills rising up from sea-level with the town on the lower slopes and gradually spreading. At a glance it looked like one of the Scottish islands with the usual wreath of mist at sea-level; then as the sun rose the steamy jungly atmosphere became apparent and one could see all the flowering trees. Everywhere flame-trees (not indigenous), bougainvillaea, hibiscus hedges and giant mimosa. I was extraordinarily fortunate in being invited to do a car/taxi tour of as much as could be seen in a limited time.

The previous evening one of my aquaintances had been hailed across the dining room by an old school mate who lives in Freetown. Old school mate, named improbably Sowerbutts, was an *awful* man, and it was a bit unethical of us to accept his kind invitation in view of our unanimous distaste. However, he collected our small party at mid-day and in a lordly manner summoned two taxis to drive us through the town, up the hair-pin road onto the plateau to the hill-club. From there we had a wonderful view across steamy forest down to the island's sandy beach. Arrived at the club our host proceeded to lower three double whiskies in quick succession while the females toyed with orange squash (give him his due he didn't force us to drink), and vast quantities of beer for the men. I saw many fairly large ants and a few other flying insects, but was not bitten by anything. The island was riotous with gigantic incredible butterflies, but also swarms with snakes. Our taxi was dismissed and we went to the host's house to collect his car. Once there he opened a bottle of champagne – no food forthcoming! We all stressed our wish to see the coast and visit the beach and this was accomplished smoothly. We managed to drop our host off to do a 'business deal' on the way. Thereafter four of us had a most pleasant few hours on the beach basking and swimming. On return to the vessel Sowerbutts appeared swaying unsteadily, plainly having topped up regularly all afternoon. The only payment exacted was an unpleasant sweaty kiss. I offered a chaste jaw-bone which was rejected, but he was so far gone he wasn't even capable of rubbing noses. I'm feeling slightly queasy today for the first time, but nothing serious – probably too much food and drink + packing in moist heat of cabin all morning. Arrive tomorrow at Takoradi where I trust I shall be met by Fergus. Hope you appreciate this effort which really amounts to something in this atmosphere, and that you and Moses [cat] are holding your tails fairly high in the air.

[It is clear from these two letters that I felt some of the shipboard activities were better omitted. I acquired two nice but pathetic male followers: one aged 46 had spent his home-leave with his mother, and was clearly never going to free himself from the maternal grasp. The other was a fat, 44 year old, dissipated engineer with memorably rotting teeth; he was, however, sensitive, widely read, and intensely interested in astronomy. About the latter he was strikingly well informed and would take me out on deck at night to treat me to drunken maunderings on the glories of the heavens. We went to the ritual fancy dress evening together – he dressed as a porter and I as a 'piece of baggage' sitting on the trolley. There was also the incident when I decided to visit the ship's doctor to ask what he thought about my swollen leg; he was an amiable, black-bearded, heavily built man and I was somewhat surprised when asked to strip off and walk to the end of the room and back so that he might assess my leg function. When I mentioned this to my new friends, they all collapsed in mirth, this being yet another demonstration of his notorious interest in any remotely comely female. Drinking began in mid-morning and continued throughout the day, reaching a climax during whatever dreary functions had been arranged for the evening. This voyage was enough to put me off 'cruising' for the rest of my life.]

1960

KINTAMPO
ASHANTI REGION

Medical Field Units, Kintampo, 13 June 1960

I AM SURE YOU will be anxious to know whether I was met or not! I was swept off the boat at about 8.30 in the morning and quickly 'facilitated' through immigration authorities and customs shed. From one of the circular letters which Elder Dempster lines dish out to passengers at frequent intervals, I had learned that *positively* nobody would be allowed on or off the boat before 9.00 a.m., so I was surrounded by considerable chaos and not a little gunked when Fergus appeared in the cabin at 8.15. The two Africans who were 'facilitating' were waiting around, so I had to cram bottles, shoes, wet bathing things etc. without method into the nearest receptacle, and leave the ship amid hurried good-byes, one glass of tomato juice and half a roll and butter! The weather, on arrival, was very similar to Belfast's on the night I left. The long rainy season which ends about October is just beginning so I shan't be subjected to extreme dry heat for some time. So far my impressions of climate, people and insect life have been favourable, but I realize this is largely a matter of luck, and that I'm due for some unpleasant shocks sooner or later. We drove through Takoradi, an extensive 'harbour' but in reality a vast agglomeration of fuel storage tanks, new well-designed warehouses, timber stacks etc. There were the usual flowering shrubs and the ground was carpeted with a thick petunia coloured creeping plant (*Portulaca*). This was virtually the last colour – apart from the ubiquitous red laterite – we saw till we reached Kumasi about two hundred miles north. We collected Adda at the Govt. Guest House in Takoradi, where they had stayed the previous night, and dispatched some of my luggage and the trunk (quite intact) by

MFU Land Rover which formed part of the reception committee. Unfortunately Fergus said they were to take this stuff to the Guest House at Kumasi, but omitted to say *when*, and they didn't arrive till next morning. F says they were probably doing a line in providing public transport facilities on the trip up. Luckily I had all necessary toilet articles, but no change of clothing. Drive to Kumasi was uneventful with not a great deal to see but mile after mile of lush green bush. It does not encroach on the road as I had imagined, being well cut back most of the way. Saw one squashed snake on the road and numerous hideous bald-headed vultures which are part of every village scene. I don't see so many up here in the north. They scavenge around the compounds in much the way hens do at home. [*I wonder why I do not mention the numerous wrecked Mammy lorries which were always part of the wayside scene, or the weird progress of those with distorted chassis which were still going, but had clearly previously been in some serious impingement.*] When we arrived at Kumasi one was sitting companionably on the roof of the guest house. There are lightning little wall lizards everywhere and one is afraid of stepping on them. They are harmless insect eaters and come in various sizes: the ones here at Kintampo seem disappointingly small and not so numerous. [*Just beginner's ignorance – we were well north of the coastal forest zone and into savannah scrub land.*] We have ants of varying sizes everywhere, but nothing (so far) like the plague we had at Portnoo. Ours are not belligerent and spend the day industriously making little piles of red soil which they excavate from a small hole in the ground. There is one enormous solitary one sharing the step with me just now: he is conventional ant-shape except for his behind which is black velvet with two large white spots. We have the odd millipede which I don't really warm to, in spite of assurances that they are harmless. They are so big and relentless in their progress – about 8 inches long and three-quarters in diameter I'd say. There are enormous butterflies everywhere, the commonest being a black and yellow about 3 inches across.

The heat in the middle of the day is intense and the slightest exertion causes one to sweat copiously, but the early mornings are delightful especially when there is a fresh breeze blowing as there is today. The noises which come from the bush are incessant, merely reaching different pitches at various times. There is the background chirping of cicadas which never ceases, but reaches a very high intensity as dawn breaks and night falls. Then there are continual exotic bird songs throughout the day – they do a noisy chorus at dawn too. The birds are to me incredible, though so far all I have seen have been termed 'common'. There are small flies which bite me a lot and the lump itches a good deal, but it is a tiny bite and does not cause watery blisters, so it can be borne with.

I forgot to tell you that my foot, and indeed the left one, too, began to swell badly when I was on the boat – this in spite of the fact that I was leading a leisurely life. The ship's doctor was absolutely adamant that it must be rested completely till it stops showing any tendency to swell. So I'm having an easier time than ever before in my life. Fergus is a very strong disciplinarian in this respect, and I only just managed to get permission to play a short game of tennis last night. Actually there is quite a lot I can do here and time is not dragging. The garden is making rapid progress and needs constant attention, curtains have to be hung, some more have to be made (tediously by hand), some typing has to be done, letters and diary written, some things I wash myself. I can see that I shall be forced into familiarity with screwdrivers, drills and nails soon!

Apart from this there is obviously a service to be performed in helping some of the African staff at MFU [*Medical Field Units*] with their efforts at the School Certificate English language papers. This means correcting their efforts (which can't be done well without doing the questions oneself), and making constructive comments. So far it seems that even where the command of words is quite good, there is an inability to grasp the central idea, and this of course stems from the varied cultural backgrounds. There is also a risk of having the house inundated with eager pupils so I shall have to try not to be too helpful. F says the African sense of privacy is minimal, and it would be easy to create a precedent whereby one had no time left to oneself. Can see this regarding tuition in tennis which he has offered to give to any promising children at the local school. Almost every afternoon a small messenger is sent to enquire if he will play, or, more important, lend a racket. The court is really dreadful – cement with great fissures and spasmodic growth of weeds, but it provides exercise, and the numerous ball-boys, some stark naked members of a northern tribe which looks almost pygmy-like, make wire netting unnecessary. Apart from all this we are both brushing up our French with the aid of Assimil records and their text-book: this is quite fun with two people, but demands considerable concentration which is exhausting in the heat. Trust you will in time appreciate the effort involved in putting pen to paper. Certainly I now appreciate F's past letters to me rather more than I did before experiencing the climate.

It now strikes me that I have told you nothing about Kintampo. Well, it is some 150 miles north of Kumasi and the drive's monotony is broken by occasional slight rises in the land surface – there are two plateaus on one of which Kintampo is situated – and infrequent villages. Mud brick dwellings with palm-leaf thatches, vast piles of fruit, pineapples, bananas, corn, mangos, avocados heaped on the roadside. Men selling the local palm-oil 'hooch' from old beer bottles, not even corked, but with froth spilling down their sides. Mostly it is wiser not to do one's shopping by the wayside as it leads to protracted negotiations or palaver. However we stopped at one village to buy pineapples and were immediately surrounded by people all selling the same things. One exception was a girl with a little leaf-wrapped package which reminded me of one of the Beatrix Potter illustrations: 'You buy nice duck egg.' I took some photographs, but this is going to be a problem as the people either hold out a hand for dash, resent your interest (understandable), or stiffen into unnatural stances and grimaces.

I should have mentioned that relations with Adda and his assistant are cordial, a state which I sincerely hope we can maintain. His cooking and general attention to detail are probably exceptional. What precisely goes on in the kitchen I'm not sure: certainly there is often a local gathering in the afternoons, and Adda's small son toddles around the back regions most of the time. I suspect the dishes are washed only in cold water under a running tap. However, I'm not going to change anything or enquire too closely till one of us gets a tummy upset. So far my guts have been working perfectly and we have at the present plenty of fruit and vegetables. This is the exception rather than the rule here; indeed the garden was only started in April before which veg. were mostly of the tinned variety.

Sorry – I got interrupted and forgot to continue about Kintampo. It is a very small community consisting of the village, down to which I have not yet been, and the higher compound where the MFU main building and staff houses are situated. There are no sharp lines of demarcation between the houses, and they are widely spaced with plenty of trees and shrubs all around. Fergus's bungalow is at first sight a model, but on closer inspection the workmanship is very poor and a number of things will certainly not last long. I went up on the roof to see why the gutter persisted in leaking even after Works Dept. people had been to fix it, and found that the slatted wooden roof to the veranda had not even been painted on the upper surface. The gutter is not in fact a gutter, but a number of pieces of corrugated iron with very imperfect joints which have not even been bolted. Putty had been used sparingly and ineffectively to stop leakage. A new gutter is said to be coming 'soon'. The rain, when it does fall, is delightfully refreshing and seems pretty heavy to me though I am told this is 'nothing'. What is a pleasant surprise is the wonderful cloud-formations: for some reason I had expected nothing but dreary blue or blue grey.

We were asked out to dinner on Sat. by one of the Med. Officers at MFU, and had a very pleasant evening, though conversation was a strain with some of the guests owing to language difficulties. Our host is Singalese with a beautiful Cornish wife (ex. art teacher) dressed already in a sari which I must say suited her. The other guests were a medical officer from Rome whose English was adequate, his wife whose English was very limited, and with whom contact was confined to smiles of good-will, his mother who was pathetically old and palsied, never spoke at all, and two well-behaved children.

[*There then follows a list of requests for things to be sent out, ranging from more curtain material to seeds for garden herbs, tea-towels and a bath rack.*]

16 June 1960

I hope you got the lengthy letter written only a few days ago – couldn't bear to think of that effort going astray! Incidentally, we are lucky regarding postal service here as people in Nigeria say that large numbers of letters and parcels never arrive. *Nothing*, I'm told is private from Dr N's correspondence down! [*There was an element of restraint in what one wrote from Ghana at the time, as it was known that a censorship system did exist; although we suspected the level of comprehension of the censors was probably roughly of the order of my field assistant pupils, one was cautious about making any overt criticisms about how things were progressing socially, the state of the roads, reliability of transport and other public services. As Fergus was an UN employee and had a national counterpart, it was particularly important that we should keep our views apparently impartial.*]

I am beginning to notice the African habit of forestalling one's needs: well-intentioned, if a little disconcerting. Frequently I'm doing something for myself, and quite under the impression that I'm alone, when silent large black feet with pale soles appear at my side offering assistance. Planted some seeds yesterday when I was *sure* no one was in the vicinity, yet later saw gardener assiduously watering that precise spot. Two can play this game, and I'm learning quickly.

This letter comes soon after the last for two reasons: (a) to tell you that we are going to Accra for about a week. Fergus has been summoned to a top-level meeting to decide which of two areas is going to be selected for a full-scale campaign against bilharzia. Shall go to see the University College of Ghana people about my foot/leg when I get there.

Was shown around the lab. yesterday, and saw the tanks for breeding stock of potential snail vectors. Was eaten alive by something small which must have lived in the grass. The bites are violently itchy, but unlike the previous ones fairly small. Temperature continues very pleasant, and a fresh breeze is blowing this morning after torrential rain yesterday. Am getting comparatively inured to insect and reptile life, though a little disturbed by two wall lizards in the bathroom – largely for fear they might fall in the bath and get scalded. Last night was moved to cry out, '*What* is that on the arm of my chair?' – 'Oh, it's only a Praying Mantis.' Rather interesting once I knew it was harmless.

Send my love to San and thank the Aunt [*Rosemary who had disowned me during my previous alliance*] especially for her 'bon voyage' card and say I'll write in due course.

[*There follows a list of technical comments regarding telephoto lenses and other photographic problems to which I was later to learn no solution was to be found even in Accra.*]

Kintampo, 27 June 1960

We were almost a week away, though we were not in Accra all the time. The journey *can* be done in one day, but I should just hate to do it myself as it is well over 300 miles of road of variable surface and tortuosity. The scenery, on the other hand, varies little! Just miles and miles of bush comprised of giant cotton trees whose beautiful pale grey trunks sweep up smoothly without side branches from massive buttresses at ground level, right to their distant foliaged tops: cocoa trees, bananas, corn, palm trees of different types, some bearing coconuts, but mostly palm oil nuts, from which the local 'hooch' is made. There are quite a number of villages *en route*, and as one gets nearer the metropolis they become more untidy and display such doubtful benefits of civilization as corrugated iron roofs and fences, dead motor cars, petrol cans etc. The traffic is fairly heavy, largely consisting of the famous mammy lorries [*so named because they were owned by the massive Market Mammies who dominated the trade – hugely fat women, displaying all the appurtenances of financial success*] or trucks which transport both goods and passengers, and are always labelled with extraordinary titles such as 'Fear Woman', 'Only Jesus', 'Snakes and Women', 'Enlightened', 'Travel Safely' – the last is rather inappropriate as one often sees trucks overturned in the ditch with the usual voluble crowd shrieking advice and comment. The drivers are courteous enough once they are aware of one's wish to get past. But they hold the middle of the road complacently belching fumes and seldom hearing one's frantic honking. As the drivers don't look in the mirror – if they possess one – it may be a long time before one gets past. This affords great amusement to the lorry passengers who do their best to attract their driver's attention. Fergus on the whole is remarkably patient, only rarely breaking into obscene abuse. So far I haven't been allowed to drive as we have either been in a hurry, had a passenger (to whom this would not be fair), been on a dangerous, soft surface after heavy rain etc. I can see that my kindly intentioned impulse to save him stress is not going to work out smoothly. He says he gets bored as a passenger – so do I.

The dash to Accra was for further discussions prior to decision on which area in Ghana is to be selected for an intensive Bilharzia control programme. It is almost certain now that it will be somewhere north-east of Accra. WHO had not expected the Ghana govt. to come across with the necessary capital sum for the project, but now they seem to be convinced of the urgency of control at this stage before improved irrigation systems begin to provide even more suitable snail habitats. [*This was written long before the completion of the Volta River dam project and the formation of the vast lake shown on the map.*] The problem is highly complex. The real solution, as Fergus acidly says, is just to stop them piddling in the streams and pools! The selection of an area around Accra will, unfortunately, mean a transfer from Kintampo – probably in September. I'm as sorry as Fergus about this because there is plenty for me to do here, and I find the isolation very pleasant in contrast to the noise, dense population and oppressive atmosphere in Accra. I haven't yet been working in the lab., but it appears there is quite a lot of unskilled microscope work which I could do, as well as compiling an efficient card index system of all the technical publications relevant to the job. Fergus has three technicians (so-called) working for him, but he says none can be thoroughly relied on to carry out tedious, but all important, jobs such as counting cercariae (parasites) emitted by experimental snails etc. The result of this sort of thing being (like me at QUB) that he does it himself and wastes time which could be far better utilized.

While in Accra I met the librarian at University College Ghana (female, and I suspect something of a battleaxe). It sounded very much as though there might be an opening for me there as their last photographer was killed recently in a street accident, and in the meantime they have been 'managing' with one African youth. I don't want to force the pace of these negotiations, and in any case my foot is still swelling – or showing that it still has that tendency – in spite of considerable rest. One piece of good news is that F may be able to take his leave allowance at any time from 1/12/60 onwards as the present contract has been extended till 1/12/61. So this might lead to us coming home in the early spring. However there are still too many unknown quantities to say anything definite – so just keep your fingers crossed.

I have had just about every possible malaise *except* the diarrhoea I had expected. At Kintampo I was a bit wheezy and allergic at first, but nothing to complain of. But when I returned after the week in Accra where I got a violent sore throat, a temperature of short duration, bladder trouble (cystitis again), and some most unpleasant watery bites, I sneezed and streamed at eyes and nose for a solid day and a half. Have been unable to trace the cause and it disappeared suddenly.

Accra was not at all what I had expected. One approaches the town from the north descending from the Aburi scarp by a tortuous road which gives extensive views over the Accra plains. The scarp marks a change in the vegetation from thick bush to the savanna land of the coastal area. Dr Nkrumah's country residence is perched above the road commanding a fine view of the plains and Accra 20 miles away. His house is a large, flat-roofed 1930s looking one, and in great contrast to the humble mud huts which are the usual roadside dwelling. Ghana, to use a well-worn cliché, is 'a land of contrasts'. These are particularly noticeable in Accra. We drove from the plains past numerous enormous ant hills, past the very fine university buildings which cover a vast acreage, past the airport, the PM's official residence – entrance gates flanked with golden eagles mounted on lofty staffs and Black Star of Africa over the gate – something faintly reminiscent of the third Reich, through the new commercial area which is full of very fine looking buildings; then suddenly into central Accra which is just about as sordid a bit of shanty town as I have seen anywhere. This surprised me as I would have thought a great effort would have been made to clean up the capital for publicity purposes if nothing else. Apparently there is an official drive for visitors which takes in all the finest buildings, best residential areas, and neatly avoids the rest. The shops are more than adequate and many of the things I brought out could easily have been obtained here.

Seemingly Exakta cameras are unheard of in Accra, which is strange as every other sort seems to be known. The UTC [United Trading Company] stores have a Swiss camera mechanic to whom I spoke. He thought he might be able to adapt the telephoto to fit: I think it is beyond the scope of sticky tape. Shall leave it with him next time we are in Accra.

We have just had one of the MFU medical officers for lunch (Italian). He is charming and speaks fluent English with a pronounced accent. I can cope quite well in ordinary circumstances, but unfortunately there was a minor storm accompanied by torrential rain which drowned all words. There we were, each pretending to have heard and understood what the other said and smiling goodwill over the coffee table.

On Saturday we had the Ghanaian health training officer from Accra for tea. He was rather heavy going, and even more difficult to understand, but he unwound after a while and became surprisingly eloquent in his criticism of current government policy! Follies committed have much in common with those in other places, e.g. insufficient volunteers to train as health officers owing to penurious salaries offered at the end of the three year course: instead vast sums are being spent on status building hospital accommodation, rather than trying to limit the supply of patients by spreading a little fundamental knowledge of hygiene etc.

There must be many more things I have not mentioned, but in the absence of any news from you I'll reserve something for the next letter. This evening is cold, and I am wearing my 'wallpaper' pants and a jumper. Outside are toads, crickets and other unidentified emitters of noise. Inside is a large ant-like wasp and sundry other disturbers of the peace. Hope all goes well, and that you are looking after – or at least not ill-treating – your knee.

Monday 11 July 1960

[This letter starts with a lot of technical photographic queries: I am writing in the era of hand-held exposure meters, heavy telephoto lenses – no zooms as yet invented.]

Photographically, so far I have improvized and have managed without a tripod quite well. I did an experimental exposure of 9 secs of the roof structure inside an African hut just by laying the camera on its back and supporting it on the exposure meter. Plainly I'll have to get a flash gun soon. The weight of equipment is no small consideration if one is walking around in the heat of the day. A few mornings ago I accompanied F on a snail collecting trip round the dam at Tamale (more of this later). He had his long-handled sieve and collecting jar etc., I had field glasses, the Contaflex for black and white, the Exakta for colour, sunglasses and insect repellent (virtually useless). We made a slow circuit of the dam, beginning at 9.30 a.m., and were both exhausted by 11 or so. Trivial little exertions like putting the meter back in the camera case, or returning to the car, leave one moist and listless. Perhaps I'm becoming acclimatized though, because at Kintampo I feel it is sometimes cold now. Tamale is over 100 miles further north and appreciably hotter.

I never said I'd broken the news to Auntie Jo, but was *convinced* you said *you* had. As the situation is a little anomalous we'd better tell the same tale till there is something more pleasing to her to report. You can just say I'm working with MFU (true) in a variety of ways, and that I'm not too isolated as I have a former friend from Queen's University working in the unit.

I'm glad you saw the travel film on W. Africa, as it will give you a greater awareness of the scene than could be conveyed by any description. My first Kodachrome is being processed in UK now, and should be back in a fortnight. The taking of village scenes is not at all easy if one is sensitive to atmosphere (mental not literal!).

I am too diffident to go wading in, as American tourists might, to record 'quaint' scenes. This sort of behaviour is all right if one has a common language, but where little is understood, picture taking becomes an invasion of privacy comparable to snapping animals in the zoo. If Adda is there to interpret and explain that one admires the roof of this house, or that one's dress, and would like to record it – that's all right. Otherwise I feel a telephoto is the answer. Sometimes I have resorted to pretending I was taking something quite different, and have managed to record the scene when suspicion has waned.

Your late aquaintance with some of the 'facts of life' at the Wilde film amused me, and at the same time surprised me. Upstairs on my bookshelves you will find Hesketh Pearson's *Life of Oscar Wilde* (dirty yellow cover with green printing I think), and *Son of Oscar Wilde* by Vyvyan Holland (Penguin). There may also be a collection of essays and poems including what Oscar wrote to Alfred Douglas which expresses the situation poignantly. I don't imagine he was anything but a largely sympathetic softy who was undoubtedly a prey for parasites. The essays etc. are also Penguin series, but with a purple instead of orange cover – shan't be at all surprised to hear you can't find them – if so, they have been lent and are lost.

On the subject of reading matter, if you are getting the *Listener* I'd be glad to have copies sent on when you have read them. That way costs less than if we order it from Kumasi. F gets the *Observer* this way, and by the time the store has charged all the 5*d*. paper ends up costing 2/-, Where the *Listener* is concerned topicality doesn't really matter: what binds me about this 'restful' life I'm supposed to be leading is that I have no more time to read than I had before – or very little more. This sounds ridiculous but a typical day will be: get up at 7, breakfast over Fergus goes off to lab. at 7.45, then I either write letters or diary/notebook, do some gardening before the sun gets too hot, typing or editing or indexing for several hours, think about food and give instructions about this and local shopping to Adda (all still peace and joy. I think he finds me an odd mixture of absent-mindedness and acute perception, and therefore not to be under-estimated – much like Fergus). Thinking about food presents problems which are aggravated by Fergus's decision to lose weight. He has succeeded in this very well, but it restricts one's repertoire. Luckily the garden is yielding large quantities of beans, tomatoes, lettuce, green peppers and cucumber, so we have salad every day, sometimes with added fresh gigantic pineapples and avocado pear. I have had to be ingenious and have made quite passable cream cheese from sour dried milk, bread from local wholemeal flour and marmalade from lemons and grapefruit – *Hausfrau* good and proper! Apart from this, frequent washing wears holes in shirts and underwear, and nearly every day I have some mending to do. Then there is the *Observer* to be read, French to be brushed up etc. Fergus comes back from the lab. at 4.15 or so – we try to get a bit of exercise at tennis if it doesn't rain. It is dark by 6.45, then wash off the sweat, anoint the bites, have a meal, relax for a while with the French textbook or listen to records – then lights out at 11. [*The MFU generator shut down then and one relied on paraffin lamps or torches till dawn.*]

To return to our trip to Tamale. We went for three days last week principally to collect a breed of snail which didn't materialize after all, and to collect 'specimens' (urine) from school children in the area. The latter are kept in our fridge overnight. Specious assurances from Fergus that the bottles have been well washed. Didn't tell Adda of this as he had previously been shocked at snails being kept in our frozen food insulated bag. The trip north from here shows a gradual change in vegetation type from the lush dense growth with giant trees to a tamer 'orchard bush' with long grass undergrowth and fewer creeping plants. We startled a pack? of large monkeys on the road, and I was lucky enough to see the last one crashing from a height into the undergrowth. He was bull-terrier sized with long grey fur and a black stripe running down his back to his very long tail. There is so much greater thrill attached to seeing only one monkey fleetingly, but in its natural state, than in visiting a zoo. North of this the road was flanked by sizeable lakes and pools with sun-cracked shores of mud. Ideal crocodile land, but I was not lucky in this respect, and saw nothing but some exotic water-birds. The villages change too, from the rectangular detached huts to most picturesque family groups of round huts (Dagomba tribe), all joined with a connecting wall. The doors of all huts except that where the head man sits and con-templates during the day, face onto the compound area. There are separate places for the hens, goats and cattle with small holes for ingress and egress of hens, and small grain stores supported on a platform; the latter have grass hats matching those of the huts, only in miniature. I know all this because we were taken to the model village at Tamale by an African CID man who is a friend of Fergus. He gave us a very clear account of life and methods – far better than the usual guide who has to have information painfully extracted. This village had models of three northern housing types and a Mohammedan mosque – it had been specially constructed for the Queen's visit to shorten her itinerary.

This letter, as usual, has stretched and is incoherent and shapeless. Which reminds me, I forgot to tell you of the awful evening when I thought we had acquired a cat. I went into the kitchen and saw this small black morsel rooting around under tables and demanded, for the umteenth time, 'What is *that*?' Fortunately it was revealed that it was staying with us during its owner's absence on trek. The owners, I now hear, are moving to Ho in the south, so I trust they will take the cat with them. I will NOT aquire an animal out here with all the attendant responsibilities and worries. Much love to you and your three responsibilities [*Cats named Moses, Samuel and Daniel*]. Foot still showing a tendency to swell – shall get fourth or fifth opinion in Accra. Intermittent sneezing, wheezing, itching etc., only to be expected I suppose. It's lucky we are not in the Congo at present.

Tuesday 19 July 1960

I hope you got this open without tearing – they are very badly designed. I don't think I have enough to say this week to cover the usual nine pages – in any case I have only four left on the pad and can't replace it till our next trip to civilization. This may be at the end of this week if Fergus gets through his present batch of snail torturing experiments. He's testing different varieties for resistance to drying out at different rapidities, and this involves regular trips to the lab. to immerse the poor b's to see if they are still alive. Apparently some disease-bearing snails in S. America have lived up to a year out of water. Remember I said I wasn't going to aquire a cat? WELL, as I suspected Dr Rosei (Italian) and family found it inconvenient to take the animal to Ho. As well as that Dr R said he thought the children were mauling it around too much (true): this seems to be an admission of failure to discipline the brats; however, would we like it? NO we wouldn't. So he arranged to hand it over to a neighbouring African member of MFU who thought it would be 'nice' for his children. Cat – which is common and black – apparently thinks differently as it spent the night climbing noisily up our mosquito netting, and was firmly plonked on the doorstep this morning exhibiting a thin appealing neck. At the moment it seems to have disappeared and I could almost wish a snake had got it. Only hope will be if the incoming German family who are to take over Dr R's bungalow turn out to be cat lovers. Incidentally I have been pleasantly surprised by what I have seen of domestic animals here. Pi dogs seem reasonably well fed, and I haven't *seen* any being maltreated. There are a few African owned marmalade cats in the village – no doubt the source of supply. Had a fifth opinion on my foot from Dr R who implied criminal negligence on the part of the first three doctors! Foot should have had complete rest for one month (in bed). External treatment with cortisone and some other vit. tabs. may still do some good if 'condition is not already permanent'! *Not* he says cheerfully nearly as bad as a similar *arterial* condition which sometimes occurs after such an illness where amputation is sometimes the only solution. So I suppose I have much to be thankful for. I dropped this pen on the cement floor yesterday and have bent the nib disastrously. Did I say I'd been making marmalade and bread? We now have a glut of tomatoes which is pleasant in one way but a worry in another – even after giving away large quantities there are a lot left to use.

My job of starting a catalogue of technical publications and typing index cards for them has begun – I can see it will take ages. Fergus cheerfully says the last one, on another disease, took six months and contained 4,000 references. Anyhow as long as my time is full I'm quite happy: the threat is that it is a bit too full. Since coming here I have read *one* book, admittedly some 700 pages, but I'm rather bitter about all the volumes I packed in the trunk.

Have just had a delightful misunderstanding with Adda. I'd asked him to try to get some tinned cheese in the village (a friend had recommended it, and the brand name was Silver Bell). Adda returns and says, yes, he got the cheese all right, but that – thank goodness – the only silver bells available were big and cost 10/- so he didn't commit us! Who would ever have thought there would be a bell of any sort available in Kintampo which is a very primitive village. I never told you that we get quite good reception of the BBC overseas service, so we are up-to-date with world affairs. Bet you're glad we are not in the Congo. So much for my sneers at the Ghanaian army: only a few weeks ago I was saying what nonsense all these army camps were. Now they are part of the UN force in the Congo.

The divorce should be heard on Sat. 23 July, if there is no post-ponement. Rudolf said he would send a one word wire saying Yes or No. Did you give him the address? Still don't know what the waiting period for the decree absolute is.

1 August 1960

I'm saddened to see that *you* have become one of those persons we both deplore – the non-reader of letters. I *never* said I had not received some of your letters – as far as I can tell everything has come through. The parcel was here when we got back from Ho. Thanks for going to so much trouble over the herbs, and also for including another plastic box. They are invaluable for a variety of purposes. One particularly good point they have is noiselessness – they don't rattle around in the car. I have one for medicaments, one for shoe cleaning, for knives, salt, butter etc. We seldom have what you would call a restful picnic on our car trips for a number of reasons. Some of the distances are considerable: e.g. Kumasi to Ho is 250 odd miles of tortuous road and one wants to arrive at the destination before it gets dark at 6.30, or one is racing to get to the ferry before it closes down and leaves you to spend the night in the car in ideal croc. country. The suitable spots where the road is wide enough to park on and there is sufficient shade are few. We picked what looked a delightful spot recently where a minor track started off through the forest to one of the isolated villages; there was a conveniently placed fallen tree for sitting on – in fact a sylvan glade-like atmosphere with faint rays of sunlight piercing the lofty greenery of the cotton trees. However, word got around pretty quickly that some good prey had arrived! Tsetses (not very common now) descended, and had to be beaten off – they have the advantage of being fairly large so they don't bite you so easily as some of the smaller, lighter insects do. The customary infinite variety of ants appeared out of thin air and began carrying off our crumbs in a business-like way. They are quite fascinating to watch, but it is all too easy to get them on your feet or up the pants. I can't yet decide which is preferable: to wear slacks and escape a number of bites with the attendant risk that things crawl up inside and get angry, or to wear shorts or skirt and be open to all com-ers. The insect repellants are some use, but that is about all. The dragonflies were numerous, larger, and more beautiful than those at home; the birds are often most exotic though hard to see because of the dense cover. Forgot to say we sometimes have green parrots in the compound here. My nose is always much better when we go away from Kintampo, and we have traced one source of irritation to some decorative gourds which Fergus had growing up the front of the house. Nevertheless there is still something irritating which seems to come on the evening breeze. [*Subsequently identified as mango tree pollen.*] One of the rest-houses we stayed in had all the pillows covered in tight heavyweight plastic which is seemingly most hygienic. Polythene bags are not strong enough, and I wonder if you could make enquiries at home about similar covers. I carry my Dunlopillow around, but it takes up a lot of space in an already heavily laden car.

I think I told you that the fifth opinion on my foot said 'off with the bandage' – well it got worse after ten days of that, and *sixth* opinion said on with it again! It is now slim again, but only provided I don't walk on it too much. It is a *bloody* nuisance because I want to take exercise in the cool evenings. Please get it out of your mind that the climate at Kintampo is unhealthy – it is probably one of the best in Ghana. We are on top of quite a hill, the humidity is not great compared with the coastal regions, we have mostly got a breeze blowing, and many of the days recently have been grey and overcast like a warm August day at home. One does not find the additional ten degrees or more trying provided the humidity doesn't rise, and, of course, provided you keep out of the mid-day sun. Several times of late I have had goose-pimples on my arms and put on a cardigan.

I forgot to tell you that I had a wire from Rudolf intimating that the proceedings had been successful. So you can heave a great sigh of relief. I never *really* doubted the likelihood of success, but there was always a sneaking fear of his antagonising the judge. We still don't know how long the delay is before one or other applies for a decree absolute. In England it is six weeks, in Ireland six months.

The cat situation is in abeyance. Just after I wrote last its rightful owners called and claimed it. I felt a dreadful betrayer handing the poor little morsel over as it had just begun to relax and stop quaking. Every time they let it out it came back here and they persistently reclaimed it. Can't see what possible fun they can derive from a terrified animal. Anyway when we left for Ho I left instructions that it was not to be refused sanctuary, and was to be fed. This gets more complicated now ... the day we left for Ho the house next to us, previously occupied by original Italian owners of cat, was re-occupied by new German member of staff, wife, two fairly large children and *dogs*. Last I saw of cat was one of the German children carrying it in direction of rightful owner, and cat making a frenzied get-away back to German residence. Don't know where this will end – feeding problem is not as serious as it would be at home because, provided they let it out at night, there is plenty to be found.

Regarding photographic equipment – it looks to me as if the 'Ebig' should do the job, together with microscope attachment. Your ideas are, as usual, a bit ambitious. Before going ahead I must see if F can get an equipment grant either from the Min. of Health or WHO. Medical Field Units are a service entirely organized and staffed by the Ghana Min. of Health; they provide clinical services, mass inoculation schemes, anti-yaws campaigns etc. In some instances, where Ghana govt. has applied for the provision of technical experts under the UN Technical Assistance Scheme, the WHO specialist will be working in conjunction with MFU staff, and will be using MFU laboratories, viz. Fergus, but he is independent of the MFU administration in most respects.

I am glad to hear you have arranged a short holiday for September, and only hope you are lucky as regards weather. It was just yesterday that we heard how bad a summer you have had. I must cut this letter short as my devoted writing means that other deserving people get shelved from week to week.

Friday 12 August

I don't think much exciting has happened – we are having more rain now and have not enough basins to put under all the roof leaks. The Aunt couldn't live here at all – we have really violent lightning and thunder frequently – aesthetically very dramatic to see the landscape lit as with flares at night – but even I was cowering under the bedclothes last night.

You will not be surprised to hear that the CAT has finally ended up here. The awful prolific African family handed it over to the von Heller children in the end as it had made its dislike of them so evident. I thought this was just fine till I heard that Mrs von H and children were returning to Germany for the new school term, that

Pappy wasn't very keen on cats, and that it couldn't get on with their boy. Yesterday the girls came round to express thanks for gift of lettuce and tomatoes, bearing the cat and obviously verging on tears, but expressing 'sensible' sentiments that I should feed it for the next few days so that it would get used to our house and not be disappointed at finding theirs empty on Monday when they go to Accra. What the hell else can I do? Assuming that it exists, is it better to do well by it as long as we can, have it shot or hand over to doubtful owners yet again? Fergus not *too* displeased and plainly regards cat as intelligent, resilient and ornamental, but doubtful if I can put my ruthless views ultimately into practice. There is a good vet in Kumasi who could do the necessary if we can't get a good home there for it when we leave here. All the nice people are heavily over-catted already, and there are three beautiful Siamese going begging, but once again, of course, ours is common and black. The distain of the von H's, whom we visited recently, for insects etc. is incredible (they have been in Africa a long time). They leave the doors open at night and as we sat over our drinks a swarm of termites came in on their suicide flight. They are fat, brown creatures about an inch long, and periodically they swarm, ending in this ritual where they batter themselves against anything they come in contact with, shedding their wings and dying in heaps on the ground. Well, in they came battering periodically against our faces and littering the floor and all flat surfaces. Von H's apparently oblivious to all including four or five large toads who came in to have a banquet of termite. I'm not repelled, but it seems a bit messy.

Then there is Dr Scott who is head of MFU in Ghana. He is charming – owner of Siamese cats. He shares his house with not just a few, but hundreds of, bats. These swoop past as one sips one's coffee. I am learning to ignore this sort of thing – one might be thought fussy or green or something! I wonder where one draws the line – snakes hanging from the light flexes perhaps? [*Dr Scott was a widely respected loner long before the days of 'coming out', and at the time we did not suspect his orientation. He lived happily in stately old-colonial style with his loyal cook/general factotum Simba. There were silk Iranian carpets of the fiddly floral type, cut glass, lots of shimmering Cardinal polish – something we all learned to live with – on the floors, and the covers of his Public Works Dept. chairs, which normally displayed the tattoo PWD because people did not stay long enough to bother covering them,*

were neatly cretonne covered. The menu was always the same at
his dinner parties: consommé soup, roast guinea fowl (which he
had shot), whatever vegetable was currently in season and rice
(potatoes would not grow successfully in this region), followed by
a very pink trifle which came out of an imported packet, but had
been whipped to a sort of foam. Suitable wines and liqueurs to
accompany the coffee were always served outside after the meal.
David grew Jerusalem artichokes, and often made half promises to
give me some, but they never materialized. He did not know what
to make of me because I did not fit any category he had previously encountered, and he was clearly discomfited by our
unmarried status. I remember loudly proclaiming left wing views,
anti-royalist sentiments, and worse, displayed no deference to
males. Later, when our common cat was suspected of having
impregnated one of his Siamese, the relationship cooled markedly.
There was also the question of his no longer being King of the
cracked, cement tennis court – Fergus having usurped that role.
We never actually 'fell out', but there was a certain coolth. This was
all forgotten a few years later when he called on us in Wa in the
Upper Region, stayed the night, and kindly brought, as a special
treat, some guinea fowl which had been travelling in his 'cold' box
rather too long. I don't know how his guts were after he left, but
both Fergus and Adda were really badly afflicted: in fact screams
came from Adda's quarters at one time. As usual I, with my seemingly cast-iron guts, escaped.]

You would not credit how effective I have become with needle
and thread – have just recovered a collar of one of Fergus's shirts,
shortened and bound the sleeves, all by hand mark you. The collar fits without a wrinkle. I know it is not done in the orthodox
way, and I was to be heard bleating now and then, 'Thank God
my Mum's not here to see this!' Could you please send me a good
selection of Venus pencils 2B, B, HB and H: I want to try my hand
on some drawing and painting too. Also I have to draw some maps
for Fergus's next project report, and may possibly have a job to do
re-organizing the MFU museum, though this question has not yet
been broached with David Scott.

Tuesday 22 August

To explain how the morning has flown would sound unconvincing, but I'll try. In the first place Adda and Co. turned out the sitting

and dining room – this means no comfort for anyone all morning as the turning out is literal – all mats, tables, chairs, etc., being banished to the garden. 'Fraidy' cat sits on one remaining chair outside with disapproving expression; after a while he removes himself to our wood-pile to hunt the numerous small lizards who live there. This habit is just as bad as bringing in small birds or mice; he comes in with a limp tail hanging from the mouth, then lays it on the floor where it is apparent that the prey is still alive, but petrified. I can't help admiring anything that can catch one of these lizards, as they are easily the fastest movers I've ever seen. To revert – I must really be getting acclimatized for I spent an hour improving flower beds and neatening edges. How I long for your edging tool, but shall not ask you to send *that*. Instead I use a local sabre-like weapon with short handle which entails much bending: African tools would make you gibber, most are blunt and without exception involve working with rump in the air and head down. The washing in the house, despite our possessing two sinks, one bath, one handbasin, actually *all* with bungs, not to mention two plastic bowls, is done in above position in a series of buckets outside the kitchen in the sun! Anyhow, once more I have digressed – I survived the hour's labour reasonably well, or so I thought, till I looked in a mirror and was confronted with beetroot hued face with white eye-holes. After that I made some tomato aspic moulds with tinned mackerel inside, then I made up milk (powdered and really excellent), then I prepared the lunch salad as Adda, having finished the 'purge', had gone to buy eggs in the village. This afternoon I must make a treacle loaf and a pudding – all this effort is necessary if one is to avoid monotony in the diet or too much reliance on tins. Could you please send me your rough recipe for scones and the standard shortcrust recipe which is printed on the top of the Spry packet. We get Spry in tins here, but they omit the recipe – I have no scales so just have to guess. [*I have not mentioned that Adda came from Navrongo in the Upper Region, and had worked for some time for Fergus in the general capacity of cook, head house boy, general factotum: he had, of course, begun to import outlying members of his family to occupy minor roles in the garden, or to learn the basic skills required for service with an European family – known to be more lucrative than working for one's own countrymen, no matter how elevated. Most such arrangements did not long survive the importation of a wife – ours survived longer than most.*]

Nothing much to record apart from the Fight in the Garden. We had a team of compound cutters doing the long grass and any hedges in the vicinity: they are the finest exponents I've ever seen of the technique of 'just' working – no one could say they were exactly *idling* except when they all gather round the mango tree in recumbent postures for mid-morning break. Well, early in the day I became aware that something was wrong because I could hear *one* voice only going on and on, rising periodically to hysterical pitch. I looked out and saw the large wife, of one of the senior African MFU staff, accompanied by most of her ten children, 'giving off' in the middle of a silent ring of compound cutters. She 'gave off' for over half an hour, with only very occasional interjections from the accused who looked no more ruffianly than the rest. It ended not quite in blows, but grips were definitely come to before they all marched off in the direction of the village. On seeking an explanation from Adda I extracted the following: that Mrs A had lent £70 to one of the men who was employed as an intermediary moneylender (Fergus says 100 per cent interest per month is the going rate). He had denied ever having had the £70 – even in the police station – and she had come hoping to extract an admission by her own means. My feelings are that it serves her damn well right for lending the money.

Then we had a Russian visitor (high-powered WHO man) – rather like Mr Kruschev in build, though with a less porcine face; he gave the appearance initially of being a great big, good-natured, simple soul, but this must be far from the case considering his position. It was remarkable how many topics of conversation were somehow not suitable! Any questions leading to enquiry as to 'how such things are in Russia?' were evaded pleasantly or half answered. I tactfully bit back a remark, only to have it said the next minute by our host David Scott. We were breaking up after a dinner party, and as the night was particularly brilliant and clear it crossed my mind to say, 'Maybe we'll see this new Yankee Sputnik' – Scott's remark was not quite so crudely phrased, but amounted to the same thing.

I'll have to finish quickly as Fergus is dancing up and down waiting for the letter to get the collection at 12.15. More snap news – Copenhagen is very probably going to be the next place of residence, towards the end of '61 I should think. [*Nothing ever came of this plan from our point of view, though the Danmarks Aqvarium flourishes.*]

A quick follow-up on the first part of this letter which was snatched from me. Please don't go to any trouble re plastic pillow cases – it is not all that important – just occasionally it would be nice to have something impenetrable to shroud the govt. guest house pillows in: particularly the one I had in Kumasi that smelled of stale sick! My awful nightly sneezing and asthma have stopped, thank goodness – think it must have been due to the decorative gourds. This is not to say that my nose is perfect, but at least tolerable. Have met a number of Africans who clearly suffer from allergies too, but they seem able to do without Kleenex at 3/6 a box.

Copenhagen: Fergus had a letter from Dr Mandahl-Barth there a few days ago giving the good news that he has succeeded in interesting both WHO and a private benefactor in the foundation of a Bilharzia Research Laboratory. The private individual will pay for all building and equipment costs, while WHO will foot all running expenses, salaries etc. It sounds quite definite that building will be started as soon as plans, architects etc. are agreed. For a long time it had been nebulous. Dr M-B is keen to have F as his resident parasitologist, and WHO have expressed no objection. The only snag may be that F's contract here continues till the end of '61, and that WHO might want to appoint someone sooner – but I don't think that is likely to prove a great obstacle. We are both keeping fingers tightly crossed because it would be a 'good thing'. Denmark is an excellent centre for visiting other parts of Europe, and it would not be too expensive to travel to Ireland or vice versa – apart from all sorts of available 'culture'.

Congratulations on your having become a patron of the arts – even if it is only Maurice Wilks! [*My mother had bought an original oil painting by Maurice Wilks of the Atlantic Drive, near Downings, Co. Donegal – a very mediocre one, but she adored it.*] Glad you had a successful trip with San.

Tuesday 6 September

I always imagine there is nothing fresh to say, but somehow the nothing seems to ramble on into several pages. We are all breathing a little easier now that it seems clear that the cat *hasn't* got rabies. I'd better begin at the beginning and give your hair time to settle down again. A fortnight ago there was a dreadful noise of – not exactly cat fight – but just our cat, making a shortish but frenzied protest around midnight; it really sounded terrified. I was sure a leopard had got it as the noise stopped so suddenly, and it was in a way a relief as it seemed one solution of the cat problem. Then I did what now seems a little foolish considering what I thought had got the cat: I went out in my nightie bearing a torch and calling 'puss, puss, puss'. Puss who always comes obediently, did not appear so I really thought that was that. But not so, next morning he was shivering on the step with one half-closed running eye, a bad limp and great unwillingness to be touched. It turned out to be about four tooth marks in the back leg, *all* of which have turned nasty yellow and pustular. He's fine now – I think an abscess broke yesterday. Anyhow I didn't worry about this fight much till our new Teutonic neighbour, who seems to have this lack of imagination that you will recognize, came up to the tennis court one evening with his stupid yappy dog Fifi. I stretched out a hand in Fifi's direction, partly to keep it off the court, and Von H says, 'Oh, do not let him lick you, he is not well and has been playing last week with Mr Cook's dog which is thought to have rabies.' Now I ask you – the dog was not even on a lead, the tennis court area was full of people, including a lot of children, and he hasn't even the wit to keep the dog at home. The next day he drops around in the evening when we are gardening – just for a little chat, accompanied by Fifi who is still not himself! Cook's dog seems to be confined to the house which is also very near us, then one afternoon I hear a hysterical dog – look out and see dog running across the compound pursued by two shouting white figures. Thinking that this is it, I firmly close all doors and confine our rabid? animal. All however proves to be a false alarm and danger period now over, but you can imagine I worried a bit, particularly as our little sweetie is spirited and likes to bite me playfully. Von H, by the way, is a medical doctor.

Last week we had a two-day tennis match against the 'neighbouring' village of Techiman some 80 miles away. At the same time we had our friends from Kumasi staying with us. Visiting team all black apart from one reptilian Egyptian flashing immense redjewelled ring, and whose actions on the court were just like Monsieur Hulot. We unfortunately had to have him for dinner: conversation demanded a great effort and there was little or no common ground. The match, which was the first of any formality, proved a great spectator attraction and was even attended by a local Mohammedan chief who arrived with attendant servant, both mounted on handsomely caparisoned stallions. These they parked just behind the back row of seats where they swished, stamped and kicked unnervingly. Eventually they and riders departed firing a few side kicks at the cars in the vicinity. The matches were not over till 11.30 on Sunday morning, after which Dr McC and Mr Gray played what was termed on the programme an 'exhibit' match of two sets. Until then the sky had fortunately been overcast, but shortly after they started the sun came out. I had to give Fergus wrist and forehead sweat-bands which were interpreted by the spectators as being some sort of ju-ju, and greeted with a great cheer. How they survived I don't know; Fergus lost 5 lbs of sweat, something I couldn't have believed only I saw the scales before and after. When they finished at 12.15 there was a strong request that the 'ladies' should also perform. We obliged, but only in doubles which was grim enough. I certainly could not have done that when I first came out, in fact I could hardly have stood on the court, so I must be acclimatizing.

Wednesday

Interval during which we have entertained two Belgian and Italian members of WHO to lunch. Have a shrewd suspicion that neither was a salad fan, as they had most sparing helpings of the delicious 'continental' which was served. We are both so fond of them, and out here they should be a great treat as so few people trouble to start gardens that we find it difficult to understand those who choose to live on stodge. The Italian doctor we met at Ho ate *daily* for lunch – and it is much hotter at Ho – a vast plate of pasta with tomato sauce and parmesan cheese, followed by a meat dish of some sort and, always, bread. I have Fergus whittled down to a mere 13 st. from over 14 – you needn't feel sorry for him – he wanted to do it, but couldn't manage a rigorous diet when Adda was doing all the cooking and choosing menus: he also says he feels a lot fitter and certainly looks it. Our only trouble is lack of 'bulk'. My guts work all right, but I suspect his have been stretched with over-eating and are too large to convey the small quantity efficiently along. Must get some delicious All Bran or something in Kumasi. My own weight is down to 8 st. 12 lbs – you probably wouldn't approve, though I don't think it's off my face – equally it doesn't seem to be appreciably off the hips either as my slacks are still pretty well filled.

I have done two oil paintings, and am not too discouraged at the results. The first is a head of one of our ballboys – it is a bit too conventional and unenterprising – make a good cover for *Time* magazine – but it is fairly competent. My next is a flower piece of some zinnias which is either of the calibre of van Gogh's sunflowers or just plain crude – suspect the latter. Still, we both enjoy it, and our efforts are without doubt better than those of Mrs von H and Mrs Wickramasing, both of whom have had some training. Mrs von H with Teutonic assurance, 'Oh yes, I plan to exhibit when I get back to Hamburg.' I think she is colour blind, on top of which she uses a great deal of primary colour straight from the tube. All her landscapes have pillar-box red tracks and roads, whereas the laterite is a soft, bright rust shade.

Kintampo, Brong Ahafo
(It is now the fashion to replace all
Old Colonial names) 2 October 1960

You enquire how my garments are suited – very well on the whole – I have probably too many dresses for a bush station where I prefer to wear shirts and slacks if it is cool enough, cotton shorts or a skirt when it is too hot. You will appreciate that the less one's legs are accessible to insects the better, even so when I have to dress up for a function disguising the blemishes and awful colour of my legs is a major make-up job! This doesn't take into account cat scratches and bites on hands and arms. Our little sweetie is a spirited animal (now), and loves to have fierce battles with me. We had a ghastly incident a few days ago when I thought I'd see how he would behave if we took him on trek as some people do. The success of this plainly depends on starting them young. We took him on a short trip in the car, the idea being that he should accompany us on a walk (when he was with the Italian family he used to go out with them as a dog does, but he seems to have forgotten). The first thing he did was streak under the car from where I had to haul him wild-eyed and kicking. After that I carried him for some distance murmuring soft words of reassurance; when I put him on the ground he got very long and low and retreated to the nearest ditch. As soon as any local appeared, as they did often on their way home from farming outlying plots of land, he was terrified and started blindly for the bush, into which I was afraid he might disappear for good. Worse to come though – I took him protesting and struggling back to the car, but as Fergus had gone ahead to 'enjoy' his walk I had no key. Cat by this time really living up to his name of 'Fraidy' seemed not even to know me, and broke loose, streaking once more under the car, where he vanished completely. I was not sure if he had got out at the other side and that I had missed seeing him, or if he was lurking somewhere in the entrails of the car. Two schoolboys whose English was extra poor said, 'It have go up the front,' but I couldn't find of what – whether car or neighbouring rest-house steps. By this time Fergus had returned silent and looking slightly grim. Vicinity of car now swarming with chattering, gesticulating women and children avidly interested as usual in any 'event'. All calls unavailing, I knew we would have to start the car, but had visions of bits of minced cat dropping to the ground. Engine started – cat appeared – but as soon as it stopped he disappeared into the entrails again. What eventually got him out was fear of a small child who crawled underneath. From there he *did* flee to the rest-house where I finally hauled him from under a chair. The spectators had enjoyed the performance vastly. Conclusion is that terror of *les noirs* is so extreme – our own servants excepted – he will have to spend his remaining days in Kintampo.

There is now another addition to the Zoo – a sweet little baby ant-eater or tree pangolin. Fergus arrived home bearing a wooden box which he opened without any introductory explanation, so my first reaction was one of horror as it looked like a snake curled up tightly. At that time we didn't know the habits of pangolins, and Fergus thought we would just look, photograph, and then release it. It had not occurred to him that it might not be weaned. Mum had been killed in a trap, but it had been found clinging to her, and as it was considered (miraculously) too small for chop, it was brought to Fergus who purchased it for 3 shillings. Only when we found him, now christened Dr Pangloss, markedly uninterested in ants, and when we read how the babies always ride on their mothers, did we realise that he was still very dependent. For the first two or three days he practically starved in spite of my repeated efforts to feed him milk with a glass dropper. This was messy, resulting in much spilt milk and the consequent complaint that both I and my garments smelled of bad milk which had also trickled under his scales and hardened, necessitating cleaning out with a match. Quite by chance I discovered that he likes his milk very warm and that he will eat it off his own soft pink private parts as,

I suppose, being the nearest approach to his Mum's belly texture. Feeds take place at about 5 hour intervals except for the night which he fortunately sleeps through. It is all very touching, but also time consuming and I don't see where it will end. He is flourishing now, getting much more active daily, but still quite uninterested in ants. I forgot to say that his only repulsive aspect is an incredibly long thin tongue for ant probing which he is inclined to stick out without warning – down my neck or between my toes for instance. He is house-trained; at least if I take him out and encourage hole-digging after a meal he mostly responds. *But* he is distressed if I am out of reach and just sits on his hind legs snuffing and groping with small hands. This dependence is more marked outdoors while indoors he climbs on chairs and up the doors and indulges in incredible acrobatics. They are said to be largely nocturnal in habits and adapted for living most of the time in trees. My only escape from him is provided by his being quite happy to sleep in a paper nest in his original wooden box. He accompanied us to Tamale for three days last week, and was relatively little trouble apart from being a great spectator attraction. I don't know how many times I have dispensed my propaganda talk that 'these animals are rare, that they are on the Govt. protected list,' and that they are a 'good thing' as they eat termites. All falls on deaf ears I suspect: reactions being either horror, or agreement that when he has been fed up for a while he will ultimately make 'fine chop'. On our way to Tamale we also saw a small chameleon on the road which we caught and photographed. The colour changes rapidly from that of sunlit grass to shaded grass, then to grass and brown foliage mixed. The eerie thing about their faces is the independent eye mechanism – like a very bad and mobile squint. Two baby ground squirrels were brought in recently for my inspection, but as their mother had escaped when the nest was dug out, I insisted they should be released in the vicinity of the nest in the hope that she would find them. It is quite clear now how these charming books on strange pets come to be written. I may offer Pangloss to London Zoo – withholding till the last that he has to be hand fed! At the moment he's about 7 inches long with another 12 inches of tail: the adult is said to have a body of up to 15 inches. [*See Appendix letter from George Cansdale.*]

That is enough of the Attenborough stuff for one letter. We are both firmly resolved not to collect any more dependents as they complicate living so much.

We have started negotiations for a special marriage licence, but don't yet know what bizarre sort of 'ceremony' will result. It should beat the last one for eccentricity which, some would say, will take some doing. One local newspaper account of a wedding recently performed in Accra read (this is true) – 'The brides (one bridegroom) were radiant in white crêpe de chine and galoshes.'

I'll have to stop now owing to pressure of work and arrival of fleet of PWD men to attend to leaks in roof, painting of kitchen, application of putty which is the universal cure-all. I have also to do quite a lot of typing for F which must catch the post tomorrow a.m.

[Letter concludes with a long list of requests for photographic technical information sheets, developer powders, and most importantly, an efficient tin-opener.]

Monday 24 October 1960

We have just received your letter in which you describe the Music Society evening – it amused us both immensely. F said it brought back to him a concert in Portrush when he was about 12, and so ill-mannered as to be unable to restrain his mirth, particularly when an encore was called for. I am glad you had such a good week in Donegal, and that there appears to be no lack of work for you in the photographic line.

I think the last time I wrote must have been just before we went up to Tamale, and then to Gambaga which is as far north as I have yet been. We had intended also to go to Bolgatanga, but through a series of 'incidents' of the gremlin nature we didn't have time, so I still haven't seen the extreme north of the country near Navrongo where Adda comes from. To begin with the Volta was in flood so instead of going to Tamale straight north for 119 miles of good road and across the two ferries which were out of action, we had to go 70 miles south-east and then 170 miles up to Tamale by another route. Then there was no petrol at Kintampo for the Land Rover which was transporting equipment for snail collectors in the north-east; this state of affairs was repeated at Tamale *and* Gambaga! The Land Rover eats petrol at 15 m.p.g. and normally fills up at special MFU pumps. The alternative was for Fergus to pay for petrol at ordinary stations and hope to recover the cost later – this he was warned was likely to be wearing and probably unfruitful! We had gone about 80 miles when the horn stuck – it's a pretty loud one, and the time seemed interminable while in blazing heat Fergus searched frantically inside the bonnet for the connection which he eventually tore out by the roots (I had always thought that it stopped when the engine did, but not this one). So we drove the rest of the way without it and a horn is an essential in Africa. When we reached Yeji ferry at mid-day there was a queue of 15 mammy lorries and one car in front of us. The lorry which arrived just after us was inappropriately called 'Just in Time'. The heat was fiercer than anything I have felt yet, and there was no choice but for the car to sit in the full sun. So we got out and wandered around amid shouting hoards, dust, goats, vultures, refusing the persistent cries of the Hausa man who was selling appetising looking cuts of meat under a tin shelter where the flies buzzed and the vultures waited. Some of the lorries had been waiting more than 12 hours, but we were extraordinarily lucky in that the ferry is not wide enough to take two lorries, but can take a lorry with a car by its side, so we got on after a wait of only about an hour. Once across the ferry the road is wide and fairly straight, so much so that we were going at 80 m.p.h. at times, which as you will read later was a *bad* thing. Anyhow, we had lunch of warm oranges, hot tomatoes, melted butter and Ryvita in the shade of a tree, and were lucky enough to see some monkeys with a colossal pack leader before they disappeared into the bush. At Tamale nothing *much* went wrong apart from the guest-house caretaker accusing us of stealing his sheets (must say I was relieved to find we had *not* packed them by mistake, as you know my absence of mind – however his is worse, and he is mostly drunk).

Then Dr Pangloss got sick which is most wearing and distressing as he is restless, won't drink anything, and paces the floor with an unsteady gait, then sicks up curdled milk and watery stuff. I now think it must have been due to the extreme heat at Yeji and dehydration, as since we came back I have found that he will sometimes drink great quantities of plain water in preference to milk. He is still far too dependent on 'Mum', shows no interest in eating ants though he will break open an ant-hill and dig avidly for a while; then he gets soil on his nose and even a few ants, decides this is uncomfortable and starts hunting for the security of Mum once again. He is as exacting as any baby, and I have lost a great deal of sleep in dealing with him as he has no discernible feeding or sleeping pattern. If he is hungry he fistles around in his evil-smelling box or starts climbing curtains, doors etc. from which he falls with a resounding thud. Worse is when he gets into bed with us and begins 'anting' behaviour on me: his favourite sites are oxters, ear-holes, private parts or the crook of an elbow. He has made some progress though, and now eats from my elbow rather than his own parts, which was unhygienic. His intellect is a little dull, I fear, remarkable only for his persistence. Fraidy cat is both jealous and frightened – photos enclosed. I developed the first black and white film last week and found it fairly easy if all liquids were lowered to 68°F in the fridge. The temperature increase in 8 minutes was about 6 degrees, even when I used ice-cubes in a water bath, but results are reasonable. I did have real difficulty in getting a good developer and used an M & B so-called fine-grain: its tone values are excellent considering the high contrast of the subjects I was taking, but the grain is considerable. Maybe I will be able to find some Ilford developers in Accra. Most of the pictures are just grinning groups of Adda and family, tennis match and Dr Pangloss – strictly 'record purposes'.

To continue with the Gambaga trip; we left Tamale next day after an abortive attempt to procure a special licence with which to get married (further attempt perhaps more fruitful will have to be made in Kumasi this week). Thirty odd miles out of Tamale when we were negotiating a series of narrow bridges on flooded ground, the right front tyre burst – we swerved right across the road with a bridge end looming relentlessly nearer every split second. I must hand it to Fergus for quick reactions as he managed to straighten the car and stop it in a reasonable position. Comparing the incident with others, I gather one mostly overturns if the front tyre blows at any speed and we were going about 60. The corollary to this: *don't* buy Firestone tyres. The last set of Goodyear did 17,000 miles – this lot have done just over 7,000, so little in fact that Fergus had never even looked at them. The Land Rover driver said cheerfully afterwards, 'Oh yes, I knew they were like that'!

Enclosed picture of me is haggard looking, though rather like you in expression – due to having to contain myself while the photographer fumbled ineptly with his equipment.

Accra, Thursday 27 October

We are now in Accra for a few days. Fergus has to give two lectures to Hygiene teachers of the Builders' Brigade, one on Friday and the other on Monday. As well as this he has a number of Min.

of Health people to see in the hope that a personal approach may elicit some answer to the various queries raised in letters over the last few months. He is particularly anxious to know if Ghana Govt. are likely to require his services for the six months after his next leave, i.e., till the end of his present WHO contract. Then we can pursue our special licence (unsuccessful in Kumasi) still further and do some Christmas shopping.

To find a place to lay your head in Accra is almost impossible. F had wired the Min. of Health asking them to book accommodation, but this had not been done so we spent last night in a new and extremely comfortable hotel with air-conditioned bedrooms. The only snag being the cost of almost £7 p.p. per night. At the moment I'm sitting on the bed trying to get maximum pleasure from said air-conditioning before we leave for a less exalted hole. Fergus is out searching this morning, and is hopeful that he can get a rest-house belonging to an American dam-building concern. As you will gather all this involves 'contacts', and a bit of grovelling. This place is so smart and luxurious – apart from the food which is unenterprising – that I smuggled Dr Pangloss in furtively as I was afraid we might be turned out if he was seen. One has to think ahead so much when leaving him anywhere. Firstly, if it is a friend's house, he must not be anywhere unexpected, or where he can climb up and knock things over. He often gets locked in the lavatory, but this involves telling everyone that he is there and please to put the lid down when they have finished. This morning before going to breakfast I had to put him in a drawer, the wardrobe having been rejected because there was access to the water-pipe system within the walls which he could just have reached. The bed where he had curled up inside the sheets was out because of the probable reactions of the bedroom steward!

Fortunately we now seem to have established a pattern of feeding, sleeping and piddling at last. Did I say he much prefers to go and dig a little hole in the garden? This is the first time I have felt that a ciné camera would be useful as much of his charm is in his weird and skilful movements.

By a fortunate coincidence the Bolshoi Ballet film is on here for the next three days. Fergus, after 16 months culture starved, is looking forward to seeing it, while I shall be glad to see it again, even though it was not outstanding. Adda has been left at Kintampo to look after house and cat while I am getting concerned about our dwindling supply of clean clothes, and the rapidly fattening bag of dirty ones. If we get into this rest-house I can either wash them myself, probably in cold water, though knowing the Yanks there may be hot water or even a washing machine, or bribe the caretaker to do them. Ironing presents a huge problem – if there is no electricity a charcoal iron is used, but I find them too heavy, the heat uncontrollable and just all in all far too exhausting to use. [*Later at Wa I had no choice, but managed notwithstanding to make maternity clothes suitable for arrival in Knightsbridge at the end of 1962.*]

It is difficult to realise that with you the winter has already begun as names of months mean very little out here, just as days of the week and dates are hard to remember unless one is in a largish town. What news of San, Auntie Rosemary, I haven't written to anyone and think I'd better leave it now till there is some happy news to impart. There will be further snags – for instance my extended residence permit elapsed three weeks ago and officials may, if they choose, refuse to renew it, saying I can't get married if I'm not officially here. I don't expect it to be as bad as that, but you never know.

I didn't tell you about the snake: Fergus came home wearing a sinister grin, and said, 'Come here and see.' After the ground squirrels and Dr P I said I hoped it wasn't yet a further addition to the Zoo. Then he opened the boot of the car and brought out about 5 ft. of bright green, writhing snake which he proclaimed dead. It *was*, actually, but I had never seen the phenomenon of muscular contraction after death, and it is very hard to believe when it is going on. *His* story is that it is a harmless snake which the workers at the lab. had horribly injured and that he had to intervene to finish the job off. He examined the head and found no front fangs. There are, however, a few snakes which have the poison glands at the back, and are deadly: Dr Scott swears that this was one of them. In the absence of any complete fauna of Ghana it will be a long time before we find out. Its skin was the most dramatically luminous I have ever seen – far more vivid than anything seen in the Zoo at Kumasi. We also encountered a large black shiny one at the waterworks – I shan't walk in long grass without boots on in the future.

I suspect we shall shortly be evicted from this air-conditioned palace, so I'd better pack up. (Later) Arrived at Yank guest-house and immediately feel warmer towards them as a race. *All* mod. con. including a washing machine, though strangely no milk jug – only £1 per day.

Kintampo 7 November 1960

We quite enjoyed our week in Accra after all. It wasn't nearly as sticky as last time and the American rest-house was almost perfect. Fergus spent a lot of time seeing Min. of Health people (all appears to be chaotic), and I spent a good deal of time at the washing machine, but we went to the Bolshoi film again in an open-air cinema as they all are, with full moon with a clear ring around it such as I've never seen before, shining brightly down on us. We took an African from N. Rhodesia with us, and I think he enjoyed his first experience of western dance 'culture'. What I did find difficult was to explain the potty plot of *Giselle*, about which I'm none too clear myself, and at the same time to explain, in apparent contradiction, that the plot didn't really matter. Then we had a delicious dinner at an Indian restaurant after which we were both so distended we could do little but lie around groaning. Since my whittling down regime succeeded I find that our stomachs must have shrunk.

On Sunday we went to a beach about 30 miles east of Accra and spent a pleasant day basking, eating and swimming. Another of the exaggerations which seem to grip many people, including Schweitzer, is that the African sun is deadly dangerous. I'm sure it can be if one is really careless, but I sat for a long time in intense reflected light under some palms, and then for I'm sure more than an hour in the open and was not at all burned. One doesn't really enjoy swimming because the sea is so dangerous one would be a fool to go further out than waist depth, so it is not possible really to relax. Then there are always rumours of sharks – like the snakes, opinions differ – some say no shark will brave the breaking surf and will be frightened of people splashing, others cite certain unfortunate incidents.

Arrangements have been made for a ceremony lasting about two minutes on Friday 25 November. Our friends in Kumasi will witness it and have very kindly arranged to have a small dinner party of about six people only. So that will be all – which is in many ways as we would both want it. You'd better not publicize till the *fait* is *accompli*! Something might happen in the meantime.

Kumasi and Accra 29 November 1960

We left for Kumasi on 24/11 – as usual in a frantic hurry and unsuccessful in our efforts to make an early start, so I was reading your letter in the car as we bumped and lurched our way over the 70 miles of laterite we always have to cover before reaching a tarred surface. Consequently I felt a bit sick and poor Dr P also chose that morning to get sick too for the first time since going on Ostermilk, so the journey was not restful. Neither was the 25th restful for Fergus, who spent the time tearing around in the car on various errands such as making sure the Town Clerk had not forgotten about the ceremony, seeing our witness, getting his hair cut, negotiating for a dinner at the Club at very short notice, and even buying some provisions for same – he arrived hot and sweaty at 3 p.m., and had about ten minutes to change before dashing out to collect female witness at the other end of the town. One really needs two cars on occasions in Kumasi, though I would not yet attempt to drive amid Ghanaian traffic. The last minute dinner had to be arranged owing to a domestic upheaval at the Grays. Leslie had employed a cook-steward during the 12 years of his bachelor existence here whom I can best describe as a 'rascally looking scoundrel' – one Daniel, whose cloven hoof did not really show, or rather Leslie I imagine ignored it, till he got married last year. Daniel's policy was one of masterly obstruction, deafness, and resentment of Pat's presence in the kitchen, tempered I should say with occasional insolence, though not in Leslie's presence. His mistake came last week when he was insolent in front of Leslie and rashly asked if they wanted to lose his valuable services (he was very efficient) – reply to this was Yes. There was consequent extreme nastiness, threats, lies etc. before he would go – in fact the police had to evict him. Pat is now going through a succession of trial servants who last on average two days.

Our marriage was much as envisaged: we arrived at the Municipal Council Offices where we hung around on dirty, noisy cement stairs and landings for a while before anyone noticed why we were there. Then the clerk whose job it was to fill in the certificate took us into a large boardroom where many juniors were sorting forms and proceeded, with the deliberation of an Irish country policeman, to fill in the necessary information. He was quite defeated by Parasitologist which appears on two lines as Parasito-Logist. After he had breathed his way through two copies we were herded into the Clerk's red-carpeted office. Clerk was an English educated African who had been good enough to dress smartly in a black suit and bow tie, and was really very pleasant – apart from tendency to indulge in what he imagined was suitable

English facetiousness – 'You've had it now' etc. He read, from what legal publication I don't know, a passage which seemed to consist largely of threats about understanding that if either contracted a bigamous marriage during the life of the other he should be punishable by a court of law – not a word about loving, cherishing etc. Then, after a very short oath, Fergus kindly handed me the ring and I hissed, 'Put it on' – he says he was getting around to it – and that was that. We then went and had a few drinks at the Club, after which Fergus and Leslie had a very sweaty game of tennis. In the evening we had an enjoyable dinner with the Grays at the Club. No photographs were taken, and I wore the dress you made for me to attend Rosemary and Arthur's wedding three years ago.

The next two days were clouded by recurrent malaise of Dr P and consultation with the Director of Kumasi Zoo, which confirmed some of our worst suspicions, that he was probably suffering from some deficiency which would get progressively worse. Apparently there is no record of anyone having kept a pangolin for more than two or three months successfully, and even an attempt to keep both adult and baby had failed. The director thought that the mother probably encourages the young one to eat some intermediate diet, such as termite eggs, before it goes onto the full adult diet. I could have tried more ruses such as raw egg laced with tiny sugar ants, but as signs of progress were so few, and it distressed me so much to see him not well, we decided that chloroform was the kindest thing. His well-being was so convincing between bouts of sickness and one thought he was so sleek and fat, then only a few hours later his little belly would sag and go thin so that I suspect it was not real fat, but just distension. So on Sunday Fergus dispatched him very quickly, and we buried him in the Grays' garden. [*I had tried going out at night and sending Dr P up inside a tree in the hope that his instincts would lead him to find natural food, but to no avail. I merely got a nasty shock when something quite large and hairy bumped into me as it made its startled exit from the inside of the tree.*]

We went to Lake Bosomtwi – virtually the only lake in Ghana – over some of the worst laterite track we have been on, the surface eroded by recent heavy rain into deep gullies. We saw a green mamba crossing the track, which reminds me I should have mentioned that seeing snakes in the Zoo here is much more enthralling than at home where they are mostly coiled in a somnolent knot. Some in the cages are very active and just dying to strike at something, while the enormous constrictors, even if knotted up in a tree or lying fully extended at the bottom of their pit, seem much more real. Anyhow, to return to Lake B., we didn't get there till 11 a.m. by which time it is pretty hot, and before us lay a tortuous walk down – rather like the Murlough Bay track at Fair Head – we only had field-glasses, one camera and a polythene box for snails (this trip was prompted by a request from Copenhagen for snails, if any, from the shores, and there proved to be little of interest). We did not take the long-handled metal sieve, as it has always been said that there is a taboo on the putting of metal into the lake. This was found to be obsolete because the villagers had many metal buckets. at the water-side. They are not, on the whole, a pleasant lot down there, all being avaricious to the extreme: 'Massa you give me penny' or (often) 'threepence'. My reply is mostly, 'Why, what have you done?' The village at the bottom of the track is decayingly picturesque with lots of trays of cocoa beans drying in the sun, and a large purple bougainvillaea tree under which the elders sit and gossip. It was not very photogenic though I took a few record-purposes shots. The lake and surrounding hills were covered with heat haze and there is practically no shore. The boats are the most primitive I have ever seen – just a shaped log on which they lie flat and paddle along by hand. What was gratifying is our apparent fitness, because the uphill climb which we had dreaded was accomplished in 25 minutes in a temperature which must have been 85 or 90 degrees. Considerable stretches of the track were in shade which was a help, but I have known myself in far worse shape on the way up from Murlough in August. Neither of us had a hat, and I had no sunburn cream – I didn't burn and neither of us has sunstroke. So much for all those warnings.

We are now back in Accra, Fergus having been summoned to a meeting at short notice, but we are only staying two nights this time.

I shall comment on one or two things in your letter. (a) Foot at last seems to be improving, and withstood the walk to Lake B. without swelling, though with some subsequent pain. I still wear an elastic sock during the day. (b) Yes, please express gratitude at any offers of gifts, but discourage sending as in the first instance they may get pinched and secondly we do not want to add to bulk of our belongings.

We hope to know by January whether we are to return to

Ghana for another term or not. In fact so many things are complicated by not knowing for certain where we are going to be at a given time. We don't even know whether to try to have an infant or not. What I have heard of both Accra and Kumasi hospitals does not give any encouragement to patronize them. Kumasi, for instance, which is a wonderful looking modern building, has no hot water supply, and all dishes, including those of TB patients, are washed in cold water. They do sterilize the instruments, I am told! It is now too late to plan for a birth while on leave, but I am getting longer in the tooth so this must not be postponed indefinitely. Christmas – You should not have bothered sending anything, and neither should San – still it will be nice to get a surprise. I may send something small to her, but on the whole I think it better to bring things home when we come.

Kintampo 2 December 1960

This morning your little parcel containing tin-opener, pencils and pastry cutter and the transparency of your painting arrived. Can't tell you how relieved I am to have that tin-opener – I am surprised that all our hands have remained intact so long. I drove half the way home from Kumasi yesterday, after which F says he feels *more* tired than usual. We didn't have any narrow escapes apart from my nearly running over a road mender's pick-axe on which he was resting.

Tamale 15 December 1960

We don't know what will happen at Christmas. Have toyed with various ideas but will probably stay at Kintampo where we will be pestered by dear little black souls singing 'Good King Wenceslas' – true, they have been practising for weeks. There will be no escape as all is glass louvres and mosquito netting and one is *en plein vue*. If we go to Kumasi we will get involved in smart 'drinks' parties and idle chitter which we both loathe, and find exhausting. If we go to a game reserve in the north we may find all accommodation full (no telephones) and this is too risky. [*I am surprised that I do not mention that there was, even at that time, practically no game to observe – even ground-squirrels were pursued for 'chop'.*] Other nice places would involve much travelling with pots and pans in order to do rather sub-standard catering for ourselves.

Apart from this we get enough battering over dusty roads as it is. The dry season is well started which means there are bush fires, brown curling leaves everywhere, and all the flood water which was extensive six weeks ago has dried up completely. So far Kintampo remains fairly green, but up here all is parched and we return from trips ingrained with red dust.

Yesterday we went to Daboya about 40 miles north-west of Tamale on the White Volta in search of bivalves. It was blisteringly hot, but I enjoyed the trip because the bird-watching was so exotic. There was a large colony of storks breeding in trees at the village on the opposite bank: not just plain white storks, but black and white with pink legs, a cerise snout, and yellow bill. We were able to watch them closely as they prodded the sand banks for food. In flight they are positively pterodactylian. [*They were wood ibis.*]

Crocodiles are said to be numerous, the dangerous ones further up river away from humanity. I'm sure they are just as scared as *vice versa*. Where we were they said only small ones come, so everyone waded around in order to dig molluscs and cool feet and legs. The various craft at our disposal were flat bottomed canoes managed by very small boys, and a *most* unsafe square-ended punt which was shipping water at an alarming rate, so much so that we disembarked hurriedly. This was the first time I have regretted the telephoto lens to any great degree as I could have done good work on the storks. [*I got two reasonable pictures, notwithstanding, and I shall always remember the little boy who was so happy when we gave him a tin of sardines.*]

1961

Kintampo, 5 January 1961

I HAVE THREE of your letters unanswered (one with Xmas parcel which arrived intact). All the oddments will be most useful, particularly the Wettex and bite soothing cream – I'm not sure if it works, but it has a psychological benefit. Fergus has already broken two corks with the corkscrew, but it has been pointed out to him, not only by me, that there is nothing wrong with the corkscrew! The face-cream too is welcome, although I fear that in spite of applications of grease, the African climate will leave its mark. I notice that I screw up my eyes even when wearing dark glasses, and that the sides of the neck get both burned and dried. The Harmattan wind from the Sahara blew for the first time the night the bloody French let off their A bomb, so no doubt we got whatever was going. The wind can be very cold, and is searingly dry; all the woodwork begins to split and warp, and one's nose feels in need of continual picking – mine bled every day at the beginning.

[*The following shortened paragraph is an attempt to explain why it is not possible to make definite plans for home leave.*]

If, as we are beginning to suspect, all is going to be shelved for lack of funds, or in favour of more urgent public health schemes, we will have to remain here till June when the present term of service on this particular project ends. The last 18 months have been directed towards the planning of a vast bilharzia control scheme, assessment of numbers of staff required to implement the scheme, annual cost of running etc. The cost was to have been shared between Ghana Govt. and WHO, but as even WHO is getting short of funds, what with certain large countries being behind with their UN contributions and GG having many irons in the fire, it seems less and less likely that the scheme – which would be unique in Africa – will go beyond the recommendation stage.

Friday 6 January 1961

I have just written a plaintive wail to the WHO Regional Office asking if a decision has yet been made on our request dated last September. We shall be furious if this opportunity of getting accommodation during home leave escapes us. They haven't even told Fergus if he can have his month's study leave in Copenhagen.

Our Christmas was much as expected – we were prey to numerous callers all day and had many on Boxing Day too. The first contingent of Giles types in best clothing arrived very early: they professed to be carol singers and did, indeed, make a feeble effort when I made it plain I wasn't going to hand out just because they were standing there. Then two small girls were said to be at the back door 'to wish you a Merry Xmas' and were paid off at 3*d.* per head. Fergus was a bit cowardly and retired to the bedroom till he saw it was going to continue all day anyhow. So I retired to the delights of the kitchen and its black smoke-laden atmosphere, while he proceeded to paint under the stolid gaze of about ten urchins who were only separated from him by the mosquito netting. When we did sit down to relax or read we kept looking around in a hunted way to see whence the attack would come next – we are open on all sides. In the afternoon we retired to the bedroom and drew the curtains, thus excluding both light and air. Later we went to the swimming pool which was the most pleasant thing in the day. For dinner we had David Scott, who had had *us* the night before, and on Boxing Day another family (dull) were moved to have us *and* DS and the Wickramasinghs (also dull), so you can gather it was really riotous. We get on well with DS, who is not difficult and quite entertaining as well as intelligent and relatively unreserved with us on our own, but otherwise the inhabitants are conversationally pretty dim, and we find that *we* are killing ourselves to introduce new topics which are almost invariably cold-blanketed.

[I wonder why I have not recounted the saga of the turkey which had been obtained for us by Adda in the village. There were sundry horror stories about the sale of dressed-up vultures being sold to Europeans in Kumasi and Accra, so I made it quite clear

that I would be able to distinguish the real thing. Consequently Adda bought a bird on the hoof, so to speak, and tethered the miserable thing to our mango tree for a few days before the ritual slaughter. Fergus was at the lab. when Adda came and wheedled a bottle of brandy out of me in order to anaesthetize the unfortunate bird. He did a fairly good job of anaesthetizing himself as well. It was edible, but distinctly stringy, and one of David's guinea fowl would have been preferable.]

The following week-end, New Year's Eve, Sunday and Monday (which was a holiday), we had two friends and offspring, female aged 13 – *very* awkward and spoilt, to stay. This involved a lot of thought about meals aggravated by sundry fads and fancies and the fact that our stores were getting rather low. I could see that one more day would have produced some biting comment from Fergus on the food fads – no pepper for me, no mustard in the sandwiches, I'd like *mine* without paw-paw, banana, orange etc. *I* can't take fat, oh *no* salad dressing for *me*, and so on. The brightest spot was Sunday when we arranged to take them to the White Volta at Kadelso about 50 miles north of here where MFU have a boat. Normally game is very seldom seen here, having been much depleted by uncontrolled shooting, trapping, etc., but we had a really rich day. On the road north we saw a duiker, a family of mongooses, a rare vulture of enormous size and two sorts of glorious bee-eaters at close range. The rosy bee-eater is spectacular, but I had run out of colour film and missed what could have been an outstanding picture.

When we got to Kadelso the boat, which is flat-bottomed and sturdy (it has to be, we later learned!) gave some trouble in starting – nasty little 2-stroke engine. Eventually we all packed in: our party, the PWD mechanic who looks after the engine, and two Africans whom we imagined to be well acquainted with the river and its channels, but who proved subsequently just to have come for the trip. One of them kept an unalert hand on the rudder and plainly didn't know right from left. He giggled every time we shot past large rocks which were just below the surface, and appeared unmoved when we hit them. Luckily Gilbert has a boat of his own in Accra, so when after a while it became evident that the crew had no sense, he took over the steering and tried to get the mechanic to *slow* when we were all shouting 'Slow, rocks.' We were afraid of holing the boat or fouling the propeller, and had no idea if it was protected or not. Also, by this time we had noticed that there was only one paddle in the boat – the other we later found gracing the rest house. Chaos was added to by loud engine noise which made it difficult for Gilbert to hear our shouts. At the worst period we were sitting aground on top of a rock swinging around on the pinnacle. The excitement was heightened by the knowledge that there was at least one large crocodile in the vicinity. Actually this made my day because I've been longing to see one in the wild state, and they are not easy to see in the Volta, neither are the West African crocs. on average as large as those of East Africa. I saw it first submerged with just the eyes and snout sticking out – this was on our way downstream, but on our way back he had come out onto the sand of a little island and we had a wonderful view, what is more he was a gigantic specimen, about 14 ft, I should say. There was a general feeling of relief when we finally got ashore again after a last minute crisis when the engine conked.

I forgot to tell you about the bush fire which raged all day around the bungalow on Boxing Day. We thought it might encroach upon the garden, so we beat it out at one point with branches from mango trees – towards the end we had perfected a technique, but the extreme heat must be very bad for an active beater and I'm not surprised people often collapse. The cattle egrets loved it and sat on the edge of the flames waiting for the insects, snakes and other refugees to emerge.

Kintampo, 16 February 1961

I expect you have been worrying over the long silence and imaging spinning wheels in the ditch etc. If so I'm sorry, but must warn you that there may be a further silence after this letter as we are going to be on the move for the next five weeks.

After our return from Tamale and the extreme NE region, we had only a few days at home, during which I should have written to you, before starting on a trip to Ho (SE Volta Region), and Accra, from which we returned on 13th. One always has the best intentions of writing while on trek, but time is usually fully occupied with packing, unpacking, loading the car, washing, meal preparation and the eternal worry of seeing that one's cold stores keep in reasonable condition till the next fridge is available. We have just bought an insulated box at great cost, but find that it does make a great difference to the food problem. Mostly when one arrives at the rest houses someone is on bended knees in front of the fridge muttering gently, a strong smell of kerosene and smoke pervades all, and there is no ice till late at night – if at all. Some of the guest houses have adequate pots and pans, and supply sheets and towels, others do not, and one does not know till one gets there. All this adds to the luggage. We have been trying to cut down on the bulk which accompanies us, but so far without great success. The usual list is one large suitcase in which our joint clothes are packed (this leads to trouble, as in theory one just pulls out what one needs for one night, and there is no need to re-pack in the morning). In practice Fergus delves for things in my absence, and the result is considerable re-arrangement before the lid will close again. There is one grip with shoes, sponge bags, insect sprays, torch etc.; the ice-box and additional rucksack for flasks on the journey; the portable wireless, cameras, field glasses, tennis rackets, briefcase, box of Kleenex, snail sieves and bottles, the eternal large bag of dirty clothes, and of course room for an additional passenger and such boxes of provisions as we buy on our way back to Kintampo. You can imagine what it was like when we had Pangloss as well, and I was mixing his feeds in the car!

Now I have acquired another encumbrance in the shape of a baby duiker (see *Flame Trees of Thika*) which will have to accompany us on this long snail survey in the SW region. It was Monday 13th on our way home to Kintampo when Fergus said, 'There is a little boy with an animal, do you want to stop and see what it is – and we're not going to buy it.' Of course, when we saw what it was, and how very young, we just couldn't let it go to sure death in the village. The price was high, starting at 6/- and only coming down to 5/- with reluctance. The child claimed his brothers had told him not on any account to sell for less, but how the absent brothers knew he had caught it, and to whom they thought he was likely to sell it is another question, as there is very little traffic on that road. The poor little morsel can't be more than two weeks old – I should say less, as its umbilical cord is still evident. I have succeeded in establishing some sort of feeding pattern, and much to my relief it does eat some green stuff as well as milk: however it is much too small to suck from the feeding bottle (also purchased at great expense), and I have to drop from an old cortisone dropper onto its nose or force feed which is not good. It is getting enough, I think, but naturally doesn't get any comfort or joy from the feeding process. It also has trouble with our polished floors and spread-eagles impotently if it is stupid enough to go off the matting. Then I have to keep it away from the cat: this is not too hard as the cat flops around lethargically in the extreme heat most of the day.

There is still nothing definite regarding our home leave. One reason for the lack of decision is that Fergus is under the thumb of the WHO area representative who is based in Brazzaville, and whose office will currently be dealing with all Congo affairs. We have toyed with a variety of routes home if we bring the car, and have so far discarded many (you will be relieved to hear). (a) motoring from Ghana to Kano and thence north across the Sahara Hoggar route; (b) going west to Dakar and up to the Atlas mountains and Tangier. Main reasons for rejection are time involved, which is unpredictable, sand, deterioration of car and Fergus's lack of mechanical ability if anything goes wrong. Reports on those who have done it range from 'Oh, it's just like a good bush road in Ghana and lots of people go on scooters' to 'Ah yes, old so-and-so took three months on the way, and at one point they were digging themselves out every four miles or so.' Some indication is given by the fact that the French authorities demand a large deposit to cover their costs if they have to rescue you – returnable at the other end.

No, I didn't hear from Uncle Joe [*the Holy one in Derry*] at all – but can't think I'm in disgrace as Fergus's sister mentioned some equally holy relatives of theirs as saying that Uncle Joe was always talking about me!

Some of the next few weeks will be spent near or on the coast, so it will be pleasant to relax? after the day's snailing: field asssistants and Land Rover will be with us too. Sorry this has been a very scrappy letter as my mind is dwelling on finishing the final typing of two new papers Fergus has written which *must* be posted on Saturday, feeding the various animals and ourselves and trying to do some dressmaking on a machine borrowed from the workshop where it is used for mending tarpaulins. Have just 'run-up' a shirt which is either very smart or just like a deck-chair cover – depends how you look at these things.

Kintampo, 16 March 1961

We returned rather earlier than expected from our trip to the SW, having left the Land Rover and field assistants to complete the survey as they seemed quite competent to do.

Future plans are not made easier by being 300 miles from Accra and suffering a now daily temperature ranging from a mere 85 degrees in the morning to 95 at mid-day (that is inside – outside it is 105 or more). This is notoriously the most trying period of the year, but the drought *should* have broken by now: we have not had rain since 1/12/60, and then not much. Fergus's powers of concentration after 22 months are at a low ebb, aggravated by the fact that he hasn't even got a fan in his little hot-house of an office. My own powers I notice are beginning to deteriorate – not helped by my first attack of prickly heat.

Friday 17th

Yesterday's writing reads very disjointedly, so I shall try to be more lucid today. The temp. is a mere 83 this morning and I am having fun trying to get developer, stop bath and fixer down to the right level. We have been reading the WHO Staff Rules which are, in many places, a miracle of obscurity and ambiguity. It looks to me as if the African Regional Office *could* ask F to remain here till the end of his contract period. He says he would fight this strongly as he feels he is not giving good value in his present exhausted state. The only response to our frenzied enquiries has been a two-line memo from the Regional Director saying he is not yet in a position to answer any of our questions. Fergus is contemplating seeing the Min. of Health here and doing some top-level prodding. I suppose if the worst happens, and we are unable to make any definite arrangements, we can either stay at a hotel for a short time or doss down in your upstairs room till we can get a caravan if they are not all booked by then.

My film has just been hung up to dry; it looks quite good though nothing of great interest there – mostly snail habitats, villagers, poor old Pangloss, two of Adda's children. I had another tragedy with the antelope and am now utterly discouraged in attempts to rear baby animals, though I realise that it is largely because each time we have picked a 'difficult' specimen. The antelope was a Royal one – I believe one of the smallest, if not *the* smallest, in the world, not any longer common, and reputedly very delicate to rear. It was doing apparently very well, taking plenty of milk, eating greenery and its droppings were normal, though it was extremely shy, skulking and stupid – not recognising me outside its pen. It was, of course, most unfortunate that we had only had it one week before we had to take off on trek, although it seemed to have become well used to travelling in its little basket, and always ate well on arrival. What happened I just don't know, perhaps a combination of things; anyhow at Takoradi I noticed it was weak on its legs, and it became progressively weaker till we got to Axim where it began to refuse milk. Then I discovered that the end of its tongue was ulcerated or that it had bitten it and so was naturally refusing to suck or eat. So I force fed it and kept it out in the open under constant supervision. I had thought it had been inside too much, and might be suffering from sunshine deficiency. After two days it was a lot stronger and I thought it would survive, then I gave it finely chopped hibiscus and cassava leaves (as recommended by Cansdale for duikers and such like), and about half an hour later it grew very weak again and died on my lap. It may be that hibiscus is poisonous, because it had that at Takoradi for the first time just before the first weakness began, or it may be that force-feeding, which is never recommended, was fatal – I shall never know. A Yank game warden we met at Axim infuriated me by constant reiteration while I was working to save it: 'You sure got a rare little animal there, yeah, you sure got a rare little animal. Very delicate though, very hard to rear, even a loud noise may be enough to kill them!' This last was nonsense because it experienced many loud noises without apparently noticing them, and travelled with us in the Land Rover which makes a noise like an aeroplane. I just do not know how the Attenboroughs and the Durrells stick the pace, the interrupted sleep, the warm feeds and patient dropping and keeping bottles clean etc. all by candlelight. Surely they must have their failures too.

[As I read this 45 years later, it strikes me as odd that I have not mentioned how difficult it is during the early months to understand the pidgin English widely spoken in West Africa. I had found the reported speech in Durrell's early best-sellers tedious to read and unconvincing: I revised my opinion after being exposed to it for some months. A classic early encounter for me was when the remains of a brassière which had been subjected to charcoal iron treatment were sadly displayed with the explanation that 'Dis knicker for top – somehow he spoil.']

Your news about Timothy was sad, but I'm glad it didn't last too long, and that he didn't have to stay with the vet for treatment – 13 years is not a bad innings really. Our own cat problem is, of course, rising nearer the surface now. Fergus refuses to be an accomplice in terminating a healthy young life and, though not naturally a cat lover, was heard to ask what it would cost to take it home. He seems to have developed a certain respect for it. I feel that what an animal suffers in transit and quarantine is probably severe, so I am going to advertise for a good European home in the Kumasi Club. Unfortunately he is presently in *mal odeur* with the cat lovers (few) of Kintampo, having sired some very common looking kittens out of David Scott's prize Siamese, and bitten severely the tail of another neighbouring cat. Anyway, as far as I can see the whole European population here is on its way out – I should estimate one more year will see complete Africanization.

Somebody in Axim rest house pinched my precious tin-opener, but I made such a fuss about it that it arrived by registered post with the District Commissioner's compliments yesterday!

Kintampo, 7 April 1961

I am sure you will be glad to have a legible letter for once, though whether I can compose so 'freely' on a machine remains to be seen – I rather think not.

At last there is some news re our leave. Though not quite certain it looks as if we shall leave here about 7 July, and make our way home via Madeira, Madrid, Geneva, London, arriving in Belfast some time at the beginning of August. The GG has decided that it can not afford the original Bilharziasis Control Plan, but that it wishes to implement a more restricted project on the lines recently put forward by Dr Scott (Fergus for diplomatic reasons in disguise). This means that estimates for the revised scheme and an entirely new Plan of Operation have to be drafted, and should, if possible, be signed before we depart on home leave – needless to say this is another job for Fergus to complete. We have been told to go ahead and take our leave as long as we are back in Ghana by 1/7/61 'in order to comply with Staff Rule 640.2', they make no comment on our request to know how many days are due, refused request for study leave, and ignored our request to make our own travel arrangements, merely saying to tell them when we proposed travelling and they would supply tickets. Naturally there would just not be time to get the tickets from Brazzaville, rush down to Accra and get them changed (which WHO do not like anyhow), get the house cleared out, all our stuff packed, Martin

Odei (new national research graduate allocated to the project) coached, home for cat, not to mention all the admin. and correspondence done, in a four-week period. The future, nonetheless, begins to look a bit more hopeful because we thought that if GG did not proceed with any WHO aided scheme there was every liklihood of Fergus being paid off. This is no idle joke as WHO operate on two-year contracts till one has served 5 years continuously, and the contract says that it may be terminated by either side at one month's notice. We have just heard of another of their bilharzia specialists who has been pushed out after his scheme (for lack of government backing) folded up in the Philippines. The Danish job seems no nearer materializing; their Min. of Health have been sitting on decisions for many months now, and I should say there will probably not be a laboratory to be Parasitologist in for at least another year. So there is every possibility that we will be asked to return here to inaugurate the new scheme at Wa. If this is the case Fergus is going to do his best to negotiate for better leave allowance – say yearly – or a short-term contract. This is because Wa is really 'bush' and living conditions will be very trying. Look on the map in the top left-hand corner near the Ivory Coast border. They have very nearly a six month dry period, it is a dry savannah zone, there is no electricity at *all*, the nearest cold store is 200 miles away at Tamale, and all the roads are laterite. These are pleasant to drive on in the wet season (inundations excluded), but in the dry season one always arrives at one's destination looking like a Red Indian in a school play: the washing load is consequently much heavier than normal. At present there is no house available, but David Scott is approaching the Regional Organization to see if they can provide something temporarily. We know that there is an empty bungalow similar to the one we have here, and over which the RO have been fighting for some months unable to decide whether the Resident Magistrate or some other should get it: perhaps we can provide a solution whereby neither loses face.

I have a couple of little jobs for you to do 'If it's no trouble' [*family joke emanating from a friend who used to ask my mother to sort out the most complicated dress-making jobs for her*]. Can you look in the DIY magazines to see if there are any ads. for Army surplus generators? We have been told that it is possible to get for approx. £12 something which has scarcely been used, and which would provide us with enough power to run a small fridge, reading lamp etc. if we go to Wa. Can you find out something about fuel consumption, wattage one can run off them etc.? Again, like the route across the Sahara, reports run to extremes such as 'cost practically nothing to run' to 'cost 3/6 a night'. Can you also find out if any refrigerator manufacturer makes a small deep-freeze unit which could be used as an additional store to the main fridge which is run on kerosene. As far as I know it is not possible to get sufficiently low temperatures with kerosene. The other thing I would like you to investigate is the cost of sewing machines at home compared with out here. There are several continental makes available in Accra, but all are expensive and do all sorts of things I do not wish to do. I just want a lightweight reasonably portable one which can either be run off a generator or with a hand wheel.

Outside the PWD squad are running a bulldozer which has never been oiled – can you imagine what sort of noise that makes? Oh, yes, we had rain, glorious rain on 22 March. Suddenly everything looks clean again, all the laterite dust is washed from the leaves and things smell so much nicer. Strangely enough the spring foliage starts long before the rains come; in fact about ten days after there has been a severe bush fire you can see new grass some inches long, and numerous small bushes with brilliant green shoots.

Our next door neighbour in the bush behind the house is a hermit – something most unusual in Africa, where family life tends to be solid – an evil looking old man with one wall-eye, and almost stone deaf. We are on very good terms because we allow him to get water at our kitchen rather than see him walk long distances with his bucket. He has a resonant cackle and speaks no English, so communication is limited. *Well*, Adda announced a couple of weeks ago that the old man was ill, so we all trouped solemnly through the bush to see what was wrong. His farm is quite large, but his house is the roughest shack of mud-brick with a palm roof; his belongings appear to be one rickety chair, an orange-box, a pipe, an enamel dish with large hole in the bottom, a bucket and a calabash. Nevertheless, he is reputed to be rich and to have a lot of money buried somewhere on the farm. He will not use a post office account because he is illiterate, and does not understand these people who disappear your money over the counter and give instead a small book. His afflictions were, to say the least, difficult to diagnose; they ranged from aches and pains everywhere, lassitude, under-nourishment, to a hot swollen foot. The first obstacle to overcome was refusal to come to the Health Centre (he had flatly refused Adda, saying he would die for sure there): I was pleasantly surprised when he agreed to the same *order* when it came from Fergus and me. After a couple of trips to the centre they decided to open his swollen foot which was then clearly showing signs of blood poisoning. This was done in my presence without a local anaesthetic and I have never seen anything so nasty, or heard such screams. The doctor made the first incision which seemed to be comparatively painless, and which released an incredible amount of pus, but then he started to probe deeply to clear the remainder – it must have been absolutely agonising, and I thought the old man was going to rise up and strangle the doctor. I also feared he might take reprisals against me afterwards! Anyhow, after the shock the relief must have been great as he has been touchingly grateful and has gone obediently to have the wound dressed. I fed him while he was too weak to make his own food and discovered why he was *so* weak. His loving relatives had been bringing food from the village while he was sick, but he was firmly convinced they were trying to poison him, and was throwing it away all the time. Apparently this is a common, and often not unfounded belief around here.

Hair-dye not really a great success, the white ones all went orange as usual – so don't bother sending any more.

Kintampo, 14 May 1961

My memory is definitely becoming affected by the climate. I can't remember when I last wrote to you. Still nothing definite about home leave, but once we do get there it will probably be possible for me, at least, to stay quite a while as there is no accommodation for us at Wa, and Fergus says he is *not* returning here till he *knows* there is a house to live in. Of course we haven't been asked to go there yet, as somebody in Brazzaville has mislaid the new Plan of Operations which we so urgently produced last month, and until it is signed nothing can be decided.

Last week's post contained some gratifyingly long letters including one from the Js who mention they have invited you to join them at Portnoo in August. DJ says, 'We really want her to come because we enjoy her company, but we would not like her to accept for fear of hurting our feelings.' I think it is extremely thoughtful of them to have asked you, and I'm sure you would enjoy it even if the younger generation and friends become a bit overpowering at times. D says she hopes you would make an escape route for yourself. I know it is for August, but I think it would be quite safe to arrange to join them for the first week or so. Please don't refuse just because you feel our home-coming will be imminent – we are likely to be late rather than early, and you can gather strength at Portnoo.

Did I tell you I had started a weekly English class for Fergus's field assistants who number six. The standard varies from aspiring GCE to semi-literate. I find this rather more time consuming than I had intended as it involves a lot of reading on my part, drafting out of questions, correcting their exercises and writing out copy book for those whose writing is completely unformed. I know you will snort at this, but I can do it if necessary. Apart from that I have been busy typing, editing, cooking, writing letters, mending etc., and have little time for anything 'creative'.

There seems some chance of the cat problem being temporarily solved. We hear that the original owners are coming back to Kintampo to relieve one of the doctors who is going on leave and in all probability they will occupy our house. My advertisement in the Kumasi Club didn't bring a single reply. A few weeks ago he didn't return on a morning when we were going to Tamale and, in the light of the fate of one of the other compound cats, I thought he had gone for 'fine chop' – which would have been one solution. However he returned later with a sore tongue and one broken canine, so it must have just been a battle of some sort.

Our chicken brood of ten produced not one hen, so all will have to be chopped. There are still three left, and you can imagine that I can't reconcile myself to having this murderous procedure going on on the premises: we munch with less enthusiasm than were they anonymous carcases. One or two had got picked off by snakes.

Kintampo, 22 May 1961

I'm sorry Fergus's inactivity re letter writing to his family has repercussions on you. Have expressed this to him, and he has written twice recently. Actually he had written some time in April too, and the pad for a long time contained two abortive attempts – one of one paragraph (agreed by us both to be of profound dullness and therefore scrapped), and another merely showing the date and 'My dear ...'! He tries occasionally, and without great conviction, to get me to do it, saying how *good* I am at letter writing: but I have stood out against this as (a) they would rather have his effort, even if dull, and (b) if he finds it difficult, how much more so for me. Of course it is partly a matter of extreme fatigue; a large part of the working day is spent in writing involved letters, preparing documents and writing papers on his work, so I can quite understand a disinclination to spend spare time writing duty letters.

I have been thinking about accommodation for our home leave. How about a small ad. in the local press? Small house or flat taken care of in owner's absence. Trouble is most people don't go away for two months at a time. I think we will seriously have to consider buying a house and letting it during *our* absence if we are to be abroad much longer. Most people seem to find this the only solution.

Saturday 3 June 1961

On our return from Tamale I had your letter of 28 May, so we are now back in some sort of rhythm. Our trip was fraught with many gremlins – almost as if you were present! We started on Monday by the direct 120 mile road to Tamale in good time to arrive for lunch, but after covering the 58 miles to the first ferry we were met by an ominous aura of inactivity and a queue of three Mammy lorries. The ferry had 'spoil' on Sunday and the SOS to Tamale had still not been sent off. So there was nothing to do but smart about-turn back to Kintampo feeling only thankful that the ferry hadn't 'spoil' with us in mid-river. We had a rushed and horrible lunch at home (I had let all stores run down so we had tinned fish, grated cheese and spaghetti), hoping to set off at 2 to cover the 240 mile distance by the other road, and praying that our accommodation booking had been received at Tamale (telephone spoil too). As we swept out of the garage there was a pronounced lurch to the left caused by a very flat tyre: for this I must say we were grateful *not* to have to press on, and also that it had chosen to go down while we were at home. Next day we got off at 6.30 and had done about 100 miles when the vulcanized tyre spoil again (with a vengeance – good Michelin X quite ruined) and we screeched to a halt. This is the second time we have had a flat just after having a repair done, and we have been fortunate both times that we were not on a corner or passing anything. After that everything went smoothly apart from my discovery *en route* that I had broken an enormous piece, the outer shell in fact, off an already heavily filled back tooth. Here too we were lucky, because the dentist, whom we know as a tennis player, was in attendance at the hospital and was able to fix it two days later. He is a Ghanaian graduate of Durham University, which is noted for its good dental school, and has a touch with the drill which puts 'Butcher' Elliot to shame. All was then well till on our return trip Fergus began to feel griping pains which marked the beginning of a really dreadful attack of squits: we were both awake a lot last night, and it was so bad he had no control at all over his guts. Your recent consignment of Wettex cloths came in for some unexpected use, and I fixed him up with a pair of tight underpants lined with a sanitary towel. Luckily we had some pills which have worked now and he is recuperating in bed with the *Observer*.

We sent a telegram to Brazzaville saying *not* 'Please can we' but 'Plan to leave on 5th July etc.' This at least brought results and we have had a wire saying that they are complying with our request to go via Las Palmas – Madrid – Geneva etc. and sending authorization to the travel agent in Accra, to whom I have already written for a provisional booking for 5 July or failing this 12th which would put the whole itinerary back one week – or possibly more.

5 June 1961

I think you will definitely be able to have more than a week-end at Portnoo even if we get a flight from Accra on 5 July, as WHO have been, for once, unexpectedly generous in granting ten days official stay in Geneva – we asked for five I think. This being the case the itinerary will be roughly as follows depending of course on whether we leave as anticipated. I should think 13 August is quite the earliest date when you could expect us. There is also a possibility that from Geneva we might pay a short visit to Copenhagen before going to London. The renewed request for study leave has been refused, and any visit there would otherwise be at our own expense.

Fergus has been invited by the CIBA foundation to take part in a conference at Cairo next March – it will only be a four-day affair, but with any luck WHO and or CIBA will bear travel costs – wives unfortunately *not* included. This is something of a 'feather' as only twenty-five experts in all have been invited to participate.

I am frantically busy because Adda has gone off to his village in the north for a few days in order to investigate what sounds like a defiance of his rights as head of the family. He had a so-called 'sister' who used to do for him here, but some months ago his wife swept down and took the sister back home, ostensibly to look after an aged parent. It seems there was some suspicion that Adda was selling her in marriage down here. Anyhow one of the stewards at Tamale told me to tell Adda that his sister was in Tamale 'looking for a husband'. When I dutifully related this gobbet he was more than somewhat gunked – so just what is going on I don't quite know and probably never shall.

There is just a faint possibility that we may be asked to stay on a little longer while a WHO Bilharziasis Advisory Team visits Ghana – but that should not mean much delay. Have just completed an elegant cotton 'tube' with slits at the side! Am improving at dressmaking.

Kumasi, 19 June 1961

We came down to Kumasi yesterday for the week-end to do some shopping and collect some snails today at the large reservoir here. It always reminds me of the lake at Castleward if I don't look too closely at the vegetation – you will see a few palms here and there – and ignore the exotic birds called lily-trotters which do exactly that: they have enormously long legs with very big fingered feet, but their colouring is really beautiful. They have soft purplish blue heads, a small black cap, rusty red backs and a yellow ruff shading into a creamy belly. Unfortunately there was an unusual number of voracious tsetse flies in evidence and I got eaten (not yet having got a new tin of 'Off' which I can thoroughly recommend – it is a spray tin, and rather expensive at 6/- I think). Later in the day it rained and we now have a glorious Irish drizzle. You have no idea how nice this, and the fore-running grey skies are. Most of the rain here is really torrential, so the soft type is a treat.

It now looks as though we will come some time about the first week in September. We had a wire from B'ville asking us to postpone till after the visit of the BAT: this is reasonable, in fact it would be ridiculous if Fergus were not here when they come to advise on the Wa project. We both think the Helen's Bay house sounds very suitable, in particular as there is a possibility of renting it also for October: I had thought that it might become really difficult to get anything later in the year than August. Of course we don't know when BAT will come; they are out in East Africa now, but if they hear that our leave depends on their visit I think they may hurry up. It is only a two-man team, and Fergus knows one of them quite well.

After all the trouble you took over guide books we have now decided to go to Greece instead if air fares are not too excessive. Would you mind looking at my woollies to see if they are all right? Black jumpers in particular, and my Liberty wool skirt in which there is a tear at the hem – could you see if there is a piece anywhere to patch it with please.

Kintampo, 22 June 1961

A few more things to add to the 'if it's no trouble' list. Can you get me a 24 or 26 inch pale turquoise zip – Optilon for preference, but fine metal would do. I could also do with a 5 inch fine black one. My confidence is now such that I alter patterns and cut collars and facings out of my head (with varying success I must admit). I have tamed the sewing machine which normally repairs the canvas on our Land Rovers.

Adda has returned from the north plus his 'sister'. The tale is that his wife and family had done a deal in selling her to a man she couldn't stand, so she ran away to Tamale where she hadn't enough money to come on down here. When I look at some of the superior nylon underwear which appears on the line, I suspect she wasn't doing too badly in Tamale!

Do you think your dentist would take me for a check-up if he knew I wasn't likely to come more than once a year? I know he is very exclusive as all are, but this seems my big chance to break with Butcher Elliot.

This week-end and the following week look like being a little exhausting. On Saturday I had arranged to have the entire Rosei family for lunch – they were always most hospitable when we went to Ho and I feel we owe them a lot. This means five adults, two children and at the last minute a wire from the Western Area Rep. in Lagos that he is coming on the same day and can we 'arrange accommodation'. He says he intends visiting the new project area at Wa, and I suspect that (a) he will want to take

Fergus along, (b) he has no idea how far away it is, (c) he will learn nothing from looking at the area, which to the untutored eye will look much like any other place. It *may* serve the purpose of letting HQ know that it is a little isolated, and might help to get us a generator and deep-freeze unit, and (d) that I will have to go along and organize meals in the very inadequate rest house whose fridge doesn't work. The WHO Rep. is an Austrian called Spitz with a very nice English wife (hope she's not coming too!), but I can detect some very Rudolfian traits. He is extremely obstinate and blissfully unaware of the finer feelings of others, and I know if he has decided to visit Wa no amount of reasoning will dissuade him. Last time we met in Takoradi – where there are many pleasant beaches – he insisted on a 50 mile drive to visit a place the name of which attracted him, despite our assurance that it offered nothing Takoradi didn't have, and despite his wife's evident fatigue. Later he famously remarked, 'Hazel enjoyed it after all.'

Kintampo, Wednesday 12 July

We have just returned from a 5-day trip to Accra where we have actually booked our flight from Accra to Tripoli, and thence to Athens on 3 August. Unfortunately I had my first attack of malaria while there. Some of the Wa mosquitoes must have been resistant to the drug we take: it was very short and sharp leaving a lingering feeling of weakness and faint malaise *aux ventres* for a couple of days – this has now turned into severe squits rather like Fergus's recent bout, though I haven't quite lost control yet. A specimen is now down at the lab. being examined for amoebae. I don't feel too bad, only slight fever and aches, but what is inconvenient is the imminent visit of the WHO team who will stay here on Sat. and Sun. needing most meals. Then on Monday we depart for Wa taking *everything* in the way of household goods as the house we are to occupy for four nights is quite bare. Can quite see that even if feeling fully 'at myself' something is liable to be forgotten. On return from Wa, the team and Fergus have to batter on down to Accra again for a meeting at the Min. of Health. I think I'll remain here to start packing.

WHO have offered Fergus a further 2-year contract, till December 1963, and this is the only redeeming feature in their recent behaviour. After refusing the renewed request for study leave, they said (apropos the Conference in Cairo next March) that 'as the invitation was sent to you personally, we do not feel obliged to contribute in any way towards travel costs', and that any time spent at the Conference would be counted as earned leave and therefore deducted from our next leave. This in view of the fact that numbers of their staff are flitting off to the US for six months on full pay *and* per diem allowance, seems to indicate that one has to be in with the right clique. They should feel gratified that a staff member has been selected for such an international conference.

Kintampo, 28 August 1961

This should surely be the last letter – or SOS if you prefer – to come from here. I'm afraid I have to announce positively the last postponement, and that is only by one week. We should get home by 14 September. I know we are wasting two weeks of house rent, but it can't be helped.

Since I last wrote we have had BAT (both very nice and undemanding visitors), taken them to Wa for five days, rushed down here and thence to Accra from where we only returned yesterday. We had another lucky escape with the car – the contact breaker in the distributor bust on our way south, but was kind enough to do so only three miles out of Kintampo, so we were able to get the MFU mechanic, who surprisingly had a spare. If it had happened further on we would really have been in trouble as we *had* to reach Accra the same day. Later on we had a puncture to add to the joys of the 300-mile trip. The postponement of one week is because we will have to pack up everything as if it were coming home for good, After Wa seeming almost certain there is now every prospect that GG will not have funds to spare. There is a financial crisis at present which is evident from the recent very drastic budget. If you read the *Sunday Times* or the *Observer* you will get some idea. Anyhow the decision will rest with the Great One (Nkrumah) himself, and will not be known for some time. There is a possibility of additional assistance from UNICEF which may sway the balance, but nevertheless we shan't know for certain for some months.

One good thing about the budget is that second hand car prices will rocket, so if we have to sell ours we should do well. I had Uncle Joe's letter telling me to trust in the Lord once again! He comes out with one priceless remark typical of Derry insularity, i.e., that from the description of my life out here it must be dull compared with a place like – say Belfast! He says he is now 82. If parcel post to Switzerland is not too dear and moderately speedy, I would like my skates – otherwise don't bother.

Wa, on further acquaintance, now that the rains have had their effect, is really quite attractive: we have had an assurance of a generator from WHO (their expense) if the project comes off; the question of a house to attach it to is quite another matter. We are toying with the idea of buying a modern saleable bungalow at home as an investment and refuge for leaves, but as usual there will be lots of cons.

[Eventually we did depart on home leave, never visited the Canary Islands, but went instead to Greece, staying first in Athens and visiting all the usual tourist sites. It was, of course, as hot as or even hotter than Ghana, but the atmosphere was not at that time polluted. We went by bus on a nerve-shattering drive to Piraeus, and thence by goat and peasant-laden ferry to Cephalonia. The bus drivers played loud ethnic music continuously, and the gilded fringe on the windscreen swung among the religious pictures above in unison as we rounded bends blasting the horn to warn any oncoming vehicle. On one side was a steep rocky hill-side which seemed to be within arm-scraping distance of the outer passenger, on the other a sheer drop to the sea. I had made complicated plans to visit the Monasteries at Meteora, but those too were never fulfilled. Thereafter there was a duty visit to WHO Headquarters at Geneva and an autumn holiday in Ireland.

By this time I was getting very broody and worried that conception could not necessarily be taken for granted. There was a visit to a gynaecologist for what was termed a D&C job.]

1962

WA/DORIMON
UPPER REGION

Geneva, 3 January 1962

WE ARE BACK here sound in wind and limb after an enjoyable, though in some ways frustrating, ten days. The sun shone almost continuously, but there was a most regrettable paucity of snow. The result was that everyone in Verbier concentrated on the same chair lift in order to reach the snow level 2,000 ft higher, and this naturally meant valuable time wasted in queueing, not to mention heavy expense each time of mounting. On Christmas day there was a heavy fall which made skiing at low levels possible for two or three days, but after that it wore through in patches and became very perilous. We made good progress, but not nearly as quickly as if the conditions had been good. Paradoxically, every newspaper was headlining heavy snow and frost in England.

We are in the Palais now while Fergus makes arrangements re travel authorization, vaccinations etc. and, if it can be arranged we will probably fly to Copenhagen tomorrow or the next day. So you should see me again about 12 January. Naturally we are relieved to know a bit more about the future, but a little apprehensive about Ghana 5. As far as we know the Ghana Govt. has still not signed the Plan of Operations, and co-operation between the Min. of Health and others is likely to be even less satisfactory than previously. So – to coin a phrase – it is likely to be no bed of roses. Also we regret not being forced to improve our French.

Fergus's Brazzaville trip is supposed to be for only two months, but we shall not be surprised if it extends beyond that time.

Your black creation was worn twice, and the skating skirt only once. My fear of falling on the very rough ice made me wear slacks the second time. My performance, though good by standards of others, was a sad shadow of the old aplomb! We have eaten, and are eating hugely, but I suppose because of the great amount of energy burned during skiing, do not appear to have gained weight.

Hellerup Club, Copenhagen 10 January 1962

We arrived here safely on Friday night after some changes in route owing to fog and snow at Zurich and eventually flew directly from Geneva to Copenhagen where the first blast of outside air reminded us of NI on a cold, wet, February day. So far we have had only one sunny day – Sunday – when we went to the cottage belonging to the Dane with whom Fergus worked in Rhodesia. Went for a long walk through the young forest, and returned to a picnic lunch of rye bread and various pickled fishes, eels etc., of which they have such a great variety here. Last night we saw the Royal Danish Ballet doing three of Kenneth MacMillan's short ballets – *Danses Concertantes*, *The Burrow* and *Solitaire*. The Burrow I had seen before, though I can't remember whether in Edinburgh or Belfast; neither can I recall if it was the Royal Danish or the Theatre Ballet that performed it. *Danses Concertantes* was to a large extent detracted from by messy costumes and decor either of which would have passed without the other. *Solitaire* also had such a fussy staging that one wondered how the dancers steered their way through the poles which appeared to be stuck with a variety of coloured paper nylon waist slips. The choreography and music (Malcolm Arnold), however, were good, as was the dancing.

On Sunday 14th we both leave here at 10.20 arriving in Amsterdam where we have a stop of about six hours. [*We walked around as much as possible and were accosted by a seedy looking deviant almost immediately.*] Fergus leaves at 6.30 for Brazzaville and I leave at 7 for London where I hope to get the London Belfast BEA flight arriving in Belfast about 10.

Cairo, Mena House Hotel, Wednesday 21 March

I hope you got the card I sent from Rome. My expectation that you will get this is not high! This morning I listened to a couple of the papers being read at the conference before coming out here on the veranda to roast myself immoderately. Cairo is really very pleasant at this time of year, and there is nearly always a fresh breeze blowing. So far I haven't gone outside the gates – it just isn't any fun battling with all the offers of a taxi, camel, donkey, guide, curio, or even 'my brother' for purpose unspecified. Everyone says 'Just ignore them', but it is a little difficult to ignore a full sized fez thrust right under your nose. Fergus, being taller, does better in the line of ignoring, and goes around with an expression rather like one of the camels or Gen. de Gaulle. Tonight we are being taken to see the Son et Lumière show at the Sphinx and should have adequate protection from the touts, who aren't so numerous at night anyhow. Poor Fergus has to present Don McMullen's paper this p.m. (it is bad enough presenting one's own in a stimulating manner, but where one is not fully familiar with the content, more difficult). The Chief Med. Officer at Geneva refused Don permission to travel right at the last minute after everything was arranged. He is <u>Hungarian</u>, and notoriously addicted to asserting his power. It wasn't that Don was any worse – just the MO said he wasn't a 'good risk' from WHO's point of view. Don had a slight coronary around Christmas time, but all the other medics had OK'd him. [*I have underlined Hungarian because the fiercest personality conflict I had suffered in my own career had been with a Hungarian refugee appointed to the QUB Library, and nominally in charge of my department.*]

We have eaten steadily since arriving here. Yesterday a huge lunch in one of the ex royal palaces in an *entirely* gilt-encrusted room with immense chandeliers. I took a picture at 1 sec. (handheld) leaning against a pillar which may give some idea. [*It came out well.*] We started with a huge shrimp patty, went on to roast meat, two veg. and spuds, then as I sat back feeling replete, all the dragomans marched in, each bearing a huge turkey surrounded by highly seasoned rice mixed with pine kernels. After that we had great slices of pink-glazed gateau covered with whipped cream and large marzipan strawberries, followed by fresh fruit and viscous coffee. That over, we were taken through Prince Mohammed Ali's two palaces, one a museum and the other his ex residence. I have never seen anything like, or indeed could have conceived, the latter. It was apparently built not more than sixty years ago. *Every* available inch was a triumph of intricate craftsmanship, some of it really beautiful inlaid work in mother-of-pearl, ivory and wood, some silver inlay, ceramic tiles everywhere – complete walls of them: all the ceilings were either gold encrusted elaborately carved beams with lashings of red, blue and green paint thrown

in for good measure, or they were covered all over with a succession of udder-like protruberances in similar colours. All
furniture was ornate with the exception of the heavy leather stud-
ded stuff in the sitting room which was pure Victoriana. Our dear
Royal family's photographs were all over the place (affectionately
signed). Naturally there were Persian carpets, marble floors and a
fountain in the entrance hall. Collectively it was really awful, but
singly there were some beautiful textures and patterns. Needless to
say the surrounding grounds were also effectively laid out, well-
established and impeccably maintained. The night before we had
attended a 'traditional style' dinner in one of the big restaurants in
Cairo. The decor represented the inside of a Bedouin tent, and the
atmosphere was heavy with smoke and burned fat fumes. Once
again there seemed an endless procession of dishes most of which
tasted of this burnt fat, and nearly all of which were tough by our
standards. The *pièce de résistance* was pigeon with the head still
on!

We expect to leave here on Sunday by United Arab Airlines for
Accra where we shall stay for a short while before going north. In
the haste of parting I forgot to thank you for all the slaving you
have done, and for suffering one or both of us. All dresses very
successful to date and I am in no way outshone by the other
female participants – competition practically nil in fact!

Accra, Tuesday 27 March

I do hope you got my letter and card from Cairo though, as I said,
it seemed most unlikely in view of general inefficiency and
screaming chaos. Ghana strikes one as being highly organized in
comparison, and the officials at the airport so much more willing
and cheerful. We got in here at 12.30 a.m. on Sunday night after
a journey of unequalled length, frustration and general tediousness
which had begun at 10 in the morning when we reported at Cairo
Air Terminal. The joys were added to by us both being very tired
from the previous day's activities, and my having incubated an
Egyptian cold which was at the feverish violent sore throat stage.
I can only repeat – let no one ever travel by UAA – aptly named
Misrair. Otherwise we enjoyed our stay in Egypt this time, and
were able to see that it is as great a dictatorship as many other better known ones. Some of the delegates were quite outspoken in
private. Egyptians are not allowed normally to leave the country:

if they decide to emigrate they may do so, but may not take more than £500 out and thus lose their nationality. Well educated parents are not allowed to send their children to schools in other countries, or for exchange visits etc. The conference went well and F delivered Don's paper extremely well in spite of preliminary nervousness.

The Egyptians are just as accomplished as the Russians or Chinese in evading embarrassing questions, and even managed to prevent us seeing through one of the villages near a health centre, in spite of the visit being part of the official programme. I have a good photograph which was taken of me fratting with the Communist China delegate. All the delegates felt they had seen nothing of the irrigation systems or the extent of the bilharziasis problem in Egypt. On Thursday we visited Memphis where little now remains but some temple columns, a sphinx and an immense statue of Rameses II; our guide, who was a highly cultured Egyptian woman with some French ancestry, then took us to Sakkara where we walked through the desert from one tomb to another (dull), descended into the heart of a pyramid and saw the hieroglyphics, which might have been cut yesterday: then hoards of men came with donkeys, camels, ponies and horse gigs and proceeded to fight insanely for our patronage. I've never seen anything like such a scrum before – they beat not only each other, but their rivals' animals as well, and would almost have torn you apart in their efforts to get you on *their* steed. In the afternoon we went into Cairo and had a surfeit of mosques and little shops. It was quite chilly so my mole stole came in useful – though rather overshadowed by preponderence of mink on the Egyptian women.

Basic stores are in very variable supply now, and things will be even more difficult for us as the Catering Guest House at Tamale, where we used to stay, is now occupied by Russians (permanently), and to hell with the rest of the Government officers who may need to stay there. Fergus has recovered the car and is now tearing around taxing, insuring and re-licensing it.

WHO Bilharzia Control Unit,
c/o Medical Field Units,
Wa, Upper Region, Ghana
24 April 1962

We have been here for ten days now and this is the first time I have had either time or energy enough to write. All has *not* been going smoothly and I think we both feel slightly 'end of tourish' already!

First of all I forgot to mention that we stayed two nights in Kintampo where we slept in the MFU rest house which is the bungalow next to our old one in which the Roseis are still living with our cat who seems in rude health though somewhat battle scarred. He has obviously undergone some further traumatic experiences with the children who haul him around and generally harass him – what pleasure they get from it is hard to say, as he is quite the most unresponsive brute imaginable. He does seem to have overcome his horror of the children – I suppose he had to or get out. The Roseis and Dr and Mrs Grant (Ghanaian successor to Scott, who is returning for one more tour only) fed us regularly and were in every way kind and hospitable. A great deal of time was spent in being 'greeted' by various old acquaintances, including the old hermit who was delighted to see us and promptly gave me two dozen eggs. We shared the rest house with one of the new influx of doctors from the East, some of whom are remarkably outspoken about affairs behind the curtain. There are indications that some at least are in danger of becoming more old colonial minded than the true species. 'These people are so ... ing lazy and unreliable,' being frequently heard.

To revert to Wa, we stayed four nights at the scruffy little Water Supplies rest house now administered by a young Nazi type German who so loathes the British that he normally refuses to accommodate them. He was furious when he discovered that instead of Dr Grant (OK being Ghanaian) we were staying there. On our second day we went to look at the old bungalow which has been allocated to us, and which is so awful at present it hardly bears description. After first inspection we just sat hotly drooping on the dirty, torn cushions in the scabby, cracked old chairs and moaned at each other for a while. The first thing we decided was that all would be lost if we moved in, as this would be taken as accepting such a sty. [*There were holes in the inner roof and a mountain of bat droppings in the middle of the sitting room; the kitchen was literally a black hole joined to the main house by a walkway which was supposed to be roofed against downpour, but was not.*]

Accordingly we have come out to the MFU round house at Dorimon which is an inconvenient fourteen miles from Wa, but has a certain charm of the primitive thatched cottage type, over-looks the pretty little dam, but is certainly not suitable for long-term occupation. A good house had been intended for us, but was given to a recently arrived Czech couple about four days before we came. Even it would not in some ways be suitable, as the kitchen premises are minute, but it is new and has PVC floors and wiring *and* fans – if one could get a generator installed.

As far as we can tell WHO are going to be reasonable about providing a large fridge and eventual generator, but it is bound to take frustrating months of negotiation before either materializes. Our residence has in its favour a very pleasant tree-planted, old established garden, but is designed on the old plan which has a separate kitchen happily, unlike here, not miles away across a snake-infested compound.

What we feel is that even when we have waited for all our requests to be carried out, the house will still be neither conven-ient, hygienic nor cool. It has been a repository for various odd bits of cast-off Govt. furniture all ringed, scratched, split and not uniform in design, the mosquito proofing is torn, louvred windows are caked with a happy mixture of ochre coloured paint and wasps' nests; all floors are surfaced with pock-marked *green* Cardinal (makes a change from the hitherto ubiquitous red so beloved by Adda) – any request shopping list of his always begins with 'Calendar' polish and Marmite. I have oft reiterated that Marmite is a forbidden product in any kitchen overseen by me, and this is not popular, nor is my refusal to buy jelly cubes. Shelving in the 'kitchen' is sagging rotten, cockroach-infested wood; both 'Belfast' sinks are chipped and bunged up. The lav. is so caked I'm doubtful if it will ever come clean (and have said so), there is no ceiling other than unproofed asbestos sheet, and virtu-ally every surface is covered with bat droppings. The main roof of the house is full of termites which deliver a fine coating of red dust over all (roof, said by others who have endured a short stay, leaks badly in the rainy season – now started.) There is a minute, much-scarred fridge with no deep-freeze compartment, and not in any case working. No Calor gas cooker and only two small paraffin lamps provided – not even a Tilley. The District Commissioner, who emanates sympathetic vibes (middle-aged, Ghanaian mother, German father), has said he will do his best to get things moving, and the PWD has also promised quick action, but we shall be sur-prised if we are in before two months or so have passed.

Meanwhile at Dorimon it is a constant battle for survival. I am doing all as Adda probably won't come till the middle of next month, and I'm already feeling very tired as the climate is not as good as that at Kintampo. We both spent an hour in the middle of the night cleaning flues and wicks, filtering kerosene etc., in an effort to find why the two ancient fridges have both gone out of action. Last night began with the slaughter of a spitting cobra: I was enthroned on the outside privy (which is a little thatched round house on its own, some distance from the main building) tranquilly contemplating the beautiful moonlit scene through the open door, when a large snake nosed around the entrance and slithered around the inside perimeter wall behind me, emerging at the door again to proceed across the compound. 'Frozen to the spot' would aptly describe my state, as you can imagine. Anyhow, I raised the alarm and felt rather bad about it when, in the ensuing hue and cry, the snake was decapitated while making a futile effort to climb up the wall of the main house. It seems that snakes are numerous hereabouts. Other residents are house martins, who have a nest directly over our bed, so they deposit droppings on the mosquito net. Termites everywhere, a toad lurking somewhere, as yet not detected, in the bedroom, and a mouse (large unspecified breed) gnawing at the front door. We are sleeping on the veranda on camp beds at present because it is much too hot inside. One of the compensations of being here is that we get fresh fish from the Black Volta which is only a few miles away. Fruit, unfortunately, is unobtainable, so we will have to see if we can have some sent from Kumasi.

Dorimon is a very small place with only about thirty adult males: the inhabitants are mostly Lobi people who originally came from Ivory Coast across the river, and are not very advanced. The field dresser who has a small dressing station here, and was trained at Kintampo, refers to them in contemptuous tones as 'these Lobis'. It has already become known that we pick people up *en route* to Wa – there is a very occasional lorry, mostly on market day, but most are too poor to pay 2/- to travel fourteen miles. Sometimes I fear the people we take are so overcome that they don't like to ask to be put down, and go past their stopping place. The women are ancient by the time they have a couple of children: we took one the other day, who at first glance looked ancient, but when I saw her face it was evident she was probably only in her early twenties.

The insect life is fortunately not so fierce as at Kintampo, so one can sit out and sunbathe early on before it is too hot, neither are the mosquitoes so numerous as in the south, though this may well be seasonal. We have a crocodile in the dam at the bottom of the garden, but he is not particularly entertaining, of a skulking nature, and not large enough to be really inspiring – only about 6 ft.

Please send in next parcel: spiky rubber or plastic thing to rest soap on, Wettex cloths, a copy of the recent 'Report on Smoking and Lung Cancer', and one of the new fast Kodachrome films just to try. I could also do with the close-up bellows attachment for the Exakta, plus a copy of Ilford Technical Information Book which I had left on order at QUB. We wear the minimum of clothing, and Fergus has taken to wearing a fetching pair of mesh underpants as suitable dress for the evening meal. [*So much for the old colonial rule of always changing for dinner in the bush!*]

Adda arrived from Accra yesterday, having left in slight *mal odeur* I gather owing to having got very drunk, and also because of an episode involving not giving sufficient notice. I must say I'm relieved to see him, as drudgery has been pretty incessant, and several nights' sleep have been interrupted by forced attention to fridges which get upset each time they are filled up with kerosene. Nights are also interrupted by severe electric storms preceded by violent gusts of wind. As we are sleeping outside this means we lie semi-awake under our whipping mosquito nets wondering whether or not to take the beds inside: sometimes, as last night, there are violent gusts and some lightning, but no rain. At such times the heat becomes even more oppressive, so I decided to lug my bed inside, only later having to lug it out again as no rain had come, and heat was unbearable. The roof of the main house leaks like a waterfall in several places so why bother?

You would just loathe the evenings as insect life is much more varied, and on a larger scale than at Kintampo, though mosquitoes not so bad except near the river. If one sits out in the lamplight reading near enough to the light source to see, one is bombarded by huge shelly beetles determined to commit suicide; the alternative is to move outside range of light. The noise of whirring wings, violent cracks as the heavy bodies whang into walls and lights, insane buzzing, as they lie upside down trying to right themselves, allied to the loud frog and toad orchestra from the dam and the owls, makes one long for a tape-recorder. However, I feel we have enough odd pieces of expensive equipment without adding to the load.

Actually we have settled in quite comfortably and many people would say life was one long rural dream of the Portnoo or Murlough Bay order – ask DJ just how restful that is! Working hours in the extreme north are normally 7 a.m. till 2 p.m., which is all right if one is living near the laboratory, but makes for a very short day with oddly spaced meals when we are fourteen miles of rough laterite track distant. Often F doesn't come back till after 3. Naturally we have begun collecting lame ducks, and have started an unofficial ambulance service between here and Wa. To date two cases of snake-bite, one trypanosomiaisis (sleeping sickness), one poisoned foot, and today a huge hernia above the navel – looks like the entire stomach. I don't know if they will be able to operate as there are no facilities for transfusion, and the Czech doctor says many who would otherwise survive die because of this. He is learning painfully fast. One of his first dramas was when the steward of a friend 'borrowed' his new Volkswagen and crashed it just outside Tamale (he then reluctantly had to resort to the wicked old-colonial practice of sacking his own intermediary servant on the spot). This was Karel's *first* car: he and his wife – a paediatrician – had previously lived in a small flat with shared kitchen and bathroom in Prague, and his only means of transport before taking up a post in Ghana had been a motor-bike.

Last week Karel was called to examine a decapitated corpse found a few yards from the Wa-Dorimon road: it was very 'high', and only on the hands and upper chest did any flesh remain. In his innocence he thought that the pool in which it was half lying had dried up, exposing it to view, and that dogs had decapitated it. We suspect it was a cutlass job, and was parked there. So far nobody seems unduly disturbed and nobody has been reported missing!

It is now 9.30 a.m. and already too hot to sit in the sun typing F's Congo report. Nominally there are two typists at Wa, but one is on leave and the other doesn't type – he only clerks!

Bird watching is quite good, so last night I was down at the dam trying to stir the crocodile into action, but he was somnolent, wearing an evil smile and with a suspicious bulge under the throat. Their camouflage, like that of seals, is incredible when they are motionless, but again if you know where to look you will nearly always find them.

Rudolf's announcement does not surprise me – hope springs eternal. She must be pretty malleable if she is of suitable age and still unaware that she is being 'moulded'. I wonder how *her* AP [*aged parent*] is reacting! I suppose I should write a magnanimous letter of good wishes, or would silence be more appropriate? DJ says *he* chose the ring but does not reveal details – turquoise matrix I suspect.

Fergus is getting around to writing home, and I'm sorry if you have been plagued with enquiries. I really can't blame him for not having done so, as he has been very busy and pretty well exhausted most of the time. However I detect greater signs of determination over the last few days – or rather he says more frequently, 'Right enough I must.' How are San, the Aunt and Uncle Arthur? Give greetings from us both. Really must stop as I have spent over two hours writing. The brain works much more sluggishly here, and there is apparently a well-recognized medical condition known as West African memory or lack of same.

Dorimon, Upper Region, 17 May 1962

After a long interval two letters have come dated 5 and 9 May – before that nothing since 19 April. All the time I have been hoping that the missing letter *must* by now have reached you. It makes me gibber to think of the wasted industry, as it was the longest one I have written – something like fourteen pages, and took three days off and on. It contained, as far as I recall, an account of our gruelling flight, various ailments, Adda's misbehavings, dull dinner parties, etc. – doesn't sound very entertaining I must admit, but as far as I can recall it was.

I can see you have quite the the wrong impression of life out here: in reality this is a delightfully peaceful little country cottage (with the usual attendant minor drawbacks). We have quite got accustomed to it after an initial period of incessant battle with defective fridges, lamps, etc., and in many ways we shall be sorry to move to Wa. The grass cutters have killed nine snakes in two days' cutting, but on the whole the snake is just as frightened as one is oneself – and if one looks where one is going the risk should not be great. All the gruesome carcases are brought to us for inspection and identification: one was particularly nasty as it had just ingested an unfortunate frog, and had been decapitated. [*Illustration follows of main part of snake with frog's legs protruding from site of decapitation.*] After inspection all heads are buried lest anyone should extract the poison for an illegitimate purpose.

Some of the people here use poisoned arrows to kill marauding cattle which trample crops. The idea is to catch the beast before it has actually died and slaughter it in the usual manner for the village market – one can't help wondering if there isn't some residual poison, but I suppose not enough to do more than give a minor bellyache. On the whole I prefer not to buy meat here in Dorimon: they say there is a young inspector who is just learning his job, but one day I was down in the market and, not looking where I was going, almost trod in the middle of a supine pig's corpse spread out like an anatomical textbook illustration. Flies were abundant as it had been killed the day before.

The villagers hereabouts have been most generous with their gifts of eggs, so much so that I am distraught to know how to use them up: no sooner do I use a sizeable quantity than somebody appears holding a lumpy bundle from 'the Chief of Buka' or 'this coloured woman who is selling cigarettes and who you lifted in the car', 'Da wife brother', or 'this woman you have take to hospital senior husband', and so it goes on. Da is the caretaker of the resthouse here, and is one of those people whose lot it is to be imposed upon by others. He has a colleague, Simbu, who is *only* a labourer (lower caste than watchman), but as Da speaks the worst English I have ever heard, is almost blind (spitting cobra), rather dirty and none too bright though most willing, everyone thinks Simbu is in charge. Adda was only here twenty-four hours before he had Da fetching and carrying, washing clothes etc. Anyhow Da wife (nobody uses possessives in speech) had a poisoned foot and we took her to have penicillin injections etc. at the Health Centre in Wa. Now we get eggs from Da, Da wife mother, Da wife brother and a variety of distant connections. Luckily many are bad, though this means one can't chance boiling them. I have made egg custard, small cakes, mayonnaise, incorporated them in all sorts of things and they still keep pouring in. [*In retrospect I do not know how this was achieved as all I had to cook on was a Primus stove.*] Eggs are not eaten here even though the people are very poor and don't eat much meat. They just collect them and sell at Wa market, or to people from the south who have taken to egg eating. I should like to start an 'eat more eggs' campaign, but I think it would be unrewarding. The African field dresser who has a small first aid post here (he hasn't received any drugs or new supplies from his local council for three months now) is quite frank about the difficulties of educating 'these people', as he calls them, to new ways of water-use, hygiene etc. He is the most frank and entertaining man I have met so far, and makes one long again for a tape-recorder. He never stops telling anecdotes, giving information about customs, experiences etc., and his turn of phrase is quite unique, but even if one reproduces it in print a great deal is lost without the intonation.

The heat is really pretty exhausting and we don't have the cool nights we had at Kintampo – also the humidity is higher. I have not recorded the temperature but intend getting a thermometer. F and I think that it might be better not to send the trunk after all, but merely a parcel which can come straight here by post. I feel we have more than enough cases and boxes already. From the list I am extracting only those things I really would like which cannot be found in Ghana. Box file, washing-up brushes, table mats, Wettex, Kodachrome + two black and white films (FP 3), the report on smoking, correspondence, white sandals. I am wearing nothing but the playsuits you made at present – and the cotton is rotting almost while you watch – and could well do with another light-weight one. I can't even wear a bra most of the time so I just sag! Buttons, if you can run them to ground, would be a good thing.

We are getting the Sunday papers quite quickly and regularly now. I arranged this in Accra, deciding to bye-pass Kumasi where they used to go astray. There were two very good articles recently in the *Sunday Times* by Aidan Crawley on the Russian Gamble for Africa.

Glad to hear you are going to Portnoo again, the weather could not be quite so bad two years running surely. There were two articles recently – also in the *Sunday Times* – by E. Nicholas on holidaying in Ireland. She speaks glowingly of the Beach Hotel at Downings, now run by an artist, the Amethyst Hotel on Achill and of Portnoo which she considers a real find. She was there in September last, so probably did not see the caravan camp. PS Fergus has finally written home!

Must stop now as there is great pressure of typing with F's Congo Report which has to be done in quadruplicate.

Monday 28 May 1962

We had a letter from you on Saturday which was proudly marked 'Missent to Gambia', but it took only ten days in all, so not too bad – we are lucky to have got it. It crossed one of mine saying not to bother with trunk after all which I know will make you gibber. I said F would not be recouped at this late date, but that is not quite correct. Apparently up to two months after entering Ghana we are allowed a limited quantity of unaccompanied air freight, after that there may be difficulties in clearing it at Customs. However if you have sent it off we will just hope for the best. I am assuming, of course, that you have now got my letter saying what to send by surface post instead! Another problem is that things may wait ages in Accra before we can get them sent up here. The tin trunk, for instance, is still there with all tea towels and bath towels. We are managing with two towels which are more hole than solid and one bath towel. As things dry quickly in the north it is possible to wash and dry in a couple of hours, but in Accra one can wait all day and still have a nasty, moist, and sometimes smelly, bundle.

Now – not a *word* till it's in the bag so to speak – I think I may be pregnant at last. Neither of us has great faith in our fitness as breeding stock, so we feel rather incredulous. Probably I shouldn't have told you till it is confirmed, as there are no symptoms (nasty) as yet. In this case the bathing suit and playsuit will look a little odd, though I shall continue to wear the latter as long as possible. We haven't liked to make definite plans yet – I'll wait two months – but in all probability will come home to NI about the end of November, as one is not supposed to travel by air at more than seven months pregnant. Pat Gray had hers in Kumasi in a newly opened clinic run by an eccentric Dubliner who has married a Ghanaian woman. She seemed quite satisfied with the attention she got, but there were some questionable details.

Dorimon, Friday 1 June 1962

No further developments since I was interrupted by sundry demands on time last Monday. F says he won't be convinced till there are visible signs. Nevertheless we have begun to discuss how best to arrange our next leave so as to cause least disruption and maximum benefit all round. As far as we can see *no* solution (as usual) will be ideal, and nearly all are going to involve considerable planning in advance. Even if I did decide to have 'it' out here we would still have to get me away from Wa in good time, and this would involve a waiting period in Kumasi or Accra, neither of which is a pleasant place to wait. One certainly wouldn't want to be 'bringing forth' *en route* south from here. If I come home to NI, which I think we both favour, it means leaving F for something like three months, and not having him around for the event. His leave will not officially be due till March, and who wants to be at home in February anyway? Infant should arrive mid or end of January. We could spend two months at home, and then could all have a holiday in May in Spain or Italy.

Just to add to the uncertainty, the Plan of Operations has still not been signed – in fact the Brazzaville office has not sent the most recent copy, which F drafted while in the Congo, to Accra yet. F is now sending acerbic wires and memos to Brazzaville to the effect that he is wasting his time here without a mandate to get cracking on the project. Actually he has plenty to do writing up papers. You may recall that at one time *last* year it was said that Dr McC will positively not return to Ghana if the Plan of Operations is not signed by 1.1.62.

We are still at Dorimon and so settled in now it will be a wrench to tear ourselves away from the lovely view of the dam. Every morning at 7 all the primary school children are taken down for their morning bath. This consists of stripping off and huddling together in a compact group while the teacher throws several buckets of water over them. It is sad they are not allowed to bathe in the dam, but that of course is exactly what would spread both bilharzia and guinea worm – an horrible affliction with infinitely more dramatic manifestations than bilharzia which is normally debilitating, but not terminal, unless the worm-load is excessive. The eradication of guinea worm should be simple as it involves no more than boiling and filtering drinking water, but as resources to boil water, much less filter it, are non-existent hereabouts, many villagers display the distressing symptoms of the disease. The very long worm can emerge from such favoured sites as the lower leg, the nipple, the end of the tongue, and even the penis I have been told. With patience it can be laboriously wound up on a match-stick, taking infinite care not to break it because should one do so there is risk of an abscess. With this threat in mind, nobody is allowed in the dam above the ankle, and there is a boy on duty all the time to enforce the rule. The village women detest him, and there are loud arguments almost every day because he insists on their taking their water from a special place which involves walking much further than they think necessary.

This place is seething with animals though none as yet of the bush variety. We have two Pi-dog pups (a white tip to the tail and a diamond flash on the forehead), and one lamb in the house at the moment, tripping us up at every turn. The lamb is an orphan brought by one of the MFU Field Assistants from a nearby village. I lent him my plastic feeding bottle and teat, but soon 'somehow' I was doing most of the feeds. It starts bleating shortly after 5.30, so I am forced to get up to provide sustenance just to stop the noise. The owner, who is rather a nice man, had an accident on his motor bike a few days ago, so lamb and pup feeding are largely my duty. When he crashed his bike into an unmarked hole where 'they' were road-mending, he must have been slightly concussed, because it wasn't till some hours later he remembered leaving his gun behind. A gun here is a *very* valuable possession, so every effort had to be made to recover it. After Fergus had taken him into Wa hospital late at night a gun search was organized, but there was no sign of it. Eventually it was said that two road workers had helped Mr B. when he crashed, so then they had to be traced. This meant a search from compound to compound in Dorimon at midnight to find where the road workers were staying. They were finally traced and admitted to having the gun which they had been 'going to bring in next day'. This may or may not have been true, but it is much more likely they would have sold it in the Ivory Coast. Everyone exhausted after trailing around in night attire in light of hurricane lamps, but a certain sense of achievement was felt on recovering the gun. All they got away with was a 10/- note.

Today is really delightful as there is a fresh breeze blowing, not for once the prelude to heavy rain, and even though the heat is intense it doesn't feel quite so oppressive. Did I ever tell you about the macabre life of the mud-wasp? There are many species and they are highly skilled, industrious builders who make a sound like a minute circular saw. They fly into the house with a small ball of sticky mud which they quickly form into the foundation of a little tunnel. The synchronization of 'hands' and mouth which seems to produce a sticky stuff for mixing is incredible: the first step is like this [*illustration of tunnel, elevation, roof and circular entrance*]. Then the nasty bit begins, she starts coming in with anaesthetized spiders: first of all she lays her egg at the back, then a spider; every time she goes out for long she puts a neat little mud door over the hole and cuts it out again the next day when returning with more spiders for the nourishment of the hatched larvae. Eventually, when she thinks her 'fruit' has enough for survival, she seals it off and starts another tunnel beside or on top of the first. We broke one open a few days ago and found larvae in all stages of development. Obviously the spiders' legs are considered unappetizing, and had been eaten only by the most advanced larvae which had then pupated. In one tunnel we found twenty-three spiders all quite fresh, but immobilized. Other related wasps deal with caterpillars in much the same way.

I think I'd better fold up now as I don't feel too bright – probably salt deficient or just plain too hot. Fergus asks, 'Will your Ma be pleased?' I said probably, in an odd sort of way, as she will see in all this a prelude to being used to an even greater extent! We expect to go to Tamale next week for our first shopping expedition in six weeks.

Dorimon, Friday 22 June 1962

Nothing eventful here except I had another short attack of malaria – this time resistant to Nivaquine, but the doctor says we were not taking a heavy enough dose for this time of year. Two days later I went down with a nameless ailment last suffered at Kintampo, aches all over, temperature, followed by a day's deafness. Sand-fly fever or something. Now I'm feeling more or less *compos mentis* again, and no miscarriage or anything nasty – one doesn't like pumping down too many drugs at this stage.

We intend going to Kumasi and/or Accra some time in August so that I can see a gynaecologist, and get our blood groups checked: otherwise I think all can be left till I come home. We want to time our trip south so that I can get material to run up a couple of dresses *before* the need is urgent, and also before the height of the rains when one can be held up by the Volta flooding and making the roads impassable. One thing annoys me – I had some literature relevant to pregnancy which I thought was coming in the trunk. Did I leave it in the air-freight one? As far as I recall some looked useless and out-of-date, all about surgical, buttress-like bras etc., but all the same I'd like to have a rough idea what is happening each month, and when to step up the vitamin intake. My testing time will be arriving in London in late November: as far as I can see the only garment which shows *any* maternity potential is my grey suede coat, and *it* has its limits. [*It did the cover-up job right to the end when the midwife argued that I had my dates wrong because I was so slim.*] Maybe I can find something thickish in Accra where the stores keep a certain amount of woollen clothing for people who are returning to Europe in winter. Fergus enquires, 'What about the lay-out?' not having got the term quite right! Please look up Mr Boyd's address – I'll write when three months are up to make an appointment. In some ways it is quite well managed because January, February and March – even April – are pretty unbearable here, and I think that to have a new baby would just about put the finishing touch to the general discomfort.

The lamb disappeared while we were in Tamale, and I suspect it has been 'chopped' although they normally would consider that uneconomical, preferring to wait, as they said of Pangloss, 'till he get bigger'. I am told he is running with the sheep in the village, but *I* haven't seen him. I find all sheep, and even the antelope, very dull – even the little Royal antelope never showed the slightest signs of intelligence. The sheep-owner, who is a field assistant working here on tsetse control is that very rare thing among Africans, a dog lover. He has a huge dog, a medium sized one, and three pups who just live in this house. They are highly intelligent, and revive my long dormant interest in a dog as a pet. They are very amusing to watch at play: the shape is rather like some of the repulsive Dürer dogs, thin long bony legs, narrow chest and hip and, if they are fortunate, a great pot belly full of some farinaceous stodge. I'm sorry to say some of the tribes in this locality still 'chop' dog – though I get the impression it is becoming a bit non-U. Likewise teeth are still filed – or rather they are not filed, but chipped off with a chisel. This I have from a reliable indigenous source – all plus points for tearing tough meat with!

Did I tell you about the field dresser giving me the locally favoured treatment for poisoned foot? 'Oh, we make a paste of squirrels' entrails or sometimes we use donkey dung' – this with a straight face, and he clearly believes in its efficacy.

There were never any developments re the decapitated corpse, but fresh in local memory is a similar incident three years ago when the assailants were subsequently caught. The men who had put them up to the job are still living near here and respected by all it seems. They just wanted a head to bury with somebody.

We now have a baby crocodile in the dam, as well as the larger one, but with the advance of the rainy season, the grass around the edge gets so dense, and the water lilies so prolific, they are now hard to spot. We are so attached to this mud round-house that we take an interest in improving the 'garden' which is semi-wild. A few red rocks here and there, flame trees now unfortunately over, many larger trees and now we have imported some cacti from Tamale – huge pieces of prickly pear which you just stick in – at the moment they have a lovely red flower.

The house at Wa is nearly ready, only needing shelves in the kitchen and bathroom. It is transformed by having dark grey floors throughout (the choice being red 'Calendar', green ditto or grey paint) very light grey walls and white paintwork. The kitchen is no longer depressing, and I have won my battle for a new sink, so we should move in shortly and *finally* get completely out of suitcases. Fergus is getting tired of the thirteen-mile trip, and the very odd hours – 7 a.m. till 2 in the afternoon without a break – often he doesn't get a meal till mid-afternoon. Then if he wants any tennis for exercise it means returning those bumpy miles to Wa. Mostly we just have a snack at night, as preparing food by Tilley lamp with attendant insects all round is no fun. I have whittled F down to reasonable proportions again, but no doubt if left to Adda's ministrations at the end of the year he will quickly swell again.

To revert to the former theme of maternity clothes: yes, would you please try to find some sort of pattern which I can make up in wool for November. I'd like to have the patterns before going to Accra in mid. August, so that I can get material. I *would* like a fashion mag. from time to time. In the meantime I hope to go on wearing the 'playsuits' as long as possible because they are very cool and comfortable: without a belt, however, they look quite hideous, and with a bulge as well don't bear contemplation. Sometimes in the evening I wear them with my high-heeled mosquito boots – rather like the principal boy in those old pantomimes that Jimmy O'Dea brought up from Dublin.

I'm sitting on the veranda in the light of the hurricane lamp watching a toad having his evening meal of small hard-backed beetles; to date he has eaten 74, and is still going strong – now 80 – he paused for a burp at 23, 36, 46, and a slightly longer pause at 51, but he is still going strong. He has just finally given up a few short of 100!

Sunday

Another day's aches followed this time by only half a day's deafness so I hope I am on the mend. At the moment I am rather distracted by a series of blood curdling screams which are coming from the workers' compound which is about 100 yards away. I don't want to be caught watching with field glasses, and from what I can see it looks as if a dog is being washed in a bucket, but surely that couldn't account for the noise – maybe they are castrating it. All is now quiet. On feast days round here one just can't avoid nauseating sights and smells. A few days ago a benefactor came to me with a huge blue enamel bowl with lid – he removed the lid with a flourish and said he brought this just killed this morning – it was an entire cow's liver and so fresh it was positively steaming and palpitating, draped with those accessories normally removed by the butcher. After dissecting it, savouring the aroma and concocting a delicious meal of it, Fergus wondered why I seemed a bit off my food. One always wonders What Next? Would I have graciously accepted it had it been a head?

Eggs are still pouring in, sixty was the last gift – of course they are very small by our standards, mostly being from guinea fowl, and have very thick shells.

By way of rest from the exertion of writing, I have just been down to the dam with the intention of taking a picture of women with calabashes getting the evening water supply. During my twenty minute wait all comers bore two large enamel basins, a red plastic bucket and a petrol can. Now sweatily returned here, I can see four large calabashes and two hugely picturesque head-loads of wood trooping along the dam wall. Photography presents much the same frustrations wherever one goes.

Adda is ailing today, but as usual his symptoms make diagnosis difficult, so he is being treated for malaria and squits. I suspect plain food poisoning and over indulgence in Petoe. The Czech doctor – Karel – tells some incredible stories of the misinformation he receives from patients in hospital who seem to think that if they conceal the *real* cause of complaint, and just say they have 'pain small' in the head, he will treat them successfully for dysentery or gonorrhoea. [*Known as 'milking'.*]

Last week he had a woman with a huge belly who swore 'no not pregnant – last menstruation two months ago, small pains.' They couldn't hear anything, and the swelling appeared one-sided, so he decided to operate – giving first a very heavy anaesthetic. When opened up there was an almost full-term child who just survived the anaesthesia after much hard work. We suspect she wanted it aborted. The doctor was furious and confessed that he cut and sewed with some venom. To complete the week's drama there were two more murders (one semi-decapitated, the other a skeleton on a mat in the bush, but as usual safely left for five days before being reported), plus one suicide.

We have heard from three different sources that the Rosapenna Hotel has been burned down. Portnoo got a great write up by Elizabeth Nicholas in the *Sunday Times*, so I expect it will shortly be quite unbearable – likewise the Amethyst Hotel on Achill made her almost lyrical – DJ said it was scruffy and none too clean the last time she was there. I'll write when there is either something to say or a letter to reply to. Life is so uneventful here that it is difficult to write an entertaining letter.

Friday 29 June 1962

There is nothing fresh here except the weather is really quite pleasant now – we have had several days of lovely grey skies and incessant rain! The bridge just outside Dorimon has half subsided into the stream, and other bits of the road are like a deeply ploughed field so there is a possibility that we may be stuck here for a few days if the bridge finally gives way. The house in Wa is almost finished, but they haven't yet produced a gas-cooker. The wood burning stove is a very inferior small specimen and I'm definitely not going to move till we have something better to cook on.

The three pups are out of favour just now: some time yesterday they quietly chewed through some of the plastic straps on our garden chair. How they did so much damage in such a short time I don't know, but when I discovered it there wasn't a pup in sight and they were noticeably absent for some time afterwards. Now I shall have to find some canvas webbing which I think I saw somewhere in Kumasi.

We are still often called upon to minister to vague ailments and mostly dish out malaria pills. Yesterday the Agric. Dept. garden boy, who is perpetually drunk or drugged, came expecting me to do something to prevent his rapidly swelling eye from closing. 'Oh, he have small fight with his brother.' I was a little brisk about this and remarked that there was nothing to stop nature taking its course, not to mention it being better not to fight with one's brother. There are some really menacing looking types in some of the smaller isolated villages around here; they come from miles around to visit the market, sit around drinking Petoe and then drift home in a quarrelsome frame of mind.

Dorimon, Wednesday 18 July

Your two welcome letters of 1st and 9th arrived safely, though my great industry in writing to sundry friends at home has not so far brought any dividends. The Technical Information books came all right without any customs charge or query, and I am eagerly awaiting *Vogue.* I keep forgetting to ask you to include a packet of seeds *in* your letters as I don't think this will be discovered, and even if it is, the loss will not be great: parsley, fennel, leek, carrot, spinach please. F's birthday card came yesterday and I think he was 'touched' considering last year even I forgot about it.

Regarding pregnancy news-breaking – F has already mentioned it in a letter home last week, so you may expect effusions. I still haven't decided whether or not to come home, but will wait till I have seen the Czech gynaecologist in Kumasi next month when he can take sinister measurements and pronounce on the inelasticity of my ageing pelvis. Fergus charitably says I don't have any stomach muscles to strengthen. In some ways it would simplify things to stay here, but as with everything else there are numerous conflicting factors. I have been taking vitamin tablets and have just got some calcium from the local hospital.

The swallows in our bedroom suffered a tragedy with their brood right under our noses, so to speak. The eggs had all hatched, and there were three vociferous young birds growing rapidly; then one night I noticed the parent bird wasn't sitting on the nest, though the other parent was sleeping nearby apparently unmoved. The squabs were making no more noise than usual and quieted down after a while, so I thought perhaps the nest was now too full to hold Mum as well. In the middle of the night there was a bit more chirping, though nothing frenzied, a bit of adult fluttering then silence. Early in the morning we knew something had happened as there was no morning feed, and even though the parents were flying in and out to visit the nest there was no response. I think it must have been a small rodent who was responsible, because I was able to reach up with a pole and knock one headless corpse to the floor; the others must have been entirely eaten because there are no flies around the nest. [*Adda was delighted because he had been longing to demolish the nest.*] There is a lovely little bushy-tailed dormouse resident, but I don't believe they are carnivorous. During the nights one hears frequent fistlings, ganchings and flutterings as bats sweep past the mosquito net so there is quite a lot of wildlife resident in the thatch. A mosquito net gives one a remarkable illusion of security even when sleeping outside.

Simbu dog, who loves me much more than he does his master, has just passed by with a worm sticking to his behind. On inspection it is the flat variety that Mortimer had – perhaps you could send the odd pill in your letters. Of course he will get reinfected – *everyone* has worms – hook, round, tape, Ascaris, Guinea etc., but according to F the severity of one's malaise depends on the *load*. Simbu dog is a very appealing animal of high intelligence, and he is going to miss us very much when we go to Wa. I could make Simbu a handsome offer for him (5/- is the going rate), but I can see it would only lead to complications later. [*I shall regret not having done so to the end of my life.*] The local dogs have very short, rather sparse coats and I think they would perish if brought to Europe. Simbu – as we have unimaginatively named the dog – has a sharp-faced sister called Fu-fu who reminds me of Auntie Rosemary's Susan, snappy and calculating, quite unlike her brother, who is wildly jealous if she comes near me, and if I pat her he starts biting her *and* me and thrusting himself between us.

As far as I know our cat is still extant and will no doubt be offered back when the Roseis go on home leave shortly. Perhaps the Russians (now occupying all spare space in Kintampo) will take him on. We shall probably stay one night at least at Kintampo on our journey to and from Accra. We have to go fairly early because in September or October the rivers may flood and put – at the very worst – all the ferries out of action. I realized only recently that we could be completely isolated from the south if all were out of action, but this is not likely to happen though it could mean one hell of a long journey. [*Sketch map follows explaining the routes.*] F1 is the one which most frequently 'spoil', but F2 and F3 also spoil last year. F4 is mostly reliable but rather a long way round. There is another way round to the north from Wa to Tamale, but only in the dry season.

Fergus is still thumb-twiddling with no official staff, no Land Rovers to do surveys, little liaison with Brazzaville, and with an escalating sense of fury and frustration. Thus are international funds spent. Oh yes, and the start of the financial year has again been put forward three months to October, so heaven knows when funds sanctioned last year will become available.

Fergus too has had a short attack of malaria which was definitely resistant to Nivaquine as he started dosing very early and had been taking quite a heavy prophylactic dose as well. It seems that more and more drug resistant strains are appearing. As far as we know this is the first resistance to Nivaquine recorded, so F has written to his WHO colleague in Ho who is head of the Malaria Control Project there.

P.S. Could you produce a working drawing of your ironing board which would be comprehensible by a carpenter of the *meanest* intelligence?

WABRI Rest House, Accra, Thursday 16 August 1962

This is the first opportune time for writing since we left Wa last Friday on our 'holiday'. Anything less restful would be hard to imagine, but it is a change anyhow as we can have the odd meal out at the Ambassador hotel, and at an Indian restaurant which is very crummy but full of character. Unfortunately I hatched a first class filthy cold on the journey down from Kumasi and have not been enjoying food since yesterday – all sense of taste having left me. It is really maddening as one doesn't expect to get common colds out here – like the Cairo breed of virus it is a particularly vicious one: I have *never* sneezed so continuously or wetly for twenty-four hours without cease. Poor F is clearly incubating it now, but has gone out to play tennis with some vague theory about exorcizing it that way. This has got me out of one of the drinks and lunch parties which neither of us wanted to attend, but has precluded me from seeing people I *did* want to see, as well as curtailing the shopping. The search for ready-made maternity garments was quite simple – there just aren't any at all though there used to be plenty of attractive ones when one wasn't looking. I have got one *Vogue* pattern which, though not intended for the purpose, will do if cut straight at the sides and I have ordered another directly from their pattern department in UK. I got quite a nice length of German rayon which looks like wild silk and have a length I bought in Cairo as well. If I feel strong enough I shall trudge around some of many poky Indian shops and may pick up something there. Almost everything is heavily patterned but I want to avoid the cretonne covered sofa look if possible. The bulge is

only perceptible to an over enquiring eye. I did receive some pregnancy literature – I think you might have left out the one by the Glasgow health authority for working class mothers! Actually by far the best books, which I bought ages ago just in case, are by the famous Spock and Dr Winifred de Kok. But please *don't* send as I am alternately saturated, bored and assailed by waves of feeling unfitted for, and incompetent to, perform 'Nature's finest task', so I have decided to forget all about nipple-scrubbing and belly-greasing, and leave all to fate. Some of the advice is laughably inapplicable – 'Always consult your doctor before undertaking any long journeys.'

The trip down wasn't too bad as we got a grey overcast day as far as Kintampo. We risked going the short route (only five hours continuous driving) via Bamboi ferry as we had been informed that it had been fixed the previous night, and was working again after a five day cessation. We took this as gospel, not without slight misgivings, and were not in the least surprised to find 'they' were still working on it when we got there, and a queue of mammy lorries about twenty vehicles long. 'They' said ten minutes and I think we were fortunate indeed to get through at all, albeit after a two and a half hour wait. We drank beer in the local 'Love All' canteen and ate cold guinea fowl, stale bread and cucumber in our hands under the enquiring gaze of about a dozen children who probably thought they were watching classy feeding habits. We had expected to have to go on to Kumasi (another three-plus hours) the same day, but again we were fortunate in being able to stay at Kintampo. David Scott has managed to keep one house out of the clutches of the Russians – one of whom actually spoke to us, and quite courteously asked if we would like to rest at their bungalow where we had called for the keys. He was clearly relieved when we refused and scuttled off. Some of the younger ones will frat on occasions, but never if there is a group leader around, and they will even ignore people with whom they have spent the previous evening if there is a senior present. Most of the groups have a female interpreter who also provides other services. For the most part, however, they are plain dreary looking females, apart from one at Tamale who was modelled on the late Marilyn: she is said to have had a nervous breakdown and been sent south for a reindoctrination course. At Kintampo we had a delicious meal with the Roseis, and met a Belgian white father who has been living alone in one of the nearby villages for the past year; he was very interesting and never stopped talking – he obviously saves it all up for his occasional trip to semi-civilization. He has been in Africa off and on for fourteen years, and amazingly enough looks quite young *and* fit even though he insists on eating only what is locally prepared, and has only very recently been persuaded to use a water-filter.

The next day we pressed on to Kumasi accompanied by a 'funny noise' which proved to be a front wheel bearing seized up, but we got there on Saturday and stayed over till Monday morning to get the car looked at. Car maintenance is one of the major worries at Wa – ineffective servicing and the knowledge that there are no spares nearer than Kumasi – probably not even there. We saw the Grays and their infant, which is pink and not very attractive. Both seem exhausted but content with their lot.

Wa, 27 August 1962

This will be a scribbled insult if it is to catch today's post. Looking back on the morning's activities there doesn't seem a great deal to show though it is now 2.15 and F will be home for lunch shortly. Our eating hours are most unsatisfactory; we are both so ravenous at 3.00 that we stuff ourselves to the point of near immobility so are not really ready for another meal at night. Evening meals have to be ready-made earlier in the day because we still have to grope around with Aladdin or hurricane lamps.

Our trip back from Accra was uneventful though we had to come the long way round from Kintampo as we were told that a French lorry was stuck half on, half off, the ferry. On our arrival in Wa we were told it had been fixed and we could have come by the short route after all. I recall my last letter was a bit downcast owing to the heavy cold, but luckily I recovered enough to finish the shopping and even to enjoy a couple of excellent meals at the Ambassador. Hot lobster in cheese sauce late at night (a whole *huge* one each), and a very good cold buffet last Sunday. No after effects, and both slept soundly: so far I seem very fit, the only symptoms being inconvenient night rising and slight tendency to have headaches. [*The latter more likely due to malaria.*]

We went to see the Czech gynaecologist in Kumasi who was very pleasant, prodded around a bit and then announced, 'Oh, here it is'! Not a word about extreme age, in fact he didn't even ask. He has given me a note for Boyd at home as he strongly advises 'bringing forth' in UK. Not so much from the viewpoint of the mother as that of the child. So I suppose we had better make a provisional booking, particularly as we still know nothing about the future here. There is a possibility of F being sent to Togo in November to do a two-month survey and the visit to Accra, as predicted, decided precisely nothing. Two days ago he had a peremptory summons to come down again, but the notice was too short so he has not gone. More bungling, this time we suspect at the Regional Office in Brazzaville.

We eventually got the parcel cleared duty free and I am delighted with some of the small items such as soap saver, Wettex cloths and a decent pair of scissors. The sandals are a good choice and fit perfectly. The same cannot be said of the bathing suit (as regards fit), but it will come in handy next year.

We have had torrential rain every day since returning from Accra. Wa has double the NI rainfall, but also a 5–6 month dry season. Tell San she'd better get ready for babysitting the next generation.

Wa, Saturday 15 September

We moved to Wa about six weeks ago – we had to as the bridge outside Dorimon had 'spoil', and the alternative route is almost thirty miles. They began to demolish it the day we left, and said they couldn't delay work by even half an hour to let the car through; six weeks later the job is not finished, so the initial zeal was short-lived. We have been back only twice since to collect vegetables from our small garden, now almost flooded, and to pick grapefruit which are elsewhere unobtainable in the north. One of the American agricultural officers says citrus will grow quite well in the north provided the baby trees are nursed for their first three years, and given water during the dry season, but the philosophy here is, 'Why should I plant trees for another man to reap the harvest?'

Simbu dog was delighted to see us, and looking surprisingly healthy in spite of worms and loss of my additional grub. Though almost fully grown, he has got only one testicle. When F remarked on this Simbu said, 'Yes, and I would like to take it.' F has threatened to do the same to him if he carries out the threat and has done some sweet reasoning about not castrating dogs – certainly not when so large. Simbu's theory is that he will grow fine and big and not run off wenching when he risks being chopped by 'these Lobis'; this may be so, but I still think it drastic, and not calculated to make the dog any fonder of Simbu, as the methods used are crude. During labial operations to female children the operator often 'cleanses' his hands by rubbing the fingers with dust from the ground.

The portable Singer sewing machine F bought for me has been in almost constant use for curtains, letting out bras etc., and during the last fortnight I have made two very successful dresses. The fashion journals harp on about neck interest and back fullness – why be full both sides? Anyhow so far the pregnancy is advancing quite aesthetically, though I am warned the obscene bulge can develop with remarkable speed from the fifth month. Sorry to 'arp on about clothes, but it is so necessary to think ahead.

There is now a rumour that the financial year is to be shunted forward a further three months. As Fergus has now written up all he has to write, he is reduced to brushing up his French and sucking Trebor mints during office hours *and* fulminating of course. He still doesn't know if he is to go to Togo in November, but has written a personal memo to Brazzaville explaining that for personal reasons it would be convenient to know where we are likely to be at the end of the year. The nicest thing that could happen would be if he could wangle a course at Geneva.

Yesterday we went fifty miles north to a small station called Lawra, taking four members of the tennis club to play a match. The road was good except for two patches which had been under water and subsequently deeply rutted by heavy lorries. Coming back we were extremely lucky to get through at all, as it was a race against a heavy storm and we knew that five minutes of tropical rain would make it impassable. We just beat the rain at the bad patches, and then saw a huge tree in the headlights which had fallen across the road. This is not the usual time for tree casualties – mostly they come down at the end of the dry season after damage by bush fires. By a lucky chance there was no deep ditch beside the road, and we were able to drive into the bush grass around the tree just as the torrent was starting. If we had not got past we would have been stuck for the night. Rain is not to be trifled with in this season, and many people get washed away trying to cross what looks like a shallow flood. About two weeks ago a Ghanaian doctor, his English wife and two of their three children were drowned just north of Bolgatanga when their car stuck half way across a drift (sort of causeway in the road over which excess dam water flows). Apparently something had burst further up and released an exceptional flow just as they were investigating the route.

We are living in hourly fear of a visit from the new Barclay's Bank Manager. He is 22 and a resourceless, colourless young man who is finding bush life dreary after his gay social whirl in Kumasi. Pat Gray had thoughtlessly mentioned our names, so he had an excuse to introduce himself, though I don't think he feels the need of an excuse as he has been inflicting himself even more often on the Korabiewiczs whose house is more accessible. He just drops in and sits for hours, giving *nothing,* apparently unembarrassed by his non-contribution, and oblivious to noises of food preparation and table laying. His favourite time is 11.30 on Sunday, and he doesn't go till about 3. Korab says we are fortunate as with them he comes about 4.30 and stays till 10. We have tried all topics ranging through literature, politics, art, cinema, wild life, commerce and sport: the last two subjects being the only ones which elicited any contribution. He unerringly lets the subject drop flat by making a monosyllabic reply. Us – 'What sort of books are you most interested in?' Him – 'Oh, all sorts.' When he finally departs we are exhausted and just groan at each other wondering if *we* could possibly have been like that at one time. Of course he is far too young to have been sent to a station like this, and the Bank is largely to blame for sending him here. They have no idea of conditions here. That's about it at 2 p.m., the hour at which one really crumples.

[*As this marks the end of our sojourn at Dorimon I must mention two things which have strangely been omitted from the letters. My attempts to establish a more nutritious regime in the hut of Da. Da wife had one toddler to heel and an infant at breast. She was very young, but both breasts were already razor straps, and the toddler used to pass by making a hopeful grab at the swinging dugs: he exhibited all the signs of kwashiorkor – distended belly and reddish hair. Full of the missionary zeal of a new arrival, I thought to make subtle additions to their diet, but had not allowed for the numerous tribal taboos of the area. Women did not eat poultry – nor eggs if I remember rightly – fruit was not normally a part of the diet, and such vegetables as were consumed were stewed to dark mush in a pot to which more produce would be added on a daily basis. I got some US powdered milk, but found* very quickly that the mixing of this was likely to produce dire results, as water was not boiled, and feeding bottles left lying around with flies crawling over the teat.

Nor have I mentioned that our own diet consisted largely for many weeks of what could best be described as ratatouille. Red and green peppers, small round egg-plants, large deformed tomatoes, local spinach and shallots were always available, so I used to concoct a mess of this with local cooking-oil and we would eat as many of the eggs as possible. The whole liver presented a real problem as I knew if I was spotted dishing any of this out to the dogs it would be a grave insult to the donor. For many years afterwards neither of us could face either liver or ratatouille. Some staples were always available in the market, no matter how small: tinned tomato puree, Blue Band margarine, sugar, tinned sardines and matches.

Korabiewicz was one of the field medical officers under the aegis of David Scott and was David's chief bête noire. Korab's main interest was in the collection of primitive carvings for the Warsaw museum, and he would go to any lengths to procure something new. His medical qualifications often came under suspicion – his philosophy being that if two pills were good, three or four might be better. His long suffering wife was not unknown to follow him around countermanding what he had just prescribed. David expected a quarterly report from his field officers and, as Korab's command of English was basic if enthusiastic, the necessity of producing these reports hung over him continually. We all helped one way or another to keep David placated. Our first meeting with Korab was on arrival at Wa – he hailed us into his house, clad only in a loosely wrapped towel, announced that his wife was crying, the fridge was broken but we must stay for lunch. Lunch began with some sort of schnapps which had to be downed at one gulp. His physique was weird – about 6′ 8″ tall, short of body and with enormously long legs. The latter caused problems when he bought a second-hand camping van from some missionaries with the intention of transforming it for the trip he intended to take through Togo, Cameroun, Congo and round the bend to Fernando Po. His legs stuck out at the rear of the vehicle. Whether they ever made the trip I do not know. What I do know is that he had published a book of his travels down the Black Volga with his first wife who did not survive the voyage.]

Wa, Wednesday 3 October

I am beginning to feel that time is running out – mail takes an average of ten days between Kintampo and here. We still know nothing definite of our immediate future, but it looks more and more as if the project will fold up, so I think you can assume that I shall return home about the first week in December. Fergus has just arrived with more mail although nothing from you. One from Don McMullen at HQ indicates that it is not so likely there might be a job there – lack of funds again, or possibly the ever-present bugbear 'geographical distribution'. [*Too many Brits and Americans on the staff.*]

Mandahl-Barth's laboratory is after all going to materialize and he has written asking F for his terms. These are difficult to assess without an intimate knowledge of cost of living, Danish income tax etc. Whatever they are they would involve a considerable drop from our present munificent screw, but that could be suffered if there were other compensations. We have to think also that travel to and from Denmark to UK is costly, and the job is impermanent. The only other possibility is something short-term in the Republique Centrafricaine. Your grandchild has been kicking for the past fortnight – a sensation which (contrary to maudlin literature) I do not find pleasurable.

We do not intend going to Accra if we can help it before I leave in early Dec. No joy to be had there at present: 6 p.m. to 6 a.m. curfew and machine guns all over the place, not to mention the customary traffic blocks which are aggravated by various stops and inspections.

What about the worm pills for Simbu dog? He is still untampered with, but we suspect the idea is still in S's mind as he says he wants a big dog. Today we were presented with a new fridge just arrived from Takoradi – it is a vast improvement on the dented, chipped, rusty one we have had in use which doesn't even have a cold compartment for meat. Hope it works as we haven't yet had time to let the wick soak long enough.

Wa, Thursday 25 October

Your letter dated 14th was waiting here on our return from a short trip to Kumasi (tennis match v. Ashanti, visit to doctor and shopping combined). We went the whole way in one day – only stopping for a two hour break at Kintampo in the middle of the day, and strangely enough we weren't too tired even though we were up at 5 and didn't reach Kumasi till 6 in the evening.

Monday, 29 October

I hadn't the energy to get this finished in time for the post on Saturday – now it is 12.30 already, and I am in much the same state again having done the usual variety of jobs starting with dressmaking, a couple of hours' typing, roasting coffee beans (and self), and making biscuits, at the same time having constant war with the hens who are always in the kitchen. They clear up all the crumbs and leave droppings instead. Please don't ask why not shut the door – it is already so hot that one needs every breath of air.

Just yesterday we heard the news that the Cuban crisis had abated for the time being thanks to Mr K's apparent reasonableness – I'm sure it will be only a temporary lull before the next incident.

Really in some ways I am most reluctant to come home to NI as I feel it may well be the start of a separation far more protracted than we want. There is still no news re the project, apart from an informal note from Don McMullan saying the last file he had seen looked more hopeful – direct contradiction of what the Accra office thinks! Fergus is very despondent for a variety of reasons, on top of which two weeks ago he saw in the *Observer* that his best friend from NI (Walter Caughey who was working on tsetse control in Rhodesia) had been killed in a car accident at Gatwick while he and his wife plus three children, one of only two months, were coming home for their first leave in three years. His wife has had more than her dose of tragedy: a few years ago her newly qualified doctor brother got polio on the way to his first job in Australia and died on the ship; then their first child died of poisoning (it got hold of anti-malaria tablets) in Rhodesia about four years ago.

Nothing much of interest to report here: we are making rather half-hearted efforts with the garden and have some beds of sickly looking lettuce seedlings which are losing the battle against predations of hens and insects. Your parsley seed germinated very quickly, but thereafter grew so slowly that after nearly two months it is still too small to pick. One either has unqualified success and a glut for about ten days or nothing. However we have a really very healthy diet with a bit of careful management. We can mostly get local spinach, there are some cabbages and aubergines at the Dorimon garden, and we brought huge quantities of grapefruit and lemons from Kumasi.

We may go to Tamale principally to visit the dentist there as I am overdue for a visit, and F's *only* plate has a marked crack down the middle. Also I want to see if anything can be done about my ears; for the last four months I have been having gradually increasing periods of semi-deafness every day (new symptom of pregnancy so far undocumented?!). At first I thought it was a side-effect of anti-malaria tablets, but as I have since changed to another drug I don't think it is that, but probably my Eustachian tubes need a blow out. It is not painful, but very irritating and makes one feel so stupid as one has no idea how one is speaking. The curfew in Accra has been raised and all is quiet *pro tem,* but like Cuba one wonders what next.

I have just got a note from the PO saying there is a packet containing a belt and two bras; unfortunately we have a 'new broom' sweeping at the local office who thinks he should charge duty on old clothing too, so we are now waiting for official judgement from further afield before claiming the parcel. Actually I got two bras in Kumasi, but yours will come in later if I return to my original meagre proportions. I am now taking a 38B. The gynaecologist looked rather disparagingly at my milking equipment and said, 'Oh, well, many European women have breasts like *that*' – just another to add to my private list of insults dished out by shop assistants – 'Nothing as small (bosom) or big (feet) as *that.*'

Wa, Monday 5 November

I am writing from a convalescent bed after yet another bout of malaria – the worst I have had so far, and hope never to repeat. [*It was later thought to have been Blackwater fever.*] The drug which the malaria experts in the south insist is infallible has already had several recorded breaks through in Wa, and the trouble is that though there are many drugs to choose from, only two are recommended in pregnancy. I had two days of aches all over that put any 'flu pains in the negligible category, there just wasn't any position to lie in that was tolerable, then a day's apparent recovery followed by relapse into violent fever. By the time we got hold of a thermometer, of which there seems to be only one in the hospital, my temperature was 103, and had definitely been higher.

Fergus was wonderful and rallied around with a succession of ice-packs and tools for clearing up sick as everything that went down, even soda water, was liable to come up without giving time to reach a basin. Karel Sin gave me a very strong intra-muscular injection which lowered the temp. dramatically, and I am now on the second day of upward trend. It is really very worrying when there is an infant inside as one is so afraid of it coming unshipped: however it is well known their tenacity is remarkable, and even if the mother isn't eating it will manage in true parasitic manner to extract nourishment. Kofi brothers came and sat in the outside room keeping watch in the African custom, very touching, but inclined to make one feel that they are waiting for one's imminent demise as voices are suitably hushed.

Nothing much else to record – the usual gory incidents as a result of differences of opinion and injudicious use of cutlasses, the odd incident of poisoned arrow wounds, and a horrible lorry accident where a drunken driver managed to kill no fewer than nine people. Admittedly the passengers knew he was drunk, but with true Ghanaian optimism, insisted that he drive on as they were anxious to get home. It is a universal characteristic here and, no matter how often the optimism is proved unfounded, it is just the same next time. When we went to Kumasi to play the inter-regional tennis match Francis Kofi expressed complete confidence – despite F's warnings – that we were going to 'drive them into the ground'. Afterwards all sorts of explanations were offered for our defeat, apart from the obvious one that we were not as good as our opponents.

Incidentally Francis's wife has brought forth a daughter named Ajua Elizabeth; now he says he has to get one called Fergus before he stops. [He did get a son by the same wife, but rather than stop, despite his Catholicism, took a second wife.] By the way we won the battle over the bras and paid no duty!

We can't do anything about booking a definite flight for me till my travel authorization comes from Brazzaville, but I will probably leave very early next month as I don't want to get involved in the Christmas rush. One can either fly direct in nine hours by Comet from Accra overnight, or go by Viscount Safari staying one night in Las Palmas. I might do the latter just to see LP even though it is said to be most uninteresting. [I have never yet visited Las Palmas.]

We have not had any orphan animals brought to us here –

partly I suspect because everything has been chopped, but also because the other Europeans have done their best to discourage the trade. I saw a beautiful skink with an orange belly spotted with white and about 1" long in the kitchen a few days ago, this morning a little beetle pure gold-leaf covered, with an outer frill of transparent plastic. I never have the heart to kill them, and they probably lose their lustre after death in any case. I nearly walked on a snake a few days ago, but it was fully engaged lowering a toad at least three times the size of its head so it wouldn't have been able to do anything much to me. One walks cautiously for a few days after such an incident, then forgets.

Has the QUB 'Filum' Society started yet? [*I had been on the Committee.*]

Wa, 10 November 1962

Before I forget – Happy Birthday – which we shall have to celebrate when I get home. Fergus is loafing around miserably, painting a bit, switching the wireless on and off, sucking peppermints and oranges or periodically retiring to bed to escape in sleep. He says, however, that he thinks the tablets are a help: I try my best with tempting little morsels, which of course will increase the girth. [*The first of many attempts to stop smoking – final victory ca. 1971 I believe.*]

No need to worry about my European cover-up clothing. I got some beautiful pure wool suiting in a restrained shade of grey and black shadow check which exactly matches my suede jacket. With a few 'little touches' of colour it will be quite smart. My dressmaking is vastly improved, and I can now knock up a dress (with collar) in a couple of days. I enjoy it more now that I have time: previously it always seemed to be squeezed in after work when one's brain was far from alert. [*My memories are of crawling around on cement 'Calendared' floors'* with sore knees, and of spending hours trying to iron bits of fabric with an almost uncontrollable charcoal iron.*]

Tomorrow we are supposed to go to Tamale, but as there is no battery in the car and no acid in Wa, this looks unlikely. I have written to Air France now my travel permit has come, making a provisional booking on or soon after 5 December. Still nothing

---

*   A word derived from Adda's inability to pronounce Cardinal which never failed to appear on his shopping list.

from Brazzaville re. F's future. Mandahl-Barth is offering a salary about a quarter of F's present one – so that doesn't look too promising.

I had a letter from Stanley [*first cousin of my mother, and stockbroker in London*]. I gather you had not divulged our little secret – either that or he didn't like to mention such a delicate matter. I have sent him a three-page epistle, and said I will ring when in London, though I feel it is no great treat for him to come all the way from Reigate for one day. [*He did, and I remember him with much affection.*]

October *Vogue* came too – more decadent than ever – but I enjoy it nevertheless, as it is so remote from life here. My one smartish dress is nylon though it looks like silk. It slithered and crept and frayed, and every inch had to be sewn over paper or it gathered in the machine. It also melts into strands like hot sugar if one isn't very careful with the iron. To cool a charcoal iron you plunge it into cold water and hope for the best! You will be surprised to learn that it is a soft shade of *mud* with blue-grey flowers at spaced and uneconomical intervals, requiring careful alignment. It does look quite nice, but F still hankers after a nice tube!

In the last letter I think I said I was recovering from malaria, but I spoke too soon: altogether I spent eight days sick with splitting headache, and inexplicably varying temperature. Now I seem really better, though stuffed to the gills with pills, some of which have to be taken in the middle of the night *after* a light snack – you can imagine how delightful a light snack is at 3 a.m.

I am assured that it doesn't do the parasite any harm even if Mum has a high temp., and that all drugs taken have been recommended for pregnant women, so I hope it will have no ill-effects. It would have been even more anxiety provoking if it had been in the first three months. The hospital here goes from bad to worse – or so Karel says. He has no anaesthetics left now apart from one bottle of ether which he is keeping in case of emergency. He has not got a single dependable nurse or ward orderly, and says if he wants things sterilized properly he has to do it himself as well as little things like changing compresses.

P.S. I want to contaminate your house with a hired 'telly' to shorten my last evenings of pregnancy – you needn't look at it! [*This was the hey-day of* That Was the Week that Was *and* Z Cars *– during an episode of which I went into labour. My mother soon became a TV addict.*] Oh, I forgot to mention Janet, and don't really know what to say: one just does *not* encounter three people one seriously considers marrying inside two years. When I left in March her mother had made her promise not ever to subject the family to such an ordeal again. So you can send congratulations, with an element of reserve, which I am sure will be understood.

Accra, 3 December

We arrived here yesterday having left Wa on Friday morning and stayed one night there. Wa–Kumasi really is a deadly trip – eight hours driving with about three-quarters of an hour for lunch. This time we went via Wenchi rather than Kintampo, as it is thirty miles shorter, but it is not worth the difference as the road is laterite all the way, and the last fifty miles lumpy and tortuous.

I saw the Czech gynaecologist again and he seems quite satisfied, if a little disappointed, that I had nothing to complain of. I am still remarkably unobtrusive for seven months. Fergus says it can't be much bigger than a frog.

This morning we went to see Air France to settle the flight finally. They had made a provisional booking via Las Palmas, Lisbon, but when I discovered that each part of the journey lasted ten hours, and that one arrived in London late at night, I decided against, and booked instead an overnight flight by BOAC Comet *not* Ghana Airways. I don't know how long I'll stay in London as I know the streets and shops will be crowded, but I might as well see the decorations, do a little shopping, and possibly meet Stanley. F bought me a crocodile skin for our wedding anniversary, and I want to see what can be done about having it made into shoes, bag etc. There are two specialist firms which advertise in the *Sunday Times*, but I'm quite prepared for them to pour scorn on it. [*They <u>had</u> reservations, but condescended to make a handbag which I still have – it is too small, because I economized, and ordered one which cost a mere £25, rather than the larger model at £35.*]

Last night we had dinner with friends and the fellow guests were Dr Alan Nun-May (now working, after his release, at the University), and his Austrian wife. Both were good company and easy to get on with, though there was that usual feeling of constraint when some subjects provoke evasive responses. From sundry subtle indications I should not be surprised if he is still travelling, and probably part of the spreading organization over here.

[*I am almost certain that it was during this short period we went to a reception held at Achimota by Conor Cruise O'Brien, who was then Vice-Chancellor. We enjoyed his company, and that of his new wife – there having been a marital upheaval which had provoked raised eyebrows in provincial Ireland.*

The cultural shock of Knightsbridge with all its extravagant illuminations was considerable, but I braved Harrods, and bought one of the first Kruschev/Yeltsin type fur hats to hit the UK market to top off the maternity suit. I also visited Lorna Gore-Brown* who had worked with Fergus in N. Rhodesia on one of WHO's early Health and Nutrition Schemes at Fort Rosebery. and who could sympathize with my sense of temporary disorientation.]

*Lorna, author of *The Africa House*, died in 2003.

1963

THE WINTER OF early 1963 broke records for cold towards the start of February, but before that I remember many lovely sunny days on which I went with my mother for short trips down the Ards peninsula to watch the varied birdlife. In particular I recall a slate-blue sky against which a huge flock of lapwings wheeled and turned opposite the entrance to the Mountstewart estate, their white undersides gleaming in the watery sunlight from time to time. When I finally went into labour – three weeks late – it was a particularly unpleasant night, and I had stuck the pains till the end of a sinister episode of Z Cars in which two innocent motorists gave a lift to a young man who produced a gun and forced them to drive to his destination. Tame stuff by today's standards, but gripping at the time. My mother drove me through a heavy snow-fall to the hospital where Katharine was delivered on St Valentine's day.

Fergus was on a protracted tour in Gabon/Cameroun and Congo Brazzaville. His letters give a vivid idea of how similar life was 'up-country' then as now, although at the time the District Commissioner, irrespective of race or nationality, reigned supreme at the small stations, followed in influence by the Mission Fathers.

Giving birth to one's first child in the absence of the father is a less joyous event than it would be in normal circumstances, no matter how loving and concerned other relatives may be. It proved, however, less stressful than the next birth, exactly a year and eleven days later, for which I decided that I would not be feeble 'like the rest of those European wives' and would 'bring forth' in Ghana rather than return to Northern Ireland again.

Fergus came home on leave two months after Katharine's birth, and we managed to snatch a few glorious days in Donegal, as well *as a week-end in London during which I discovered to my horror that I was again pregnant. We met James Pope-Hennessy and Lorna Gore-Brown, went to Covent Garden and the Tate Gallery, and prepared ourselves for a future life totally different from our hitherto more or less carefree one. It seems I did not fly out to Ghana till early August, which is when the next batch of letters begins.*

Accra, Monday 12 August

You will be relieved to hear that all went – if not entirely trouble-free – well, and we were met by Fergus early on Sunday morning. He never got the letter I sent to Brazzaville, but he had one waiting at Accra which mentioned the date of our arrival. The journey would not have been at all bad, had it not been for the episode of the rose-hip syrup which was with us stickily all the way to Accra, and is still occasionally to be found lurking in unexpected crevices. I'm sorry we were rushed off so swiftly, but it didn't allow any time for tears. The plane to London was fully booked and I was the last person on; there wasn't room for the cot next to me, so Katharine had to sit on my knee the whole time. She was very good dispensing smiles all round, and I had a forbearing neighbour who didn't flinch – visibly anyway – even when she upset the supper tray on the floor with one of her smart upper cuts. Luckily there wasn't any liquid on it to join the gradually spreading snake of rose-hip which ran down the centre aisle. When the staff had time they took the bag down to the lav. and inspected the inside. They reported that it was all over the paddi pads and Kleenex, but they were able to give me two small packets of pads to replace them. At London I had a session in the lav. removing splintered glass and washing out my jewel case, glasses etc., not to mention re-arranging the cot, all of whose blankets were contaminated. Katharine threw a scene in the lavatory, but quieted down after a while and eventually went to sleep at 10.30 as we were boarding the Accra plane whose engines were in full cry by that time. Bookings seem to have been most uneconomically empty – probably no more than forty passengers altogether, and I could have as many seats as I wanted which makes all the difference. Anything more awful than a long flight with all seats full and no room to spread I can't imagine. [*I was to experience many such in subsequent years.*] Sleep evaded me for most of the night: I had *just* dropped off in an upright position when the stewardess boomed in my face, 'Wouldn't Madam like to lie down?' After that I remained restless. Katharine, notwithstanding awful vibration on the floor where she was, and icy air-conditioning, slept right through. All the baggage arrived safely and Fergus had managed to get the WABRI guest house for us (West African Building Research Institute), so that was a relief because the fridge is reliable, there are fans, mosquito proofing and a factotum to provide tea and breakfast. Adda is back though he doesn't have much to do when we stay here, but he is useful for small jobs of washing in the early morning after which I mostly tell him to buzz off. Katharine has shown no signs of dismay at black faces, dispensing her usual charm. We took her to lunch at the Ambassador Hotel yesterday and survived the ordeal; she is not quite herself in that she is demanding much more food instead of losing appetite as I expected, and there has been a tendency to whine at times when one is convinced she couldn't be hungry – only to find in the end that she is. She lowered a whole bottle of ice-cold milk at the Ambassador only two hours after a half bottle here which I thought would ensure peace while *we* ate – just as well I brought it. We are due to go out to dinner tomorrow and out for tennis this afternoon, so I can only pray for good behaviour.

Adda brought the glad tidings that all ferries were flooded in the north again, so I can foresee trouble. I didn't even have time to thank you for enduring us so long because of the excess baggage crisis; however we do so now sincerely.

Accra, Monday 19 August

I hope you got my short letter telling of our safe arrival. Fergus was very lucky to have got out of Brazzaville before the violence began – it broke out a few days after he left. He imported a filthy cold which has lasted over a week and which I *thought* I was escaping, but now fear the worst. Judging by occasional coughs and sneezes the baby has, or has had, a minor version; according to Spock they seldom get a severe one during the first year. She developed prickly heat only two days after arrival, but it has disappeared again, either due to cooler weather or to a powder I applied. Accra is relatively pleasant at this time of year – temperatures often remaining below 80 and with quite a lot of grey sky to shield the glare.

Yesterday we went down to the beach for a few hours; it was

one of the less popular ones, but only because the shore is largely rocky and bathing unsafe, which is a bit tantalizing. However we enjoyed lying in the sun from which I protected Katharine too much so that she didn't get any colour, and myself not enough so that I have a very tender back.

Our stay here has become protracted on account of the many small things which have to be attended to: car servicing, stores for Wa, packing cases and arranging transport for same, driving licence etc. Shopping is complicated with the infant, but we manage somehow, and all the Ghanaian girls are only too pleased to carry and admire her. We have now had her out to lunch at the Ambassador three times and have not been disgraced; she sits much more steadily now, and doesn't need wedging into the cot any more. We have also been out to dinner a couple of times and had no trouble till we got home again when she woke up and wouldn't go off again for ages. We will try one more evening sortie, but if there is trouble again shall confine ourselves to the middle of the day. Fergus demands why can't she just lie naked on the rug? So I am trying this experiment and have counted three pools in about half an hour. Karel came up from Cape Coast a few days ago and says Katharine is more advanced than their Karel who can't yet sit, and has no teeth – with true continental tactlessness, he says, 'I think your methods must be better than ours.' I can only hope he doesn't repeat these sentiments to his dear Marta – the child specialist by profession!

Interval for dressing hideous ulcer on leg of Adda's son Yambah who has joined us during his school holidays. The independence of children here is striking: he sets out from their village, which is in the extreme north-east, with a friend of the same age seemingly with no doubts that he will be able to trace his dad in Accra which he has never visited before. It is like a child leaving John O'Groats for London. Anyhow the bush telegraph operates even down here, and shortly after his arrival Adda got a message saying his son was staying at the army camp and please collect him. We might just as easily have gone to Cape Coast where no doubt he would also have caught up with us. I happened to glance at his leg today when he came to 'greet' me and saw this volcanic crater – 'Oh, a stone hit it about a month ago.' I then 'gave off' in true NI form, as both he and his dad should know better than to leave such a thing open, and painted a vivid picture of gangrenous limbs dropping off through such neglect – 'Oh yes, I have seen in the north.'

I'll bet he has. There is (needless to say) a plan behind his visit, not just devotion to us. He has a list of expensive items to be purchased for his entry to the Catholic secondary school at Navrongo, and clearly our assistance is expected. [*See Appendix*]

Tuesday: Last night I stayed here and nursed my throat while Fergus went to dinner with the Roseis. This morning I feel much better, but expect the next stage will be sniffles. Katharine took both soup and chocolate pud. from a small cup yesterday and is much more co-operative and *slightly* less messy than with a spoon.

Kintampo, Thursday 29 August

We seem to be marooned here in transit for Wa. The lorry with Adda and quantities of stores, grapefruit, suitcases etc. left here at 5 this morning in torrential rain; since then it hasn't ceased and we are afraid the roads will be quagmire, and that we might get bogged down on the way. F is down in the village getting petrol and we will decide when he gets back whether or not to risk going on. The danger of waiting is the roads and rain may worsen and the ferry close through river flooding. What one never can tell is whether the rain is really widespread or purely local. Sometimes it is dry *at* the ferry, but the river is in flood owing to torrents much higher up. Anyhow we have enough stores with us for a couple of days, the fridge is working and there is a good caretaker in the rest house (the bungalow next to our old one) so things could be much worse.

Wa, Sunday 1 September

One loses all sense of time here, so I've had to do lengthy calculations to get the day and date. We didn't go on last Thursday, but stayed an extra night and left the next morning at 8.30 which is late for Africa, but good going with an infant. Katharine's timetable gets reorganized to suit our travel, and has worked very well so far as she is hungry earlier in the morning. When in the car she sleeps far more than usual and will go for six hours with only a sip of rose hip. She gets slightly disrupted the next day, usually making up for any loss she may 'imagine', but it really has been remarkably painless so far.

I'd better begin from when we left Accra. Our stay there was enjoyable but exhausting, involving much shopping and subsequent careful packing of all in crates for the long journey. The Min. of Health gave us a huge lorry for the purpose which accompanied us to Elmina for the week-end taking also Adda, Yambah (complete with vile tropical ulcer now responding to treatment arranged by us). We were given an empty house, lent cups etc. for breakfast, but otherwise fed very kindly by the Sins who seemed delighted to see us. Apart from slight contretemps with the water supply which ceased overnight all went well; a visiting lecturer in engineering from Kumasi spent a sweaty morning blowing through the system both orally and with the aid of our car pump without avail, but eventually fixed things after climbing up into the outside tank where he spent about half an hour up to the waist clearing out the silt, dead geckos etc. and expending much unnecessary energy cursing local 'plumbers'. We had a couple of very pleasant days on the beach, handed over the polio vaccine and disparaged (in private) young Karel, who is a stolid, unresponsive lump without teeth (K has two now) and unable to sit up!

Last Monday we came up to Kumasi and were lucky enough to get one of the rest houses on the University campus. They are infinitely better than the government catering one where we used to stay, but one has to do one's own cooking – no real disadvantage as the catering house meals are mostly nauseating. One does, however, miss the constant chittering, bartering of Hausa men and gaping at the new visitors which one has at the more central venue. The new hotel – very much needed – is due to open in October and if it compares favourably with the Ambassador will be a great amenity. Kumasi is much as before: the Grays are on leave, the shops are better stocked apart from no butter, but there are many unfortunate middle-school leavers who can't find jobs plaguing one to buy: nylon socks, Biro pens, Drummer lavatory freshener (which has 'took on' in a great way), oranges, grapefruit, razor blades etc., so that one's patience is sorely tried and sometimes sinks so low as to tell a black brother to bugger off.

The long journey from Kintampo went off smoothly enough: we had to go the very long way round through Damongo as the Bamboi ferry is out of action. We reached Buipe ferry about 10, but had to wait ages as the river is higher than we had ever seen it, and the crossing consequently takes longer. Katharine behaved very well sitting in her cot on the bonnet of the car, and holding court to a large audience to whom a white baby was a novelty. We stopped at Damongo rest house for lunch and finally reached

Wa about 4 p.m. It was fortunate that Adda had preceded us as he had been able to do some minor organizing; even so the first two or three days were exhausting chaos.

Delay in finishing this letter has been due in main to the knowledge that the post was unlikely to go out as we are at present cut off from Tamale by flooding of the northern ferry. However I hear that some mail is going via Kintampo, so I'll hope for the best. So far no letters from you have reached here, and I wonder if you sent one to Ankaful which went astray. Fergus's boss in Geneva has threatened a one-day visit to Wa at the beginning of October. He is one of the more congenial ones at HQ, but clearly has no idea of the distances involved as he proposes arriving at Tamale at 11 a.m. by plane (Fergus will have to go all the way to meet him), proceeding to Wa the same day, staying here the next day, and returning to Accra from Tamale the day after by a plane which may well leave at crack of dawn. All this will involve about 800 miles of driving for Fergus on top of which it is likely that the ferry south of Tamale will still be *hors de combat* if the present torrents continue. The Bilharziasis Advisory Team are also coming later on in October which will involve more fetch and carry, plus providing full board and lodging.

Great progress has been made, thanks to the persuasive powers of Fergus, on project houses for junior and senior staff as well as a rest house, and we hope to move into the nicest one shortly. It will be a vast improvement on our present shack in that there will be good mosquito proofing throughout, PVC floors (though they haven't heard of silicone sealers yet), and should be a bit better ventilated. It is also wired and has fans ready for the arrival of a generator. [*If I recall correctly the generator was finally in action only a few months before we left in 1965!*]

The man in charge of building has been most co-operative, having made a number of alterations and additions speedily. The plan of the house is reasonable but, as usual, the workmanship deplorable, but one just tries not to look. Unfortunately some bod. not over endowed with taste had chosen the floor tiles and laid them before we came: they could, however, be a great deal worse and at least are not gaudy, but have a fancy pattern around the edges, without which they would have been better. We have asked them to build a low wall around the porch and veranda which will enable us to confine the baby, and should be almost snake-proof. [*It was not.*] The walkie-pen has come into its own now and

Katharine spends quite a lot of time in it. Progress with solids is still minimal. One gets encouragement one day, then flat refusal the next, but I suppose she will survive.

Wa, Friday 6 September

Last night was horribly interrupted: despite our going to bed about 8 to catch up on lost sleep, there is some unidentifiable thing in the bedroom which is giving me asthma, itching eyes etc., such as I had at Kintampo, but not before at Wa. At first blame was put on the rug which had been stored in your blanket box which no doubt has been moth-proofed. This was banished, but there was no improvement. Then we decided it was the sheets which had been stored beside it – banish and wash sheets – still no improvement. I don't see how it can be the pillows or mattresses which are the same as last year. The only thing I think possible is that some well-meaning person has sprayed bedroom and bedding with a residual insecticide. Anyhow, if it is not the asthma it is Katharine needing to be turned over, or the windows having to be shut against violent storm. There are three bedrooms in the new house, so we shall be able to put the baby in another room and confine her accessories to one area which will be a 'good thing'. There was no sign of the trunk which went by sea when we left Accra, so we may have to wait ages. Naturally I find I put all the Wettex cloths in it, and we are using one which has had Adda's treatment, which almost equals San's and is now in shreds. Of all the things I brought, I think the Nobactin bottle steriliser has proved most useful for keeping bottles clean where boiling is inconvenient or impossible. If you are sending *Vogue* or *House & Garden* you might stick a carton down the middle.

Just caught Adda conscientiously boiling the tea-towels in with the nappies. All is peace and joy so far, but no doubt we will have our quarterly dust-up soon.

Wa, 19 September

Both your letters (the one forwarded from Ankaful and the other sent here), came by the same delivery. The mails have been even more unreliable owing to disrupted communications; the record being one from Accra which took a month. There seems to be a subtle change taking place in the weather and we have had several days without a downpour, but rumour has it that the river is even higher than before, and that when coming from Kumasi one has to cross a bridge which is already under water. That can be really dangerous: if you remember, a local doctor and his family were drowned last year crossing under such circumstances. We haven't heard any more about the proposed visit of F's Geneva boss; if he only wants to talk and not in particular to see the project area, F will go to Kumasi to meet him. If the Czech doctor has returned from leave I will go too, as I suppose I should be looked at: if not I'll just stay here with K. I think you would see a great change in the latter; she has been sitting without support now for about two weeks, has two large teeth and is generally taking even more notice of things (solid food excepted!). We try various ruses and get a certain amount down, but there is never any real enthusiasm, and I'm sure I get far more rusk, cereal etc., on the 'one for me one for you' basis, than is good for me.

We are going through many frustrations over the project houses here. The Ghana National Construction Corporation is raking in £31,000 for building three houses, a rest house and some junior staff quarters. They are not, or should not be, a profit making concern so considering that, not to mention the deplorable standard of work, the price is high enough. However the bungalow, even if imperfect, will be a great improvement on what we have had. Daniel's description of the house: 'Oh Madam, it is very splendid' – Francis, 'As befits your status.'

Tomorrow is National Founder's Day and there has been intense activity on the football ground opposite all week. A bunting embellished pavilion has been erected for the DC and other important persons, a Freedom and Justice arch has been put up, and the police band has been practising their repertoire of old colonial tunes – 'A hunting we will go' among them. There will also be local music and – I hope – some dancing, otherwise it will probably be a rather desultory marchpast of local government servants.

Tuesday 23 September

Founders' Day was much as expected: I put in a nominal appearance at 8 a.m., but retreated after half an hour owing to heat and impending bath and meal for K. Fergus survived till 10.30 which was pretty good as the dais for important persons, while lavishly decorated, didn't provide any shade at all, and faced directly into the sun. It was the usual march and parade-past of official servants and services, MFU Land Rovers, Agric. Dept. and Pest Control sanitary squad (bucket collectors) etc., a little dancing which I missed and a few heavily caparisoned horses.

This morning's mail brought a welcome letter from you. So far no papers or mags have come either from you or Accra, and we haven't seen a Sunday paper for about five weeks. It is hard to believe our house in NI is going up so quickly, I only hope the builder isn't seizing the chance of the architect being on holiday for covering up things [*he was*]. I'm dying to know if it proves as spacious as envisaged. It would be preferable from the point of view of making the sites look less cramped not to have a fence between our two 'estates', but on the other hand, if we were to get awful tenants at some time in the future you might not like that idea!

By the way as the sea trunk has not appeared and may never do so, the Wettex situation is desperate, so please send some inside a magazine. I now use muslin nappies folded to Paddi-pad shape and lined with Kleenex – this is very successful as they are cooler than the towelling kind which are also too bulky. Of *course* I have only twelve muslin but numerous towelling ones – that is the sort of thing one is bound to discover on arrival. Maybe you could send some as they weigh very little.

Sorry to hear about Stanley [*stockbroker cousin of my mother who lived in Reigate and had developed cataracts*] – will try to find time to write to him. I find rather less time for correspondence as K though quiet and undemanding most of the time does have to be bathed, bottled and have feeds made up in addition to the usual chores of cooking, bread making etc. I'm looking forward to moving house as the new one is properly mosquito proofed, while here we are eaten alive every evening. Have you broken the news to various? You made no comments – or are you ashamed of the indecent interval! [*Pregnant again and baby due in February '64.*]

San's pink rabbit is still in favour, but of the soft toys the favourite is an unhygienic, unwashable equally pink dog made in Ghana and presented by the Roseis. I discovered that K has two large front teeth coming through – somehow they weren't quite where I'd been expecting them though that may sound odd. Fergus is a great success with her, horsing and generally 'over stimulating baby' every day till she is nearly paralysed with mirth.

I'm really getting to the last part now. Unreliable or non-existent communications are complicating our existence in every way. We had pretty well decided that F should go on his own to Kumasi to meet Dr Ansari when we heard there is no petrol in town, also no rest house available in Kumasi at the University to which he wrote ages ago. Now he has to wire the Govt. rest house and is unlikely to get a reply (if at all) before he has to leave on Monday. Apart from all this he doesn't know if the Accra office got his letter recommending that Dr A should go to Kumasi instead of Tamale! A camp bed on the MFU office floor is hardly suitable for important guests, but that may well be how it ends. Haven't yet finished my film, but will send results when available. [*Black and white processing was much more difficult in the north than it had been in the relatively sophisticated laboratory at Kintampo, and evidenced by the poor quality of the pictures I sent from Wa.*]

Wa, 20 October

This letter is long overdue, but somehow I just haven't had either time or energy available previously. Last time I wrote Fergus was due to go south: he set out at 7 a.m. and returned frustrated about 4 p.m. having gone well over a hundred miles only to find a large part of the road washed completely away, a long queue of lorries each side and one up to its middle down the hole: had it been slightly lower he says one could have driven over the roof. About twenty miles from Wa on the return journey he ran out of petrol, but was lucky enough to be able to send an SOS to MFU for a Land Rover via a passing truck. Nobody bothered doing anything about the hole for ages as the road workers in the vicinity were going slower than usual owing to not having been paid. For the next few days sundry conflicting reports came in about (a) the hole; (b) the functioning or otherwise of the ferries. Four days later (by which time F would have been in Accra had all gone well) we had a telegram saying Ansari's visit was postponed! The rains are definitely on the wane now, but all roads are in a dreadful state and will probably remain so for some time. However, we intend to go to Kumasi early in November if we can get accommodation which is always doubtful. We may (or possibly F alone) go on to Accra again depending on accommodation. We used to go on spec. but dare not do so now with a baby.

Last Monday we moved to our new bungalow which is an improvement on any we have had previously. At last we have completely unpacked and are no longer devoured by mosquitoes every night. The bedrooms are cooler and K can have one to herself. We have a larger fridge which is an improvement, apart from eating huge quantities of kerosene (at present unobtainable in Wa). Many staples which can normally be got in the village – flour, tea, petrol – have run out owing to the state of communications and petrol; when it does come, is being sold at black market prices.

About ten days before we moved Fergus employed a lame duck aged about 13 who came and told a most convincing and pathetic tale of coming from his village about twenty miles away because his father and mother 'have both die recently and I have only sisters who can't feed me. The people in our village are very bad.' He had such a frank and open countenance that even the experienced and hard Adda was taken in to the extent of allowing him to sleep in his quarters. He did a little daily grass cutting in return for 'chop' money, and of course I dished out drinks of milk and bananas to subsidise his meagre diet. One part of the tale was that there was an uncle who might look after him, but that a new school uniform was required if he was to return to school and that uncle couldn't afford it. Fergus made enquiries which weren't very fruitful, and cross-questioned the mannerly child who looked hurt at the suggestion that he might be lying; in the end the agreement was that we should buy his school uniform in return for small services till term began. Then one morning a 'nephew' of Adda happened to see the boy and enquired what he was doing on our premises as he had absconded from school last January taking with him the £4 his father (alive) had given him to purchase a uniform, and had apparently been living on the money since then. It transpires that all – or almost all – was lies from start to finish and Adda found one of our coffee spoons in his box, while another had already disappeared – presumably sold. He was carted down to the MFU office and further grilled before being put in the care of the Social Welfare officer till his father should come and claim him. Tears came and F momentarily felt a brute till Francis told him the boy was loudly complaining that F had promised him 30/- and had failed to pay up! So that is the last time we are going to fall for a hard luck story – at least that's what we always say.

Monday 21 October

The house is swarming with voluble and inefficient workmen each with his even less efficient apprentice in tow. The only ones worth anything are the MFU carpenter who is here undoing or altering various idiocies perpetrated by the GNCC, and the PVC tiler who does quite a neat job. Plastic tops are unheard of here, so we got them to tile a number of benches and draining boards.

I wrote to the architect immediately when I heard from you – not making any accusations – but asking when we might expect the first of his monthly progress reports, and confirming the verbal instruction that no tender was to be accepted till we had seen them. There has not been time for a reply, and I certainly never really expected a monthly report, knowing architects as I do. [*This one was outstandingly negligent to an extent that in the end I refused to pay his fees in full.*]

Infant No. 2, about whom you enquire, is giving no trouble apart from the usual stirrings, but I really *must* get looked at in case it is inside out or upside down or something. I don't think you need worry about malaria so much now that we are not being so badly bitten, and in any case we have increased our prophylactic dose.

No. 1 seems flourishing and is now menacingly mobile in the Walkie pen: it is really a great invention and keeps her quiet for hours. She shoots all over the house and pulls mats off tables, pans off low shelves and generally leaves a trail of litter which some sweating adult has to pick up. My only criticism is that I think it has delayed her crawling: she gets in the right shape but still doesn't move, so rapidly gets impatient with her immobility. She now makes lots of noises of the da, ma and ba variety, plus a repertoire of raspberries and can imitate if one gives an example. Solid food is still a problem: she will take banana and a nasty mixture of Farex, glucose, Horlicks and milk, but there is seldom any real enthusiasm, and she is inclined to let her attention wander to Dad, her toes or just flies on the netting. On the other hand she still seems satisfied with four meals at 4-hourly intervals, and can sleep through till 5 or 6, though she is often restless a couple of times during the night – probably more teeth. Her only *completely* undisturbed night from 6.30 p.m. till 6 a.m. was through one of the most violent electric storms of the season! We were both cowering under the bedclothes thinking of all the nice corrugated sheeting on the house, and the absence of a lightning conductor. However she does sleep better in the day, and has a nap both a.m. and p.m., though the latter is usually short.

Fergus and I have just been on a tour of the other two houses and the rest house. We are now depressed and irritated at various further follies which we have not forestalled. Hatches which do not slide, cupboards and shelves up crooked though they have spirit levels on site, sinks set sloping into the wall with crude brackets and wedges of wood or plaster to fill up the gap. I haven't yet investigated but I'll bet the bracket is nailed to a cone-shaped wooden plug which will be guaranteed to pull out.

[*Some time later Katharine narrowly escaped death when our own sink, which was full of hot water, crashed to the floor without warning.*]

I rescued our newly arrived Swedish water heater from the ministrations of the plumber and his two mates today. They had it spread all over the floor and were clearly completely at a loss, aimlessly fitting one unlikely part into another and then hopefully reversing them. I read the instructions which were *not* clear even to a moderate IQ, and said that as we had no electricity and were unlikely to have any for some time, I had rather they postponed the job. They all looked relieved. We can get one of the Swiss engineers up from Kumasi when the generator comes, and he can supervise all. I couldn't bear to think of such a good piece of equipment being hammed up. It is super up-to-date, and the instructions were full of ominous warnings about correct adjustment of reducers, thermostats etc.

We have been toying with the idea of asking Dorothy to come out in February to lend a hand with K when I'm in hospital. She is one of the few people who don't get on my nerves (though one never knows till one lives for a while in the same house), is good with children and young and fit enough to stand the climate which will be at its grimmest then. It would be no rest cure, but she might enjoy the experience, and if we paid her fare considering F gets 80 per cent of my confinement expenses, it wouldn't really be such an expensive baby. We haven't decided yet, and must cogitate a bit more. One copy of *House & Garden* came, but so far no *Vogues*. I'd like a *Vogue* Pattern Book too please. I'm still doing the pregnancy quite elegantly – a *soupçon* thicker this time, but nothing obscene.

You will be glad to know that F has decided he has had about enough of Afrique [*first duty tour was in 1952*], and will take any opportunity that offers after this tour. Unfortunately the Mandahl-Barth laboratory has been refused planning approval by the same Ministry that had approved some of the earlier stages, so he is at an *impasse*. F is making enquiries about study leave for a course in Epidemiology from which he feels he would profit, but that would be quite some time ahead and in an as yet undetermined country. [*We were to spend the academic year 1965–66 at the Harvard School of Public Health in Boston.*]

Tuesday

Torrential rain nearly all morning and F is at home writing his speech on the United Nations, its functions etc., which has to be delivered to a local audience of teachers etc. on United Nations Day. We have had no mail for ages and I don't think any has gone out, but last night we heard that the Kintampo-Tamale road was again open so perhaps there will be an inflow soon. You will be glad to know that I have found three Wettexes in one of our hitherto unpacked cases. Would like a *plain* imitation tortoiseshell comb please – not for combing but for keeping roll at back in place.

Kumasi, Thursday 7 November

One loses all sense of time out here and I'm not sure if this is either Thursday or even the 7th. We left Wa as early as poss. on Monday which was not early (9.30). One has to get food ready for all, de-frost fridge at the last minute, get infant stuffed full enough to last several hours, or at least until there is time to reach a rest-house – in this case it was at Damongo, something over a hundred miles away. Minimal work has been done on the road apart from the deposition of large heaps of laterite preferably sited on the blind corners, and at one place we had to wade across quite a wide stretch to make sure it was passable by car. A lorry had just come the other way and was voluble with assurances that it was OK, but past experience has led us to suspect African optimism, so we always check or double check before taking any risk. Needless to say the passage of heavy lorries helps to worsen the surface, and as the workers have presumably still not been paid, there is little hope of early improvement.

Accra, Monday 10 November

We reached Kintampo only just before dark and had a minor crisis there as the rest-house keeper was on leave: this did not mean that he was absent – just not working. During his holiday all equipment etc. is unnecessarily locked away by those in charge at the top, so there ensued a hunt for the man who had the key to the store. There is a universal mania here for locking things with a commonplace small key, certainly not effectively enough to keep out any determined thief, but enough to cause great frustration to the guest who wants nothing more than to get inside. In this case some bright spark had locked the door between the kitchen and the dining room and 'mislaid' the key which he swore he'd left in the lock. After trying every key in the house we eventually got one to fit; this sort of episode is a bit last-strawish at the end of an eight hour drive.

I forgot to mention that K had chosen this time to have her first attack of squits, but she was considerate enough to choose times when we were within reach of water or a rest-house to explode. She had it for a few days before we left and I was getting quite worried as the Ghanaian doctor didn't advise anything constructive, and Spock was alarming on the subject; remarking that in the 'rare case of a baby being hundreds of miles from a hospital rush him there at the first signs of blood or mucus.' This was the case, though very little. Mrs Grant at Kintampo [*her husband also a doctor had taken charge of the MFU on Dr Scott's retirement*] was much more constructive and gave me some carrot extract which cleared it up within thirty hours or so, much to our relief.

On Tuesday we travelled on to Kumasi and found even that road, normally good, was purgatory. We stayed at the Govt. Catering Rest House once more and did not leave till Saturday a.m. as the car had developed a clutch ailment, was consuming excessive quantities of petrol and not pulling well. Katharine proved a great attraction for the numerous children of the rest-house factotums who all have adjacent quarters. She sat out on the small veranda in the walkie-pen and held court. I came out one morning to find a snotty-nosed child offering her a dead chicken which he was dangling by one leg – whether as chop or a toy I don't know. If the former no doubt it would have been accepted: she likes lav. paper, Kleenex (preferably used), shoe laces and anything adhering to the waste bucket in the kitchen. That was how I discovered she could stand with the aid of the pen as she was making strenuous efforts to reach down into the bucket. She can crawl now, but very inefficiently, and much prefers to skite around on wheels. She is very friendly and forthcoming, still going to anybody regardless of colour without protest; she is fascinated by people's teeth, getting an exploratory hand or finger into their mouths if given any encouragement. Apart from the unhygienic aspects I'm sure she will dislodge a plate sooner or later.

The Grays are back in Kumasi absorbed or, in her case, obsessed, by their brat who is having behavioural problems due to too much travel, Ghana – Italy – England – Australia, and is far from a charming specimen. I really don't feel I would be happy to leave K with them for any length of time despite kind offers.

We had to come down to Accra with the worrying thought that we had no place booked to stay, on top of which it was Saturday when all offices are shut and most people are on the beach. At Kumasi a call had come through to the effect that our usual rest-house could not accommodate us even though we had written ages ago. Luckily enough we called in, just to make sure, found the message had been completely garbled, and they had been expecting us for two days. What a relief.

This is Monday morning and Fergus has begun his round of UN and Min. of Health official visits, while I spent a restful morning here free of household duties. I am trying to tame some of the numerous large lizards that live on the roof here, using cornflakes as bait – some of them now come within a couple of feet.

Tuesday 11 November

All our pens are giving trouble so a pencil may be better. I have developed another stinking cold (seem doomed to develop one every time we come to Accra and are in reach of delicious meals). This one came via K who seemed little put out by it, not being particularly snotty, though restless at night. F is bound to get it as I splashed away all night and had a raging throat. No idea where K picked it up – no doubt from some kind person who just *had* to hold her!

Your letter no. 5 came, also several *Vogues* and *House & Gardens* – also the most welcome Wettex and Neobactin – many thanks. The photos of the house in course of construction are somewhat alarming, but maybe it was just the angle. You appear to have acted sensibly (shades of Rudolf) about the power-plugs in our sitting room. Apropos your birthday – I'd like you to buy yourself a copy of Osbert Lancaster's recently published autobiography, the name of which I can't recall (only if you think it appeals), and debit it to our postal account. Very mundane, I know, but there isn't much else one can do at this distance.

[It is odd I do not mention Kennedy's assassination as I quite clearly recall hearing the news over the BBC overseas service while we were staying in Accra. Nor do I mention that I took so many codeine tablets to fix the cold that I suffered stomach bleeding – much to F's alarm.]

Kumasi Rest House, 3 December

We have been away from Wa much longer than anticipated as it took F nearly three weeks to get all his negotiations settled in Accra: accordingly, as we had not asked to have mail forwarded (risky) I am not up-to-date with your news, but look forward to finding a letter when we reach Wa later this week. The roads being so bloody and the Min. having sent our sea consignment, for reasons best known to themselves, to Tamale, we are returning via Tamale: the distance is longer, but the road from here north is tarred all the way and one makes better time. Fergus has managed to get a Govt. Transport lorry again to take our stores, Adda, tin sheets for roof of Adda's house in Navrongo, office supplies and furnishings etc. for the project rest-house etc. So that takes the pressure off our own car which beats its previous record for tight packing. Poor K goes on top of the pile on the back seat in her carry-cot *if* she's sleeping or quiescent, but those times are becoming ever rarer, and she mostly has to come in front between us where she is rather a menace owing to wanting to assist with steering and gear changing. The car seat I bought at home is pretty useless as same, though all right as a high-chair: it is too bulky and would be quite useless in a small car, so we have got a very lightweight second-hand one from the Grays.

K's progress since I last wrote has been more rapid than I can remember; I think in my last letter I said she was able to stand – well, after two days she was standing most of the time and is now walking with the aid of the pen. She has perfected her crawling technique though she much prefers to be on her feet and can pull herself up now. We notice that the strain on our vigilance is increasing and we feel, like the Sidwells, that this is sometimes too much at our age! Always having to keep one or two steps ahead in anticipating the next grab. She's a real dynamo – particularly if you compare with the Gray child who is a year older. Pat has very kindly offered a couple of times to look after her, once when we went to see the Mission hospital at Agogo, and again today for our last minute shopping. It's no rest cure for Pat as her own displays extreme jealousy taking the form of throwing herself screaming to the ground and banging her head violently on the floor. [*I think it was on this shopping trip that we encountered Peggy Cripps, daughter of Sir Stafford, by that time married to Joe Appiah, who was at a similar stage in one of her pregnancies.*]

On Sunday we went the fifty-odd miles to Agogo to see the Basel Mission Hospital. The MO and staff were kind and confidence-inspiring, and there was an overall air of Swiss efficiency and cleanliness. The greatest points in its favour are (a) European trained nurses; (b) that they can accommodate and feed (very well if the lunch they gave us was typical) the rest of the family; (c) they even do laundering for mother and baby, an unheard of service elsewhere and (d) they allow siblings in to visit Ma. They do, however, insist that one provides someone to look after No. 1, but Fergus should be able to cope till I am up again: if Dorothy can come to help all will be simple, as it would release F to visit Accra again if necessary. The compound is beautifully situated on a small hill in the middle of tropical forest and the grounds are beautiful – full of bougainvillaea, hibiscus etc. I fear it will be frantically hot and notice there are no fans in the rooms though they *say* their nights are cool; such statements tend to be of dubious accuracy as I think people who have lived long in the tropics eventually change their standards of comfort. There is an undoubtedly monastic atmosphere about the place and Christian goodwill abounds, but they were all quite animated conversationalists, and the Matron of the rest house and F share gardening interests. I must say we are both relieved to have made one more step in the arrangements, and to have seen and approved the hospital.

Tamale, Thursday 5 December

Yesterday was an endurance test, but we are safely installed here. I'll give a quick resumé: up at 5 to finish packing started the night before but uncompleted owing to need for light and necessity not to make too much noise as K has to share our room when we travel. Make morning feed on approx. 1 sq. ft. of available space as the rest-house furnishings are minimal (all other feeds prepared the previous day and frozen solid in the deep-freeze). Prepare or gather together cold sterilized water, bread, oddments for *us* to eat, teats, clean bottle recently used as one can't leave anything dirty or things will harden on and go bad rapidly. Breakfast, feed and bath infant, start packing car. All was ready by 9.30, but no sign of lorry which was to take the bulk supplies for three or more months (thinking of exhausting process of having bought same in steamy atmosphere on swelling feet!) Fergus then had to tear off the Govt. Transport to ask what the hell. Eventually lorry and driver appeared having been to various unlikely places such as the hospital, No, nobody had told him where to collect us. Don't believe a word, but as is always the case one can't *prove* anything – like his tale today that he had to dash 12/- to the policeman at the ferry in order to get across. This is fishy as Govt. Transport gets automatic priority.

We eventually got started at 10.45 with K unfortunately already having had her nap and very lively. Two hours took us to a place called Ejura where one forks left onto laterite for Kintampo or straight on for Tamale. A large notice said 'Ferry congested take other route via Kintampo', this both longer and rougher and at present impossible owing to Yapei ferry being out of action due to water being too low for floating ferry and too high to use pontoon bridge: this is a situation which must occur every season, but we hadn't coincided with it previously. F by this time reiterating that he had had enough of this bloody country, its organization or lack of same, and may its inhabitants roast in hell etc. However a policeman at Ejura assured us that all was well and that the notice referred to conditions long past! So we went on and found a round rest-house where we could have our snack lunch and exercise K. At 3 p.m. we reached the end of the queue for the ferry. Dust, smoke, seething yelling humanity, howling brats, odd cooking smells, mangy dogs rooting for anything that might fall to the ground (not much does except leaves in which food has been wrapped, paper and orange skins). Luckily there were very few cars, and they get across much more quickly as they can be fitted in beside a lorry, where two lorries would be too wide. Normally two ferries ply, but one had 'spoil' and the other was in the process of being tied to an inadequate looking motor boat with an insubstantial looking rope. Some of the waiting lorries were enormous cattle trucks with poor patient northern cattle inside – they have a water-hump like a camel. I felt it would be preferable to cross with same doing my best to suppress visions of ferry and motor boat parting company, leaving us to float downstream towards the coast. When they eventually got hitched up, the crossing took only five minutes, but the shouting disorganization on the river bank on each side was such that the time taken to get vehicles and passengers off and on was at least twenty minutes. There was no real 'system', so it was just a case of who could thrust the nose of his car into the most advantageous position first. I instructed F to forget any gentlemanly impulses he might have retained (few by that time) and we embarked at 5.15 much to our surprise. I had thought at one time that we might have to return the hundred miles to Ejura rest-house for the night, and was worried about what was going to happen to our box of cold stores containing about 10 lbs of butter. All went well for another hour when there was one of those alarming noises which was only a tyre going, but I have *never* seen a tyre shredded so completely – there was nothing but fine ribbons left of the outer casing. We have really had more than our share as we had another puncture just before reaching Kumasi last Friday. I forgot to mention how angelic K was on the journey – about its only redeeming feature.

Interval for distracting K who was crawling all over me and wanting the pen – reminiscent of your cat Daniel helping with the dressmaking. K now understands a lot and will clap hands to order, give one hand and then the other for standing up. She makes attempts to say 'dog', but her favourite for the last few days has been 'No'. I forgot to say her hair is now much thicker with a slight wave and is a lovely golden corn colour. Unfortunately I did not bring the camera on this trip as I thought we would be back much sooner and that I would have little time to spare. As usual, of course, I regret not having done so; I missed a lovely picture of a line of little girls carrying enormous clay pots on their heads (a type of pottery one sees only up here).

Wa, Sunday 8 December

Here we are again after nearly five weeks of rest-houses and travel. Enjoyable in many ways, but it is also nice to be out of suitcases once more. The greatest lack here is fans; it is so airless, drab and dusty now the dry season has really begun. Our huge mail contained only one letter from you describing various inefficiencies perpetrated by the builders and architect between them. Sorry you are having to do site-supervision, but you probably enjoy it after a fashion.

Our two-day visit to Tamale merely confirmed that the sea freight had been sent on to Wa (where nothing seems known of it) some ten days ago, so we may be claiming insurance yet. However, F was able to get equipment for the project rest-house at the Medical Stores there. As soon as we have a nice rest-house, no doubt all odds and sods will descend for a nice little holiday away from Accra, expecting to be wined and dined in style by the light of hurricane lamps (Oh, how quaint! No electricity – fancy!) This hospitality is often not reciprocated – when bush livers go south they often get a cursory, 'Oh, you must drop in for a drink *some time*, but when they come north it quite different – some don't even bring contributions to the larder. Fergus's new resident rep. is a butcher-like bastard from NZ with a hale and brash manner – no credit to the UN – he, wife and daughter are planning a little jaunt up here in January which we are dreading. We should also have a visit from Denis Pirrie who used to be LCC Chief MO, and who we *do* like, but nevertheless it will all add to the daily strain of dragging one foot past the other.

Mandahl-Barth's laboratory has at last congealed, but the salary offered remains very poor, and the directors want the parasitologist to sign a 5-year contract. We are cogitating seriously, but have not yet reached a decision as so much depends on cost of living, availability of housing, and many other factors such as educational facilities (Danish state system reputedly excellent), pension schemes, gratuities etc. Please tell San we got her cards and thank her very much.

Wa, Monday 16 December

I hope this reaches you in time for Christmas – it *should*, but one never knows. A long letter from you came a few days ago, and I'll try to deal with it though I don't think there was much requiring answer or comment.

Your description of our building enterprise was both graphic and amusing. Please don't imperil life or limb in order to get pictures – I can bear to wait rather than risk AP being smothered to the neck in red mud. I think it was agreed that top soil should be deposited and site left 'neat, clean and tidy', but now have little faith in the architect to ensure this is done: an amiable, but ineffective young man.

The sea trunk finally arrived here. We were both glad O. Lancaster's book was enjoyable: from the reviews I read in the *Sunday Times/Observer*, I thought it would appeal to you. This letter is being written between demands of general house chores, gardener with cut finger, Adda with ditto, infant with dirty bottom, fridge under which the flame has gone out etc., plus awareness that this must go off tonight if it is to reach you before Christmas.

We have just had a wire from Dorothy to say she can come out to help in February. She has been fully warned that it will be no real holiday, about heat, humidity, insects, lack of fans and so forth, but I suppose she feels it might be worth the risk. I must say I am relieved, even though it will further complicate arrangements when travelling, booking rest-houses and so forth.

Katharine continues her rapid progress – she now walks almost everywhere in her pen and hardly paddles at all: she can go from one piece of furniture to the next, and all around beds and her cot, but not yet without holding on. I forgot to say I had her weighed in Accra and found she had continued to put on a steady 4 oz. each week since coming out here: so in spite of apparently inadequate diet, she's clearly thriving. She now eats quite a lot of Farex in her bottle, plus some disguised in banana and orange juice, but vegetables or eggs are treated with rude scorn and skillfully choked upon no matter how finely sieved. Spock – 'Your baby will have graduated to chopped foods of most kinds by 9 months.'

Must admit my girth is greater than last time, when I was still able to wear playsuits at 7 months. I completed another tent yesterday which can later be cut down to a straight shift which is the most practical garment here being cool and loose, though no doubt 'out' by now at home.

I hear *Which* is doing a special on contraceptives so you'd better get us one if it doesn't cause you too much embarrassment. We don't want another addition to the family in Feb. '65! Must go and roast and grind coffee (grinder purchased at Boals quite useless, and have reverted to the mincer).

The next two months are going to be busy as we expect quite a number of guests and it will be no time at all before we have to set off for Agogo.

1964

Wa, Wednesday 8 January 1964

NOTHING FROM YOU recently, so I'll start another and no doubt something will arrive before I finish. Various *Vogues, House & Garden* and Wettex came around Christmas time, also excellent Italian cookery book [*Elizabeth David's first*] and a Durrell which we had not read before. Thank you both for the offerings and all the effort involved. I think we have enough Wettex to do for a while now. Muslin nappies came too, but I think I'll probably have to buy some in Kumasi as there won't be time for you to send enough before No. 2 arrives, and I don't want to bother Dorothy with numerous requests to bring this and that as baggage allowance is slender. Another tube of 'Pretty Feet' would be welcome. My feet have got into a really repulsive condition owing to going around without shoes on floors which have nearly always got a fine coating of laterite, and the extraordinary drying properties of the atmosphere at this time of year have produced deep black fissures in the hippo-like soles. Have been working on them for the last week with my remaining stock of PF, and though improvement is appreciable, I don't think it is intended to cope with such a severe case. Analagous to having clean underwear on admission to hospital, I feel my feet would be too shaming at Agogo in February.

Katharine is plaguing me at present as she seems to think the only desirable area of the room is in my vicinity, and only amusing toy this pen. We have a new labourer working in the garden (Mousa Moshi) and she often sits in the pram watching him or moves around the veranda happily, provided he is in sight, but if he moves off there are protests. He is the most awful spoiler and discipline underminer I've met to date. She just has to squawk and he comes running to pick her up, then of course when put down she squawks again, after which he will carry her round on one arm with hose-pipe in the other hand. This morning I put my foot down and am no doubt thought callous: with Adda as interpreter I tried to explain our principles of discipline in simplified form so heaven knows what was conveyed. When she can really walk independently – I should say another couple of weeks – she will be able to follow him around, but at present she still wants to hold on with one hand. That will involve wearing shoes which she doesn't like; the alternative is to develop a hard pad like the locals. She doesn't like clothes either, and I can foresee big trouble when we return home: she never wears dresses, just small pants which I made out of cuttings, but her skin has remained perfectly healthy except for the very first few days when we arrived in Accra last August. Of course the climate in the south – even Kumasi – is just that bit more trying most of the time. At present we are having very pleasant dry season weather, even though it is becoming noticeably hotter and for the last week or more there has been quite a strong breeze blowing. Dorothy has asked me if her nighties *must* be cotton and my reply is that I shall be surprised if she can stick even that during March. She will coincide with the height of the flying insect/termite/snake/toad season, but we haven't mentioned that as we don't want changed plans at this stage!

Wa, Thursday 9 January 1964

Glancing through various *Vogues* it has occurred to me to wonder what the Kendall leg [*a strong gene on my mother's side attributed to my grandfather's fondness of cycling – rather too shapely and muscular*] will look like in the currently fashionable boots (thigh length?) and diamond patterned thick-knit stockings. [*Mary Quant has a lot to answer for.*] There was one picture of a model sitting almost starkers except for a pair of Rudolfian blue ribbed knee socks and stout brogues, which I thought really deserved a prize for decadence.

Tuesday, 14 January

I can't think how the time goes so quickly in this 'humdrum' existence of ours, but it certainly does. This morning we had, for once, quite an entertaining mail. A long one from you, my Kodachrome back – most are quite good, but the entire film is suffused with an overall laterite tinge. Letters from Auntie Rosemary, Denis Pirrie in Accra (who was not after all able to come for Christmas), Ilona (the woman we met on the ski slopes at Verbier, who had briefly encountered Fergus on a ferry in the Gambia. At that time she had been accompanied by *two* males, and Fergus got the impression she would have chucked them both and attached herself to him had she been encouraged). [*The meeting on the ski-slopes was one of those remarkable 'long arms of coincidence' as it was I who approached her in an attempt to assist her beginner's struggles; she then spotted Fergus and made an unabashed bee-line for him, shrieking 'My Adonis'. She never gave up her hope of seduction, even when they met in London while her husband was on his death-bed in a adjacent room. A subsequent 'long arm' incident occurred some years later when we met one of the Sisters from the Agogo Mission Hospital in the post-office at Grindelwald.*]

By now Dorothy should have had a letter from me giving detailed instructions re inoculations, travel etc. You ask how far we have to travel to Agogo – answer about 350 miles – I try not to think too much about it! We plan to leave here on Katharine's birthday, 14 February, travel the comparatively easy 188 miles to Tamale where we will stay one night only: that will provide some peace of mind in that there is a *reasonable* hospital if an emergency should arise. Then we will travel south by the good, tarred road to Kumasi – this is the route we took on returning from Accra, and we are 'reliably' told that the ferry is now unconstipated. There is a shorter route via Bamboi, Wenchi, but there are no suitable rest houses, hospitals etc. *en route,* it is laterite nearly all the way and we think an eight or nine hour drive is too much for Katharine now that she sleeps so little. After one night in Kumasi we will go on to Agogo where we plan to arrive on 17th or 18th, i.e. one week before 'it' is due. Then Fergus will either dash down to Accra for Dorothy or meet her at Kumasi airport, though it would be better for her to go by road from Accra as it would give her an idea of the country which she would never get from the air. A 'witty' medical friend has advised Fergus to be sure to have a good sharp knife to hand in case of wayside delivery, plus a bottle of brandy as an antiseptic for knife and cord – then drink the rest.

Copenhagen is no longer on: in some ways this is a relief as there were so many reservations too complicated to detail here. At present Fergus plans to ask for leave next September and travel home via Rome to attend the first international conference of parasitologists.

A few comments on the less sunny aspects of Katharine. She *still* wakes at night – often two or three times; not wanting food, but just getting into a hysterical tizzy: mostly a suck of rose-hip soothes, but not always, and last night she was stamping around the cot at 3 a.m. muttering over her vocabulary and quite willing to be sociable. I think we have had only about five uninterrupted nights with her altogether. *She* can catch up on lost sleep during the day, but we can't. Often she doesn't even sleep then either, and once or twice has gone from 6 a.m. to 6 p.m. with only a half hour nap. She gave up the afternoon snooze – only half an hour anyhow – a few weeks ago. All rather trying for Ma. At present she is outside with the compound labourers sharing their breakfast break, if not the food, which is a nauseous looking mess of dried fish and red pepper mixed with kenke, a farinaceous mixture which smells and tastes fermented. No doubt it will be found more palatable than anything I laboriously sieve and prepare. Her daily diet, even now, seems inadequate. Breakfast: orange juice mixed with 3 teasps. of Farex + 8 oz bottle also with Farex. Lunch: mashed banana, *possibly* some Heinz mess out of a tin + bottle – quite often only banana and bottle. Supper: much the same as lunch. Egg disagrees unless hard-boiled, and she doesn't like it; I've only got it down twice smuggled into a tin of Heinz, but now she seems to detect it. Fergus has just appeared for a mid-morning cup of cold cocoa, so I'll wind up and give him the letter to post. Please send some emery boards inside your next letter.

Wa, 22 January 1964

Since 19th Katharine has been walking without assistance: it happened surprisingly suddenly; in the a.m. she was reluctant even to let go of support, but by 4 p.m. she was not just staggering a few steps but walking right across the room and now she can go all over the house. She's been even more off her food than usual – more teeth probably – there are now eight and a red bump where the first molars will come through. Either that or she is adopting the faith of her favourite Mousa who is fasting for Ramadan. While I write I am suffering on his behalf as he comes to do a hard day's work without food *or* drink between 4.30 a.m. and 6.30 p.m. I know it is a self-imposed discipline, and my pity is misplaced, but it takes the enjoyment out of one's own frequent drinks. There is a definite lessening of the extreme dryness, and although we still have a breeze on most days, I notice Katharine is getting sweaty-headed after her snooze again and everyone is drinking more.

A couple of days ago I decided to try Katharine on the ordinary powdered milk which we use (full cream as opposed to the skimmed SMA) as I thought perhaps SMA was too sweet and this might be keeping her appetite down. She took several bottles without comment, but this morning looked reproachful and implied it was poison, so 'mother worm' was reduced to 'Will you take it if I make some SMA?' and she did.

Fergus wants to make a snail pond at the new laboratories; I know that nowadays one uses a plastic sheet of some sort instead of cement, but having seen the deterioration in a plastic swimming pool here, I wonder just how it would last even supposing it were obtainable.

Mandahl-Barth's job fell through because the Board of Directors found Fergus was 'too hesitating and set up too many demands'. Accordingly they have appointed instead M-B's second choice who is a good worker, but unqualified, and lacking some of Fergus's attributes. On the other hand his wife is Danish, he speaks Danish, has lived there before, and is not suffering a drop in salary of exactly half! Our feelings are mixed: there were many drawbacks attached to the job, and as Fergus says one doesn't like to go to a new place with many misgivings, but it did offer a chance to return to Europe. However it may all be for the best: we don't feel that HQ in Geneva will dispose of him if they can help it whatever the Regional Office may feel like doing. He gets appreciation from Geneva, but from AFRO continual rebukes for 'taking too much upon yourself' rather than recognition that if he didn't do it nobody else would, and the project wouldn't even be as far advanced as it is. [*By this time Fergus – never enamoured of DIY or things associated with building construction – had been forced to take on aspects of the project which would normally have been attended to either by someone from the PWD or a Public Health Engineer.*]

Did I mention in my last letter that Fergus is going to apply for a WHO Fellowship to do a Master's in Public Health and Hygiene course at Harvard for a year from Sept. '95? The other choices are California or New Orleans which has a good course to offer, but is climatically too like Ghana. Applying doesn't necessarily mean that he'll get it, but I think after seven years with WHO he probably will, and it would qualify him better for any administrative job that might arise within the Organization. We have been without Sunday papers now for some weeks – for reasons best known to the Ghana Govt.

Basel Mission Hospital,
Agogo,
Ashanti Region
18 February 1964

You will be relieved to see the address. We came down a few days earlier than originally intended so that Fergus can have three days in Accra before meeting Dorothy. The first part of the journey was exhausting as despite all efforts we didn't leave Wa till 11, so were travelling in the hottest part of the day. Katharine behaved excellently, but even so there is a lot of wriggling and humping around that wears out the person who is being wriggled on. [*I remember that Katharine bumped herself on the steering column and had a huge lump on the forehead when we arrived at Agogo.*] We got to Sunyani, where the Sins are now stationed, having returned from leave a month ago, about 6.30 and stayed a day and two nights with them before going the remaining eighty miles to Kumasi. They were extremely hospitable, and it is a pleasantly informal relaxing house to stay in. The two babies played together well and cut down the time required for vigilance, by keeping each other amused. Young Sin is still at a slight disadvantage as he is not yet actually walking, though on his feet and a speedy crawler. We stayed one night at Kumasi so as to have a morning shopping, then came down here yesterday. It is now too late to say don't send teats, I have enough here to feed six babies, having greatly overestimated wear and tear when thinking ahead; however, I can probably find a welcoming home for them. The hair combs I said not to bother about *would* now be useful as the severe Harmattan wind made everything so brittle that two recently broke in two on falling to the floor.

I forgot to say that your long letter with news of Holy Joe's demise came about a week ago – what a bastard just to drive on – not a bad way to go provided he was immediately unconscious. [*HJ was knocked down by a hit and run driver not far from his home at Drumahoe on the outskirts of Derry.*] Have just been examined and told that all is apparently well and not twins (I was sure I could feel two heads). D-day is expected to be 23rd, but one never knows – out here being hotter it might be early. I only hope Fergus and Dorothy get back from Accra in time. Even if they don't I'm sure the 'House Mother' would cope for a short time, but she is extremely busy, and it would be an infliction. The arrangements could not be better from the point of view of keeping in touch with the rest of the family. We have a large bedroom with w.h.b., two beds and a cot; off this is a long veranda looking across a bougainvillaea planted compound towards a row of Royal palms. Next door to our room on one side a room is reserved for Dorothy, on the other side is the labour ward from which one is carted off to deliver, but to which one is later returned. The food is excellent, and they are most co-operative about allowing one into fridges and mixing up messes for Katharine with their electric mixer. Adda has come too and is coping with washing and ironing. It is stiflingly humid weather compared with what we have come from, and there are no fans. Being on a hill, however, there is often a slight breeze. Needless to say Fergus will let you know by wire as soon as there is news. Marta Sin, who is a paediatrician, says all the white babies out here cry *even* more than in Europe when new. What a jolly prospect!

Agogo Hospital, 27 February 1964

I hope by now you will have had Fergus's costly wire telling you of the safe delivery of another 'female' – Grania Mary. A boy would have been nice, but as a companion for Katharine probably a girl is better. She's not quite as beautiful as Katharine was (though as the latter was 3 weeks late it is not a fair comparison) and shows what looks suspiciously like an incipient McCullough nose! Today she is contented, but yesterday was unhappy with a stomach full of stuff swallowed in transit. Once again I'm trying the painful breast feeding process which is going better this time as she is co-operating, and it will be a help if I can keep going till we reach Wa at least. The labour was blessedly short starting about 3 p.m. and being over by 5.30, but was awful in that they don't seem to hold with anaesthetics (as I suspected – some misplaced quasi-religious idea that one *should* suffer) and it went on beyond last year's black-out stage with many more stitches as a result. No long rest accorded either after delivery – just a cup of tea offered while I was still strung up under a hot lamp awaiting Herr Doctor to finish his evening meal before coming to stitch me up. [*Three years later in NI, my gynaecologist was prompted to ask, 'Who in the name of God did that last stitching job?]* On the credit side I feel better today, and even yesterday, than I did after Katharine's birth. Anyhow, if there is ever a No. 3 I'm going to have a signed contract with the hospital agreeing to the use of narcotics as requested. Otherwise they are very efficient and kind and the food is good though the strain of conversation at communal meals is as anticipated a little wearing. [*I do not mention that Grace was always said and that if for any reason one was slightly late in appearing at the long table, Grace was delayed and glances of cen- sure penetrated deeply while one settled on the hard bench. Nor have I mentioned that I was deprived of that long sleep which is so necessary after a birth. The baby was transferred to another room, but I could hear her crying somewhere during the night. The nurses assured me she was all right, but no sleep came.*]

Dorothy arrived safely having been met by F in Accra and driven up here, so she had four full days to get to terms with Katharine. They are getting on fine, and there has been no more trouble than one could normally expect. There is a German doc- tor here with wife and child age three and a half + a baby of five months; every day Katharine goes over to visit them for about an hour at lunch time, so we don't have to worry about her where- abouts. Plans for the next week are now congealing: Fergus has been summoned again to Accra and will travel down on Sunday, stay two days and return on Wed. or Thurs. We will leave Dorothy in charge here and rush up to Kumasi to do final shopping which will be packed into the Land Rover and despatched early the next day to travel directly to Wa in one day + cold box and Adda who will prepare house, fridge etc. On the same day we will all travel with minimum baggage to Tamale where we will stay one night proceeding next day to Wa.

Agogo, Monday 9 March 1964

I have a bad conscience as it is nearly two weeks since I wrote and I know you will have been waiting for a further bulletin. That we are still in Agogo will surprise you: last Thurs. Fergus and I went up to Kumasi and did a final shopping in preparation for early departure the following day. It was tiring, but not too bad, and most of the evening was spent packing tins and bottles into card- board boxes so that they could safely go by Land Rover early next morning. Because I was tired, also because next day was a public holiday (Independence Day), and the 'Hitler Youth' movement would be on the march in all villages, we decided to delay our departure till Saturday morning. On Friday night Dorothy's hernia, about which she may not have told you, chose to come up bigger than ever before and with more pain! Medical examination next morning pronounced that it should be operated on as it was slightly inflamed and strangulated. Her doctor in NI had said it would be OK and could quite well wait. So she was carted off to the theatre early on Sat. All things considered it was well-timed, as if it had come on at Wa we could not have relied on any good medical advice.

I am feeling as new again, and can cope with both infants all right for the time being as there is no cooking to do and washing and ironing are done for us by the Mission. [*Adda had already departed.*] Fergus left yesterday for Sunyani where he was going to stay the night before travelling to Wa today. The present arrangement is that he will come to Tamale on Wednesday 18th to meet us off the plane from Kumasi. A sister of a hockey playing friend of Dorothy whose husband is working in Kumasi, has kindly offered a) to come to Agogo on Tuesday to collect Dorothy, me and two infants; b) accommodate us overnight and leave us to the airport next day. It is deadly dull here as everyone is so oppressively Christian, so we feel constrained to exude equal goodwill and concern for our fellows. We shall be delighted to escape next week. One admires their dedication and the work they are doing, but there is an intensity which, in an almost wholly female community, is unnatural. Visitors come and go, but all are of the same ilk – middle-aged to ancient, with grey buns and mud-coloured dresses of pre-war cut – one wore a solar topee and heavy men's shoes with ankle socks (the latter *all* day even when changed for an evening festivity into a limp silk dress!). Some of the talk around the huge communal table we have enjoyed – though much takes place in Swiss German which is *very* different from proper German. One has to guard one's Ps and Qs on so many topics that it is difficult to relax. A great 'thing' is made of grace saying and 'closing' at the end of the day, anyone coming in a few minutes after the gong has been sounded feels like a man in a Bateman drawing.

Another reason I'm quite glad to be here is that Katharine was done for smallpox again three days ago, and I'd rather she had her reaction here where tranquilizers and dressings are available. We are both worried about it as (which has happened before) we feel we have been bullied by the medical profession. I asked them to do it in an unobtrusive place and was told, 'Oh no, it is always better here, and will leave no mark.' Then he made *two* long scratches with a scalpel, instead of the quarter inch one recommended on the vaccine. This he explained was because she had been done many times without success (even though I told him it was when she was under six months old when antibodies are often *not* formed). Naturally *both* have reacted so I expect a really bad reaction. This was three days ago and she is very tearful already and running a fairly high temp. She has been perfunctorily examined by a female Dutch paediatrician who first of all said, 'Oh just put some talcum powder on the rash', then reluctantly prescribed some pills to give her a quiet night. She says that if the primary reaction is severe the second is not usually so bad, but that this is not always the case. So I can see I am in for a very trying few days: if one is not crying the other is, and frequently both in harmony. [*I am down-playing the anxiety here; it was extreme: Fergus was in Accra, Dorothy convalescing nearby, and I remember being as near hysterical as I have ever been – using, at one time, language unsuitable for the ambience, and insinuating medical negligence. I was also badly underslept and, I now suspect, suffering from postnatal depression.*]

No. 2 is swelling rapidly and is a better eater than Katharine was, but also not inclined to a regular pattern – sometimes sleeping five or six hours on a small feed, at other times getting hungry after two or three hours. She's getting better looking now, but has a more triangular face than Katharine had. The latter is very interested, but has to be watched carefully as she doesn't understand 'gently' yet, and gives the baby the same hearty pats that she gives to dogs and cats. For a long time she referred to anything pleasant or on four legs as dogs, but dogs is now reserved for the correct object, and has been superseded by 'burds'.

We can sit and watch the pied crows and cattle egrets from the veranda every evening when they come in to roost in a tall pine tree. The scene is exactly like one of those rather hackneyed Japanese prints of the sort popularly reproduced on Christmas cards, or hung on the wall beside the now ubiquitous Chinese horse which in time will come to bring shame to their owners – equivalent of the flying ducks of the thirties and forties.

Wa, Wednesday 25 March

I can't recall when I last wrote, but it must be nearly three weeks ago. Dorothy was skilfully repaired and back on light duties within a week: she was supposed to be taking it easy, but I don't think it worked out that way, but she doesn't seem to have suffered any ill effects. The week she was in bed was a nightmare for a variety of reasons. Fergus went back to Wa, and so was not around to share duties or anxieties, which was just as well. The first thing was the savage vaccination I mentioned in the last letter. After three days Katharine had a temperature of 103° and on the fourth day developed a bad rash which drove her mad at night. I had lost all faith in the female who had sent a message to the effect that there was nothing to do except 'put powder', so throwing medical etiquette aside I went to one of the other doctors for a second opinion, and got some ointment plus sleeping tablets which eventually put her off to sleep after three hours' screaming. On top of the reaction she got a very bad fluish cold from the child of the doctor who did the vaccination, and was staggering around in the mornings as if her legs had no strength; this was most alarming at the time, but after a few days *I* developed the same disease, only then realizing that she had probably been aching all over. We were lucky in comparison to the doctor's wife who had to stay in bed for nearly a week, while a full-time nurse was commandeered from the hospital to look after her baby. Now we are back in Wa the virus has gone almost full circle – the baby has had it – but not badly: Dorothy has had it mildly and Fergus is awaiting developments.

We were very relieved to get away from Agogo as the exhaustion entailed in keeping an eye on Katharine all the time was considerable: all the places she most liked were out of bounds – like the kitchen, various steep flights of steps and other patients' rooms. As these were all accessible from a common cloistered veranda, we had to erect barriers which of course constituted a nuisance to all foot traffic. Dorothy's friends in Kumasi could not have been more helpful: he collected us by car on Tuesday and took us to their rest-house for the night, gave us breakfast and dinner, got our air tickets and put us on the Tamale plane next day where we were met by Fergus at 11 a.m., reaching Wa about six hours later. Altogether it worked out smoothly, but I was getting pretty fed up with mixing up feeds on top of rest house lav. cisterns or in the plane where things tend to slide about a lot.

Both infants are now well; Katharine in particular looks much better since reaching Wa again, though her arm is a worry as it has to be covered to keep dirt out, and is healing slowly as a result of not having formed a scab yet. I am furious each time I look at it as I'm sure she's going to have a bad scar, and feel that Francis Kofi could have made a better job of it (that is one of the many jobs the MFU field assistants perform). She is eating a bit better now we are back on home ground, and much less trouble to watch as there are fewer hazards around. She still has the devoted Mousa with his hose to entertain her; he continues to spoil and periodically one hears a scream of naughty temper followed by Mousa's explanation that 'I want take the hose but *he* no agree.' I forgot to mention the congratulatory comments of the lab. workers – the choicest coming from Francis who is not renowned for tact, despite trying so hard, 'Oh, sorry doctor, the next will be a male, but after all girls are more serviceable.'

The heat is oppressive and the clouds that have promised rain for days past are still tantalizingly lurking in the vicinity, but no rain yet. You *can* smell it coming, as described in so many books but not fully understood till one experiences the thrill. We are all lying around 'garpsing', and looking reproachfully at the motionless fans. Mary is filling out nicely, but suffers from bouts of colic. She is a much better sucker than K ever was and tends to gulp down her feeds even through the smallest hole; this sometimes results in the whole lot coming up again at the first burp. She is also better during the night than K was and *can* do a seven or eight hour stretch sometimes. Dorothy has retracted her view voiced a few days ago that you could have stuck the heat all right. This afternoon she is reflecting on those persons who just collapse and die in New York wondering if she is going to do the same.

Wa, 15 April 1964

I think my last letter was both short and not at all entertaining and imagine this will probably be the case in future months, particularly after Dorothy departs. She leaves in a week's time. I would have had a nervous breakdown without her assistance – as it is we have all three been on the verge of same once or twice. The rain fell before we reached Wa, but was only the first of what are known as the 'small rains', since when, with the exception of one night's moderate fall, there has been a return to extreme heat and

Harmattan conditions during the day, but without the nice cool nights which usually accompany that wind.

A couple of weeks ago F was summoned to Tamale to collect two high-powered WHO men and convey them a) to Wa for three days and b) to Hamile on the border with Haut Volta [*now Burkina Faso*] where they were to be collected by the health authorities. Their mission was in connection with an inter-state co-operative plan to control onchocerciasis (river-blindness), but at present there is a border dispute going on which made it possible they might not even get across. They *did*, but such a state of affairs doesn't augur terribly well for future inter-state efforts. These two staff members are both German – one tolerable, but the other insufferably 'continental', self-satisfied, a monopolizer of the conversation, restless and utterly exhausting. Dorothy and I slaved away all last Friday preparing various repasts in advance between infant feeding and bottom wiping, as we had them for three meals a day over the week-end. After they departed we felt we had almost nothing to do and sat around groaning spasmodically and sipping coffee laced with vodka. The nights unfortunately are interrupted rather more by K than M at present: she is getting more teeth and is suffering from the heat at night. Mary has an enormous capacity for food and mostly only requires attention once during the night around 2 or 3 a.m., having gone to bed at 6.30. K seems not to be unduly jealous, but does show a tendency to show excessive affection for whoever is attending to the baby, crawling all over them, the bed and baby and thrusting herself in between. She loves music and always beats time or dances when the wireless is on: slightly vulgar tastes though, as I heard F saying disgustedly, '*Twisting* to Beethoven's Emperor'; she also spends ages in the garden hosing or playing with the large red ball. We had Adda's Yamba and his younger brother for the Easter holidays and they all played together for hours without any strife. Now they have returned to Navrongo so K has to rely on casual workmen or us for entertainment.

I must relate the saga of the termites' nest in Dorothy's bedroom. We thought she was just being neurotic complaining about 'things' crawling around and over her at night, till one afternoon I happened to open the bottom drawer of the built-in dressing table in an unfruitful search for a missing garment: there they were in teeming thousands, big ones, little ones, winged ones, unhatched eggs, empty egg capsules. As soon as they were disturbed they began a lava-flow mass exodus spreading wildly in all directions, so I grabbed the insect spray and attacked immediately, while D and K stood outside looking on, in one case with interest at Mum's antics, and the other frozen in disgust and apprehension. The nasty part is that I hate to destroy such a complex community even if it is in the house; the insecticides deal fairly speedily with them, but there are always a few bodies feebly twitching and trying to extricate themselves from the dying mass – horrible.

Last night we were all desperately tired, and I resolved to go to bed at 7; needless to say I didn't go till 8, and at 9.30 the first of the interruptions began with F getting up and blundering around with a torch and tennis racket muttering about 'something in the garden'. He went out and fistled around among the vegetation for ages, returning to say he had found a shrew engaged in trying to eat a toad which had blown itself up to unswallowable size. After some deliberation he had separated them, returning to bed having woken me up so thoroughly that I had to take a sleeping tablet. Interruption No. 2 was a really heavy rainstorm with what sounded like giant hailstones on the roof: this meant a trip around to close windows, cover infants, reassure same if necessary, back to bed hoping rain will cool the atmosphere. Rain did not cool it, so up again to open windows, uncover infants, get a drink from fridge walking in the dark on a moist Wettex cloth which nearly gave me a seizure till I saw what it was. Mary woke at 4 a.m. for a feed, then peace till 6.30 when morning tea arrived.

This morning F, D and K have gone to Dorimon and will look for crocodiles at the local ju-ju pool on their way back: after a particularly long period of bawling yesterday, F suggested that GM would make a suitable sacrifice! This morning, just to be awkward, she has behaved very well, though yesterday *and* the day before was not to be appeased. She seems to be what Spock calls a hypertonic baby and has indigestion rather than colic, starts at sudden noises and movements, but *looks* thriving. K is eating reasonably now, though seldom with much concentration, and speaks long involved sentences reminiscent of Harry Hemsley's Horace.

Wa, 30 April 1964

Today looks like being peaceful enough to offer a good chance of getting this letter done in one operation. All is peace, though far from quiet, because two of Adda's children, age around six and three, have come to visit, and they and K play amicably on the veranda for hours at a time. Strangely enough there is never any strife such as one associates with such play at home; the only sounds of distress are when Michael and David go off to their quarters (out of bounds for K owing to general grime and hot wood stove). Grime and runny noses are an integral part of M & D, but the advantages of young company around are legion, liberating me from constant 'assistance' in the kitchen and elsewhere. Bath and feed time for Mary are a signal for a slight display of jealousy and over assistiveness, crawling all over the bed, up my back and giving M loving, if rather heavy handed, pats on the loaf. K's vocabulary is rapidly expanding: she has a fair imitation of butterfly, ball, book, bath and bugger (not encouraged, and I haven't worked out to what she is applying it).

Since I last wrote various gremlins have been working overtime in the transport field and we are now without a vehicle; even the MFU bike which F now uses to go to the office and back is unreliable. Last Wednesday he made an early start with D to take her down to Kumasi, from where she was going to fly to Accra to be met by a UN staff member who was to see her safely out of the country. Half an hour after they left I discovered D's suede coat in one of the cupboards. I hoped they would not discover the omission, and began to make complicated plans to send Adda down to Kumasi in a mammy lorry with the coat. Unfortunately D did remember, and they returned two hours later – F grimly silent – having covered 120 profitless miles. After discussion it was decided they should go by another route and stop the night at Kintampo, proceeding early the next day to Kumasi. I sat back and wished them well, but at 6 p.m. a small black overloaded Volkswagen driven by a female missionary appeared with Dorothy looking white-faced and exhausted after having spent the day waiting in broiling heat by the side of the road no more than sixty miles from Wa. They had three punctures in succession, and had completely ruined two inner tubes plus one tyre (no inner tubes now available in Ghana, likewise spare parts etc. etc.). Fergus remained with the car and was rescued late at night by the MFU Land Rover, but did not get here till 2 a.m. What with that, anxiety, infants waking, and an attack of allergy, it was a memorable night.

Next day the Land Rover was sent out again with a mechanic to diagnose the trouble – something over and above the punctures – and to tow the car back to Wa. Later that day the team returned minus the car, looking a bit sheepish and confessing to having had 'some small accident' resulting in car being even more *hors de combat* than before. What the 'accident' really was nobody will ever know, but 'somehow the car went for ditch' – several indentations make this evident. It took F almost a week to get it brought back to Wa where it now reposes in the MFU yard awaiting further diagnosis of spares required. Exhausting and exhaustive arrangements for D had all to be cancelled by police wireless message as it was too late to rely on the ordinary telegram system. Eventually D left Wa two days ago with the MFU biologist who was going on leave to the south. Presumably she will write soon and let us know how she finally got on the plane.

I have been coping OK since, but feel that without D's help I would not have remained sane during the last two months, and would probably have committed infanticide. She definitely had the worst of GM who has only very recently really settled down to regular well-digested feeds at reasonably timed intervals.

Yesterday I asked Adda if he now cooked his own spinach my way – no water other than that of washing, five minutes only, conserve vitamins etc. He replied, 'Oh yes, I like it too much, first I cook it, *then* I put it in my stew. I protested, 'But then it gets spoilt staying so long in the stew on the stove.' 'Oh – I only keep it two days.'

Mousa, the spoiler, recently got a second-hand wife from someone who had had *him* five years and he no conceive. Now he have conceive after three months with Mousa and the first husband say it is his child and want him back again. Mousa is worried, but we reassured him that once divorced she was his property etc., and that he should not worry as the first man talk nonsense. A few days ago I met the wife who has a very large bulge: so perhaps No. 1 husband *has* a legitimate grievance!

Wa, 18 May 1964

Yesterday morning I was all set to start a letter to you when the insufferable little gossip who is married to the local doctor chose to call on us complete with her litter of three daughters. It had seemed for a while that my frostiness had discouraged her, but the effects are wearing off, as we have had her on two Sundays recently. Both our brats were sleeping, so F and I were looking forward to a couple of hours' peace for me to write and him to paint:

one of the visiting children walked on one of his paintings just to add to the success of the visit. They aren't even good playmates for K, as all three seem dull-witted and just moon around or roll on the floor. This family set-up is a clear case of the African student having married the landlady's daughter.

Otherwise all goes well apart from interrupted nights which will drive me to infanticide or nervous breakdown if they go on much longer. Last night there were three interruptions by K, requiring a drink and nappy changing, two from Mary, and a rain storm. All that was missing was an attack of allergy. Unfortunately I have developed some sensitivities akin to the Kintampo ones – very disappointing as I had thought to be free from them in Wa. *What* is causing K to continue like this I just don't know: if it is teeth it has been going on continuously since last November. Spock says, 'This can be quite a problem if baby doesn't go back to sleep again quickly.' To me it seems quite a problem even if baby *does* go back to sleep again, as quite often I do not, and just lie waiting apprehensively for the next outbreak. K now has all expected teeth except the last four back molars which don't usually come till they are over two, but she may be getting them early as she did with all the others. By the way, did any of our ancestors lack canine teeth in the bottom row, as she seems not to be getting any; all the others are up and evenly spaced leaving no room for canines though they are present in the upper jaw. Apparently this is not unknown, and mostly inherited from the maternal side.

Wa, 20 May

Two busy days and two reasonably restful nights have passed – not without interruption – but only short-lived and easily dealt with. Of late I have been going to bed with a sleeping tablet and a strong whiskey inside in an attempt to get a few hours' solid sleep before the first outbreak. I have almost completely cut out the evening meal as I'm trying, with no evident success as yet, to cut down my vital statistics which, if I had another 2" on the bosom, would qualify for outsize 40" – 30" – 40". I don't *look* as fat as this, but the tape measure says so. The face, needless to say, is haggard with black rings under the eyes. This morning seems to have been spent alternately making spaghetti by hand, using my lovely Italian machine to roll it out and cut to required size (the problem is keeping sugar ants off while it dries out a bit), and cleaning dirty bottoms of different interesting colours and consistencies. K, though super bright in other directions, has not yet grasped the pot idea; she is impossible to catch as there is no regular timetable, and never shows any sign of redness in the face or other effort – just a delicate forward inclination and Bob's yer uncle, so to speak. No doubt when it does finally click she will be delighted with the new idea.

A bit of good news to impart: the Brazzaville office has granted F permission to attend the Conference in Rome from 21–26 September, 'as no additional cost seems to be involved'. It does mean, however, that he will be taking home leave after only 15 months, instead of the required 18, so he is surprised that they have granted the request. He will probably get the usual few days in Geneva and London 'for purposes of discussion'.

We think it would be best if I come home ahead of him in order to do a few things to get the house more habitable: then *possibly*, you being willing and strong enough to look after M, I might fly out to Rome to join him for the last three days of the conference and thence to Geneva. D has offered to look after K if necessary, or alternatively San could be called upon, if her own committments allowed, to come and help full time – I'm sure she would regard it as a holiday! Whether or not we return to Wa after leave remains to be seen, but F is determined it must not be for long. The stores position here is steadily worsening, and the Minister of Trade (who recently revoked *all* import licences for 1964 following 'certain irregularities' in the granting of same) has been the subject of much criticism in the local press. Commodities disappear altogether from the market for weeks at a time – even essentials like flour, sugar, milk etc. Luckily I had a huge supply in stock, but even so we had used up all our flour (I make the bread which uses a lot), and we are not likely to see cheese again for a long time. So the position as a whole is uneasy, and becoming increasingly so: spare parts for cars, tyres etc. are also affected, and of course all prices are rocketing. Even on F's hitherto handsome allowance, our cost of living is high.

People and things are conspiring against my finishing this letter properly so I'll sign off in haste. Forgot to mention that K has eaten my turquoise eye-shadow (without any apparent ill-effect), so could you please send me another one?

Wa 28 May 1964

The last couple of days have been b. awful and I feel as though I am going around in a faint aura of sick, shit and sour milk. M is always a messy burper, so even with great care she often manages a direct hit! K has had some unidentified upset resulting in frequent throwing up and diarrhoea, and to crown all F spent last night disturbed by bouts of nausea, and threw up copiously this morning.* David Molesworth (head of the Ghana Leprosy Service) was staying here during all this and was also afflicted by 'something' – so no doubt my turn will come. Another VIP is due tomorrow, but only for two days, at the end of which F will have to tear down to Accra with him in time for a meeting on 2 June, using our now highly suspect car, once again moving, but only just. I don't like being left here alone, but have been lucky that it hasn't happened more frequently.

Very sorry to hear about Moses as he was always my favourite, but it probably was better that he didn't have to endure the trauma of moving to a new habitat. I wonder how long you will resist the temptation to acquire another animal. Have miraculously managed to finish a dress in just over three days. I see from the fashion mags. that hideously fud. shoes are 'in' again – so your day has come at last!

Wa, 10 June 1964

[*Much of this letter concerns the house we were building in NI, and hoped to occupy during our next leave.*]

Your reports of the general ineptitude of the workmen might well be applied out here. The local plumber is the most amiable, but least skilled, of those who have worked on this house (poss. exception the gents who cut the wood for the doors. Their saw never quite got through, so they just tore the rest of the way resulting in a decorative jagged edge). The plumber has been five times to fix a copious leak under our sink: one of his troubles is that he goes in for too many joints which always leak. After sundry ineffective tightenings with wrenches, he resorts to vast quantities of putty through which the water spurts within a few hours. Four visits

---

* These digestive disturbances were later attributed to our having eaten some guinea fowl kindly donated by our guest, who later admitted that it had been in his cold box for a few days.

did not suffice to mend the handle of our lav. which was eventually fixed by the Chief Leprologist. Several attempts to achieve a decent flow from my sink tap have produced only a wide umbrella of water at all pressures; he hasn't got any washers, so laboriously cuts one when needed from an old inner tube or something similar.

Both infants are more or less well. GM still has indigestion and requires tedious burping sessions which she produces with varying degrees of violence – occasionally jettisoning the entire feed without warning. She seems otherwise to thrive, and mostly sleeps right through from 6 till 5, or with luck a little later. She was very restless for two nights recently, and in the morning I discovered that those horrible sugar ants had been having a meal off her scalp: they must have found a patch of delicious scurf – anyhow the attack produced many tiny red sore spots. K has not been quite right for almost a fortnight, but nothing definite. Intense reading of Spock indicates that she must have had a 'feverish grippe or mild influenza'. She was sick a few times, completely lost appetite for a few days, had squits and a slight temp. She is well on the way to full recovery now and in good spirits most of the time. Her favourite reading matter is one of the the famous Bannerman series on W. African birds. She can imitate some of the more common local ones, but is a b. nuisance with the heavy volume, enjoying it only in the company of Ma or Da. K has also developed a great fear of wind and rain recently – unfortunate, as we are now having frequent storms. *Interval*: during which I have written on Adda's behalf to his wife, son and son's headmaster. After a fortnight's pot training we have got as far as K making a large pool on the floor, then going and kindly wiping it up for me with the nearest tea towel. Actually there is progress in that she has begun to show signs of distress at being dirty.

Wa, Wednesday 1 July 1964

This being yet another public holiday (Independence Day, National Founder's Day, Positive Action Day, Republic Day, etc.) Fergus is looking after K so I can get down to writing. Still no success with potty: she now remarks with simple pride, 'Oh *look* potty,' as the lake spreads. I leave her pants off most of the time as we have plastic tiles and it doesn't matter, but at home it would be more awkward.

Your letter describing the move to Craigavad came yesterday – glad to hear that all went well and that you like the new abode. You say you are now gathering strength for dealing with K. You will need it; she is mostly charming and vivacious, but in spite of eating practically nothing has abundant energy and will drive you mad at mealtimes. She has just been offered chicken and rice, chocolate cake, pineapple and a mug of Vita cup. The last she has spilled twice, she has chewed two bits of pineapple and spewed out the residue which she has wiped over her tum, eaten one small piece of cake and rejected the chicken. Then she got a bit of our lettuce, chewed it slightly, spat it out, dipped it in the Vita cup and sucked avidly: at that point, as recommended by Spock, I decided it was time to stop the meal. After a wash-down during which she drank the bath water, she is now out in the garden eating sand which she doesn't seem to like very much. [*I shall never understand how our children escaped getting some of the more unpleasant worm infestations of Africa. It was not until we were in Tanzania some years later, that Mary got threadworms. The cook's children were often loaded with* Ascaris *worms which is contracted through faecal contamination.*]

Wa, 18 July 1964

Yesterday F received one of Brazzaville's well-timed blows which may alter our plans completely. A cancellation of the permission granted over two months ago to visit Rome *en route* to home; the excuse being that he is not entitled to take leave till January 1965. As only three months are involved, this seems an unnecessary adherence to the infamous Staff Rules, and they could quite well have seen the leave situation before granting the request. F has made an official appeal for re-consideration and has sent copies of all relevant memoranda to individuals who might intervene successfully on his behalf. Taking likely postal delays into account, I do not see how we can know definitely in much less than a fortnight. It is all extremely annoying as all the bookings have been made. [*This episode effectively put an end to our complicated plans to drive from Rome to Geneva.*] F thinks the Regional Office will probably capitulate in the end, but it is all such a waste of energy. [*The Regional Director in Brazzaville was an infamous despot, one of whose rules was that only he had the privilege of positioning his desk at an angle, and that no other staff member* had the right to display a national flag in his office: consequently an atmosphere of general wariness prevailed at the Regional Office. To question the wisdom of any decision made by the Regional Director was tantamount to putting one's career at risk.]

Wa, 7 August 1964

Last week we had to take Katharine to Jirapa hospital – one of the White Sisters' establishments, and generally recognized as being more efficient than Wa – under its present MO anyhow – for treatment of alarming symptoms which turned out to be some of the many varied ones of malaria. She began the day normally enough, but started having screaming fits at approximately one hour intervals during which her temperature soared. The first fit came on so suddenly I thought she had swallowed a pin as I was dressmaking at the time. F said we were not going to take any chances, so I packed up all nappies, milk making apparatus, boiled water etc., one clean dress for me and nothing for F inside half an hour and we set off for Jirapa with Mary in the carrycot. It is only a one and a half hour journey if the roads are in a reasonable state, and so far this year the rains have not been excessive, but the car is now so unroadworthy (brakes almost entirely ineffective, no spare tyre yet) that we took the Land Rover along in our wake in case of breakdown.

K had a thorough examination on arrival and an immediate injection in her bottom which began to work the following morning. [Many purists insisted on waiting for lab. tests before treating for malaria, but the more experienced were unwilling to take the risk of that wait, having witnessed cases where the patient was dead before the test results confirmed that it was, indeed, malaria.]

The nuns kindly gave us a room with two beds and access to a sink so that I could make feeds for the children, and they provided us with food too. We stayed one night only as K was obviously recovering enough to take notice of 'orses, cows etc. on the return journey. Unfortunately the follow-up doses proved ineffective, and she had a slight relapse on the third day, but we quickly changed the drug, and since then she has quite recovered, though altogether it took about a week and she tires more easily. I think I know how she got it in spite of getting her weekly prophylactic dose: it had always been put in her night bottle and sometimes a little was left, so she was probably slightly underdosed in the season when malaria is at its most intense. She now gets a nasty dose in a teaspoon instead. [*The official line at that time was that anyone who contracted malaria had been negligent in taking their prophylactic. In point of fact we were witnessing the beginning of the emergence of resistant strains of the parasite.*]

A cable from Brazzaville which must have cost at least £5 came today authorizing F to go to Rome after all! Yesterday's post also brought K's shoes which are very nice, and just about the right amount too large. She likes to put them on, but quickly tires of the weight and restriction and demands to have them off again. We now plan to leave here on Sunday 16th for Tamale, where F will see if something can be done for the car which is rapidly disintegrating after five years of hard use. If Karel Sin can meet me off the plane at Kumasi I will stay with them till F comes down with the repaired car to collect us. If not I'll just fly down to Accra and wait.

In many ways we are glad to be coming home, though had it not been for the Rome conference F would have preferred to wait till spring when the climate is at its worst here and nice in NI. In other ways too he will pay for it, as he will probably have to serve here in March/April 1965. The wire from Brazzaville indicated that his next leave will be due in July 1967, though it could be taken in January. On the other hand if he gets the Fellowship for Harvard that would be such a change it would seem like a holiday. [*It certainly was a change, and a great experience, but no holiday for any of us.*]

Michael, Adda's second youngest who is five, has been with us for the last three weeks and has been a great boon as K spends most of the day – often in very unsalubrious places – playing with him. Her appetite has also improved with the competition, and I think she has eaten more today than I have ever seen her. Mary was weighed at Jirapa and was 14 lb. 5 oz. at 5+ months. K was 15 lb. at six months, so they are much the same though a different shape. Mary has a wide, flat back and fat arms and shoulders; fortunately her face has now absorbed the McC nose and she is quite comely.

Accra, Friday 21 August 1964

We got here on Monday evening after what seemed an interminable time, but was, in fact, little over twenty-four hours after leaving Wa at midday on Sunday. I'll give the more gruelling details when we meet, by which time they will have become amusing. Fergus arrived by car yesterday to find me somewhat recovered, having had as much sleep as one can ever expect with K in the vicinity. Luckily we were able to get our usual comfortable rest house, and can have it till the end of the month.

Saturday 22 August 1964

I am quite unscrupulous about using other people or their children to entertain K, and find that the latter are invaluable, so I hope there are some suitable little souls nearby when we reach NI. Yesterday I picked up a small child of the US Embassy, plus nanny – both were sitting dully by the side of the road near their gate – and brought them round to the rest house. The child is three and doesn't speak as well as K. She is not retarded, but it is clear that she is left far too much with the nanny who provides no stimulus at all to the intellect; she is also an only child and highly possessive. Yesterday they quarrelled a lot, but today there has been minimal strife. Adda's Michael was left behind at Tamale after making an attempt to board the plane, and was inconsolable for a while; he is by far the best companion despite snotty nose and nits. We have been invited to a succession of dinner parties given by people we entertained at Wa. Tonight we go to F's Area Representative – unpronounceable Jugoslav name – Djukanovic – who used to be their Minister of Health, presumably loyal to the regime, but said to be very charming. Other friends have returned to UK for good and Denis Pirrie left just two days before we arrived. The Roseis are returning to Rome as they are expecting a third child in October. Tomorrow we are going to the beach for a barbecue lunch: enormous effort will be needed to organize bottles, nappies and adult sustenance, but I suppose it will be worth it; last time we enjoyed it very much. Neither time nor energy to write more so I'll stop and look forward to seeing you next week.

[*There followed a protracted home leave for me and the children. Fergus, after using his leave allowance, was sent on several short-term consultantships to the French speaking parts of West Africa, Cameroun, Congo, Gabon, Brazzaville and Kinshasha, République Centre Africaine, before we returned to Wa in March 1965.*]

1965

Accra, Friday 12 March 1965

WE HAVE MORE or less recovered from the trip now and are staying at the usual rest house near the airport till some time late next week, as Fergus has to attend a conference for the first three days thereof. As trips with two infants go I suppose it wasn't too bad, and both behaved quite well though they never slept at the same time, so I had no rest at all. Mary slept a lot, but Katharine only an hour in all. Neither plane was crowded so we were able to spread ourselves around and all stewards were most helpful allowing Katharine to rampage the central aisle making acquaintances all the way. There were moments of anxiety such as when I saw a piece of hand baggage being borne off officiously in the opposite direction to all the rest, and someone coming along with what should have been Mary in the cot, but turned out to be a black baby instead. Exchange was quickly facilitated. It is very fortunate we did *not* take that Saturday flight which Fergus met, as it came in at 1 a.m. having been delayed at London till 4 in the afternoon. Also fortunate that he telephoned you as otherwise we would not have been met: that, considering the humid chaos that always prevails at Accra, would have been purgatorial. As always the intensity of the heat took me by surprise: *only* 82 degrees, but very humid: one's hair begins to form limp, sticky tendrils. Katharine recognized Fergus as soon as she saw him and wouldn't be parted without protest. The heat seems to upset Mary more; she was slightly sick just after we disembarked. The African child we had been offered was tightly cocooned in a thick knit suit, including bonnet, and showed no sign of discomfort. All were wrecks (except Katharine of course) by the time we eventually got off to bed, and this is the first time I have felt energetic enough to write. Mary remained off colour for some days, but today there are signs of improved humour though the hard floors frighten her after the carpets she has become accustomed to at home. Katharine has resumed her primitive way of life around the back door with the hangers on as if never interrupted, and all are willing slaves. She is also eating better – I think partly in imitation of Fergus – and goes around saying, 'I want some more.'

Supplies are just as short as last year, and when deliveries come they are whipped up by those lucky enough to coincide with them. I have tried Mary on some of the dried milk we use and it seemed to agree all right so that is a relief. SMA is spasmodically available, but very dear. Minute eggs cost 9d. each and a small packet of corn flakes 3/6, tinned tomatoes 4/9, though this comes cheaper than buying fresh ones. So much for your Socialist paradise

Accra, 17 March 1965

It feels already as if we had never been home, and all are acclimatizing speedily – indeed Katharine showed no signs of being upset by the transition. I am the one who feels most hot and weary. Thankfully both children sleep more during the day than at home, and Katharine folds up at 11 nearly every morning. On Sunday, as a matter of duty we took a short expedition to the beach – a rather unappetizing one nearby – with the Rosei family. All brats enjoyed it, but Katharine remains a frightful coward about the sea, although talking a lot afterwards about 'I swimming'.

On Saturday we made the huge effort of getting organized to attend a lunch invitation from Brendan Parsons: this entailed taking Abdulai (Adda's successor) along as baby minder, the idea being that all should stay in the kitchen regions, but it didn't work out like that as Katharine wanted to join the party. However on the whole it was a success and I don't think our host was unduly upset by child company. [*I can not recall the details which led to Adda parting company after so many years. The rift occurred while he was alone with Fergus at Wa earlier in the year: I think Fergus's tolerance broke when Adda got paralytically drunk and was found to have been smoking hash as well. In retrospect I think he had been on the hash for as long as we knew him: Fergus said he had become insufferably demanding and generally big-headed.*]

Abdulai, so far, has not revealed any cloven hoof, and has a more pleasant personality than Adda. He is just as good at washing and ironing, shows that he is open to teaching re cooking, and is infinitely better with the children. Katharine has adopted him with enthusiasm, and goes around chanting his name just for the fun of saying it. Last night we went out for the first evening engagement, having given Katharine an aspirin, but even with that she woke at 11 and cried till we got in at 11.30. It was a pre St Patrick's Day drinks party with the usual vacuous talk, and I got so tired of being 'amusing' about our forthcoming trip north and answering well-meaning enquiries about the dear children. Afterwards we went to a Lebanese restaurant recently discovered by Fergus with Denis Pirrie and a Polish ENT specialist. We had a delicious meal of various garlicky sausages and a variety of different kebabs. No squits to date – a real restaurant 'of the people' on an open courtyard with small metal tables and chairs, a large cage of budgies, a fish tank and lots of lush greenery. Unfortunately there was a pervasive smell of African drain as it is in one of the less salubrious quarters of the town, but after a while one forgot about it. The 'toilet' was unique in my experience: it was reasonably clean but sited at the top of the stairs and had a window of unobscured glass (uncurtained too) looking onto the landing so there was no need for an engaged notice. Inside one had a choice of three receptacles: a) an ordinary lav. which was working all right; b) an enamel chamber pot (full) and c) what is known locally as a thunder-box – a box with hinged lid and bucket within (also full, but largely with paper).

It now looks as if Fergus will leave here by road on Saturday arriving at Tamale on Sunday night, and that on Monday morning we will fly from here to Tamale, going on by road the same day to Wa, after having transferred our stores to a Land Rover which should meet us at Tamale *if* they get the wire in time.

Katharine asks periodically where's Grannie, Dodi, Fiona, etc., but doesn't seem unduly disturbed by their absence. Mary seems to like black faces, and is not at all shy any more – also turning into a back-door type when given the chance. I can't say I'm looking forward to the trip to Wa, but it will be over fairly quickly, and then we can settle down to a routine again.

Wa, Saturday 27 March 1965

We are safely installed in glorious Wa once more, and have adapted remarkably quickly to the new routine. Needless to say our generator is still not hitched up, so those much needed fans remain tantalizingly immobile. All that is needed is a pole, 100 yards of cable plus a few hours' work, but we can see that Fergus's successor as project leader will be the beneficiary of his three years' toil. Mary is 'helping' me to write this letter while Katharine is flat out. Unfortunately they are seldom asleep at the same time during the day, so letter writing is very difficult. Mary would sleep throughout the night if not disturbed, but mostly one of Katharine's outbursts wakes her.

I fear you are not going to get such frequent or lengthy letters as before, if the last two days are any guide. Demands are incessant from 6 a.m. or earlier till 6.30 or 7 at night when one thankfully collapses amid mosquitoes buzzing and bats squeaking, to drink one's hard earned beer on the veranda by the dim light of the Aladdin. We had a pleasant enough flight to Tamale apart from Mary quietly emptying half a tin of pineapple juice over my seat while I took Katharine to the Elsan. We decided to stay the night in Tamale after all so as to ensure a really early start the following day before the heat became devastating. Standards continue to deteriorate gradually at the Tamale rest house: now only one of their fridges works (in the bar for drinks), and the kitchen is without. We had an omelette for breakfast which rather surprised me owing to the extra labour involved: when I went to see the cook about Mary's boiled egg, I discovered why. He was busy breaking obviously bad eggs into a large bowl, while pleasantly explaining that the only way to serve them was as an omlette because they were too bad to fry, and that many more would be broken before we found one good enough for baby!

The journey here was dustier than ever previously, but both children slept quite a lot: even so there were some trying passages and ill-timed demands for rose-hip drinks. We got here about 3 p.m. which is early enough to get everyone cleaned up and some of the unpacking done before dark. It is still very hot and no rain has fallen yet, though there have been sporadic showers in the vicinity. Fergus's Uganda kob, which Daniel had been feeding, is in good condition and devoted – though not in any intelligent way – entirely to him even after an absence of nearly a month. [*I do not remember the circumstances in which Fergus acquired this animal, no doubt so pathetic that it could not be refused.*] It won't take its bottle from me at all, and Fergus finds its constant leg licking, snuffing and dunting slightly repulsive, but feels responsible.

It is in or around the house most of the time, otherwise going to the office with him where it spends most of the morning lying under his desk. It is a beautiful, elegant creature, but just as stupid as Pangloss if not more so. It is not house-trained and never will be, so what with that and Mary wearing no nappy, the floor cloth is in constant use. The antelope freezes when peeing so one can thrust a potty quickly underneath if one is nearby. Katharine suddenly decided in Accra to use the pot while one of the WHO wives was having coffee with me; she dashed onto the veranda clutching her behind while proclaiming loudly, 'I have to do a smelly'! I find the house much more pleasant without Adda and Abdulai works just as hard if not harder.

A young American overseas worker called socially yesterday; his opening remark to Fergus was, 'Say, you're kinda old to have a little girl like that,' an inauspicious opening ploy if ever there was. Fergus has been offered the job of Biologist in the new advisory team formed by WHO, but unfortunately they have chosen Ibadan in Nigeria as the base and we do not want to remain in West Africa. In addition Fergus thinks the job not as interesting as one which may come off in Southern Rhodesia where a Bilharziasis team wants his services on loan from WHO for a three-year stint.

Monday 19 April 1965

Today is the Muslim equivalent of Christmas, so there is a general holiday and Abdulai has departed in his finery to the Mosque. Before doing so he did some washing, cleared up the breakfast mess and made beds, so I will only have to cook and clear up any subsequent mess. There will be a general slaughter of unfortunate beasts, and if there is a repeat of last year, Mousa will appear tomorrow with belly-ache – what Fergus aptly terms 'protein poisoning', so unaccustomed is he to any quantity of same. [*Mousa's staple mid-day meal was of boiled cassava which is of low nutritional value, liberally sprinkled with red chilli powder.*] The schools have a holiday and there are already four small boys playing on the veranda with Katharine, Mary and the kob. If they go away they will quickly be replaced by some of the numerous children of the newly appointed rest house keeper next door: Katharine will join them in a feast of mangoes and dawa-dawa seeds till eventually she will be so exhausted she will come for a sleep about mid-day. [*The dawa-dawa tree produces fluffy red balls which dangle like Christmas tree decorations, and subsequently long pods inside which the seeds nestle in a yellow powder-like substance which one sucks off rather like sherbet.*] Neither of them is any trouble provided there are other children around, but if not boredom sets in with consequent demands on Mum's time and patience. Some heavy rain has fallen at last and cooled the air delightfully, but the temperature and humidity are rising again.

Yesterday we gave an Irish lunch party with one of the Catholic brothers from the local mission whom we mixed with a Presbyterian surveyor from Dundalk who is working for the Overseas Development Dept. The brothers do a five-year tour here; it used to be seven, and there remain some of the older members of the Mission who remember a time when they went home once in twenty years, or even longer: so when we are feeling discontented or inclined to complain we think of them. Nothing much of moment – Fergus has had a slight attack of malaria. Mary, Katharine and I something suspected of being amoebic dysentery which used to be very serious, but can now be treated successfully, though if neglected can be nasty and is likely to recur, so we will all need a good check-up when we get to Boston in the autumn. Mary decided to walk properly shortly after we got here, and has lost her fear of the hard floors. Her personality is improved with seeing so many new faces, though she will never be the extrovert that Katharine is. She is feeding well and was not unhappy about the dysentery apart from a fever one night: *I*, on the other hand, feel as if I had been wallowing in shit for the last few days. Various little sample bottles destined for the lab. are lying about the house, there are numerous accidents and to add to that the antelope which, though kept largely outside, is very fond of coming in. Katharine, however, always informs me if anyone has so far forgotten him or herself as to do a smelly on the floor. The Sunday papers are much missed though I doubt if I would have time to do more than glance at them; please send some Brillo pads and a nylon pan brush next time you are rolling one up, otherwise we are well stocked with supplies, indeed we will probably have a surplus. There will be no difficulty getting rid of stores as even in Kumasi deliveries now come very infrequently and are sold out within a few hours of reaching the shelves. We have a great sense of relief at the prospect of clearing out for good in July, and fling each emptied tin with satisfaction in the dustbin as being one less item to get rid of when the final clearance takes place.

Interval for capturing antelope who was uneasy because of so many noisy children and was tearing around the house and garden; it cannot be trusted to return unless Fergus comes to dish out reassurance. I have been pursuing it squeaking frantically with San's pink rubber rabbit to the noise of which it responds.

Sunday 25 April 1965

This is a very pleasant morning – more rain fell a few days ago and there is a slight breeze stirring all the foliage, so though hellish hot in the sun, it is quite pleasant in the shade. Mary has just gone off for a snooze while Katharine and Fergus are disporting themselves with five neighbouring children and a football. They are part of a huge family who live in an adjacent bungalow – 'educants' [a word coined by Francis Kofi] more or less: father is a nominal RC with two Muslim wives and a total of seventeen children as far as we can work it out. Two small girls of probably seven and five called Amina and Alamina come every day accompanied by a ten year old brother called Adam who is invaluable as he looks after both Katharine and Mary, and exerts himself pushing Kinky [stuffed donkey on wheels] and the pram. I wish you could see Kinky and the pram speeding through the bush in a sort of chariot race; the former is showing signs of wear and is now laterite coloured: he will collapse soon owing to constant overloading.

Our healths and tempers are variable according to the amount of sleep and whatever disease is current. Fergus is presently suffering from bad backache at night, but has got over the malaria. I had a most painful, but unidentified bite on the foot last week: swelling and intense itch for 48 hours, then gradually subsiding. Dysentery is in abeyance at the moment and we are well stocked with suitable drugs. Katharine still wakes at least once at night – often twice – while Mary mostly goes right through. However, should we be blessed with a good night childwise, there is some other disturbance like a rain, electric or wind storm, or recently a mouse in the bedroom necessitating frequent, ineffective sorties with torch or hurricane lamp. Torch batteries are now 2 to 3/- each if obtainable at all.

Monday 26 April

Yesterday was far from a day of rest, so I didn't get your letter finished. In the morning two of the RC Mission brothers called for a chat and a drink, and one of them has kindly volunteered to hitch up our generator. He thinks very little work is now needed to get it going, so perhaps after all we will have a few weeks of benefit. In the evening we were invited to dine at their Seminary with a French Canadian Father, an African one, two brothers (one Swiss and one German) and a visiting Swiss architect who is designing an extension for them which they will build themselves. They are a lively, much travelled, highly dedicated group, and I have great admiration for them. The local American Baptists, in contrast, seem a churlish uneducated lot, desperately narrow in outlook and frightened to mix with any other group even if Christian. The other denominations get together from time to time, but apparently the Baptists refuse all invitations. They have, however, just acquired an antelope of another breed than ours, and came to ask advice on rearing. (Fergus had previously refused it, though I thought two would not be much more trouble than one.) On further reflection, I am sure it would, and would add to the already vast quantity of powdered milk that has to be laboriously mixed with an egg whisk, and the large number of puddles and smellies that have to be cleared up. [*The other thing I recall about the Baptists was that their children were always ailing and looked pallid and undernourished. They were not allowed to play with the locals either. So far my letters contain no mention of the contingent of Russian geologists who were based some distance outside Wa. Karel Sin knew something of their existence as they would sometimes require medical treatment; it seems they were under strict orders not to mix with any other ex-patriate group, and had to report at regular intervals to a Party official based in Tamale.*]

If time permits today I must make an effort to write to G. Durrell at his Jersey Zoo to see if he would like our kob. This will be yet another headache associated with our departure – still, it could have been a hippo or croc. Katharine is trying very hard to learn how to carry things on her head, but straight, shiny hair is a disadvantage. Her favourite load is her potty (full) into the lav. for emptying – so far no accidents, but it is just a matter of time.

Friday 30 April

Mary is fed and Katharine is flat out having played furiously all morning with her numerous friends who at times seem like taking over the house: one finds them reclining on the floor, sitting in odd corners all over the place, or just watching my operations in the kitchen with wide eyes – rather like the antelope – hoping for the odd hand-out. These I give, partly because it encourages Katharine to compete, and partly because I think they are undernourished. It doesn't show in the smaller ones, but from about seven onwards, they look thin legged, thick jointed and a bit ribby.

We have had electric light since last Tuesday thanks to the labours of one of the RC brothers, and it makes such a difference, in effect lengthening our day by three hours. Previously by the time the children were off and there was any chance of peace, one could not read in comfort, and excursions to the kitchen were a groping irritation; added to that mantles for Aladdin lamps are now almost unobtainable, so we were threatened with reliance on hurricane lamps only.

Postal services are appallingly slow and seem to have deteriorated again – internal post often takes ten days and it is just not worth the expense sending wires.

Last week I got another horrible bite, on the finger this time, but so far am the only victim. I want Fergus to have a proper overhaul before he goes to the US, and he agrees for once. He has had bad backache at night for the last month, various aches in the diaphragm, neck and back and a general feeling of debility so we suspect some tropical ailment. It might be just suppressed malaria, but should be diagnosed. I forgot to tell you that the first night of the 'electric' we had to extinguish all but one bulb owing to an invasion of thousands of flying ants, moths etc., nothing is perfect. Have even read a book – about the third since Mary was born – Rebecca West *The Harsh Voice* – Penguin edition. I think you might enjoy it even though most of the characters are nasty. We'll be home in no time, but not for long I suspect. Love to San and yourself.

Monday 17 May

We are still waiting for Part I of your last letter to arrive. Part II containing a detailed and all too convincing bank statement came late last week.

We had a two day visit from David Molesworth, the Chief Leprologist, who was making his annual grand tour of the north; he is an undemanding sort of guest, with a fund of amusing anecdotes, which is just as well as I was stricken with some nameless and debilitating ailment the day he arrived, managing only with great effort to prepare lunch the following day before crawling off to bed in a state of collapse. Ailment – as usual – responded to blasts of anti-malarial, so I suppose it *must* have been that despite my conscientious pill taking. Katharine was assiduous in making frequent visits to the sick bed, bouncing thereon while saying, 'Poor Mummy's sick,' in deeply affected tones. However the strain of infants has been lifted somewhat by the acquisition of a male nanny who looks after them or supervises activities on the veranda, takes them out in the pram etc. He is a 'brother' of Abdulai, i.e. same tribe and unemployed, presently sponging on Abdulai for odd meals and general sustenance as is the custom. Should Abdulai fall on evil days he can expect to sponge on some other member of the tribe to an equal extent. Yakubu will receive a small salary at the end of the month, sundry discarded garments and so forth. Katharine has just returned from a morning sortie to Adam's house and smells unmistakeably African – one of those undefinable smells – slightly sweaty with a dash of charcoal fire about it. She still eats very little at home but seems to get enough by scrounging Abdulai's unhealthy white bread which is infinitely preferred to our own wholemeal variety. She also likes groundnuts, shea nuts which have a high fat content and from which the local butter is made, mangoes and the ubiquitous dawa-dawa which leaves all the children yellow mouthed: the season is almost over and I am rather glad as 'House & Garden' are littered with spat-out seeds and discarded pods.

Mary's vocabulary is much the same as Katharine's this time last year: book, dog, turkeys, down, out and bad. She has been a bit off colour for the last week and very wakeful at nights which, with Katharine still rousing at least twice, wind and rain, though no more mice, has been a little trying.

Antelope still doing well and now coming when called – horns so far not emergent. I can bear the delay quite well: they will be two feet long and lyre-shaped and he often shunts his head hard up between my legs! Have written to G. Durrell offering him, but so far no reply. WHO has approached Fergus to do a survey of molluscs in Togo and Dahomey before going to the US, but he has told them it would be far too rushed and not, in any case, the best time of year to conduct one. There are many other problems too, such as accommodation for us, technical equipment etc. So he has said that he would be willing to undertake it after the year at

Harvard, i.e. late 1966, and that it should last for approximately six months.

The record-player is now going and we have been playing *Peter and the Wolf* (narrated by Peter Ustinov) almost every evening as both infants enjoy it. Unfortunately it is the only record really suitable for them, and we are getting a bit fed up with the repetition. Please see if you can find my battered old copy of *Peter Rabbit* and send it out.

Monday 31 May 1965

I am going to sell my Singer sewing machine here, they are much in demand as they are no longer imported, and I never felt the same about it since the mouse ate lumps out of the wood and used the base plate for a 'latrine' which removed all the enamel. Can you do a bit of research on lightweight models with a free arm for getting inside small armholes.

Fergus has been writing profuse reports and papers, so this has meant nose to typewriter during my 'spare' time. Nights continue hellish as Mary is now waking once at least which I hope is due to eye-teeth and will pass. She is a marvellous 'chopper' and can now be left with minimum supervision to pack it in herself: almost anything is acceptable – even a dead dragonfly found on the floor. The funny thing is she doesn't look any sturdier than Katharine did at the same age – if anything lighter. K's appetite continues capricious and she still likes her bottle – slight jealousy, I suspect. She gets quite a lot of unwholesome stodge at Adam's house and Abdulai says she demands her cut of anything going in his quarters. Her table manners are wholly African: 'I *want* to eat with my fingers, I don't like a spoon.' She and two other dear little souls were playing a singing game on the veranda a few days ago, chanting Ai Ai Assin. After much enquiry we got a sheepish translation – it means 'Do not urinate on the meat.' Another amusing anecdote from last week. A local acquaintance came asking for a loan of £20 (which he did not get), but Fergus enquired why the sum was required. It was to pay the police to persuade them to discontinue an action which his wife was taking against him, as he and the wife had, after the heat of the moment when she made a formal charge, agreed to patch up the quarrel out of court. But what was the dispute? 'Oh, she refuse to do my washing and when I made a row she pull my testicles and they have swell. Then I was angry and "somehow" her ear got in my mouth and I bit it.' Relationships around here tend to be at about that level. Abdulai tells me that he have two wife, but no get good one yet. The first, though daughter of a good Muslim, drank and smoked wee (Indian hemp) and the second one just lay around the house and refuse to cook. So he 'finish with women – all be the same.'

Mousa is in the process of purchasing another after last year's fiasco. This involves further borrowing from Fergus whose interest-free loans are much sought.

Fergus has been summoned to Accra for a few days and I don't look forward to being here on my own with the infants, but don't see that he can get out of it. It will be a chance to get a few extra supplies, though we have done remarkably well since March, only recently running out of butter and still having some bacon.

Monday 14 June

A long, interesting, letter from you came last week telling of progress with your garden and visit to Rowallane [*National Trust garden in Northern Ireland*].

Fergus is at present in Accra – or I hope so anyway as he left here last Friday – mainly to see his Brazzaville boss who stayed here in April last year, and to clarify the last stages of his assignment. When he returns we should have a much more definite plan for the following few weeks. Fergus's back has been a bit better, but is still perceptible, and the local MO, in whom we have little faith, said it sounded like an ulcer which is quite probable considering family history and the pressures and general tension over the last few months, not to mention the future prospect of going back to school again at Harvard, where he will have to study bio-statistics with little more mathematical ability than I have at his disposal!

I forgot to tell you about the enormous spiders we had in the house one evening after a heavy rainfall: you would have hung yelping from the fans I think. They were a sort of cross between a lobster with huge hairy pincers and a spider – probably harmless, but we sprayed them with No-Bug before they had a chance to run into the bedrooms.

We are having days alternately very hot and quite chilly, but it still requires no great courage to get into a bath run straight from the cold tap and we haven't had a proper hot bath since coming here. Last Wednesday we had a send-off party for Daniel who is going to Kintampo for a six-month training course. There was lots of beer and a large stew with rice, yams and fried plantain, plus a cake, custard and tinned fruit – all much appreciated. The guests were ill-assorted, but as Daniel had chosen them, we couldn't complain: as usual they ranged from well educated down to near natural ju-ju men. Rose, his fiancée, with whom he had a nice little domestic set-up, was present. She is a primary school teacher and while largely silent, was able to contribute to the talk if positively brought in – more than most do.

Both infants are reasonably well, though subject to a succession of cut knees, stubbed toes etc. which in spite of washing and Cetavlexing nearly always turn red and are slow to heal. Mary, though much slower than Katharine in taking off into the wide open spaces, made up for it last week by just setting off and walking down the road to Adam's house, before which she had never ventured further than the veranda step. She was furious when retrieved.

The kob despite low intelligence has shown signs of missing Fergus and went completely off his bottle for three meals running, which has never happened before. Hunger got the better of him yesterday and this morning he did a bull and toreador act with me to get some more. Horns still only about half an inch long, but head like a rock and strength unbelievable considering his slender build.

Katharine is a shameless shower-off now – not in all company, she has her favourites, one of the brothers at the Mission and a Swiss architect who is designing their new technical school. 'Look, me are running and me are jumping, I nearly fell down, I am reading my book.' etc. She is definitely at the Beatrix Potter stage now, but the two you sent will do till we get home. *Two Bad Mice* belonged to Auntie Rosemary [*b. 1910*] – that's why it is so worn. Katharine still obviously remembers all at home, but most importantly the 'bull' which licked her hand.

Wa, Friday 25 June

I have no idea when I last wrote, but know it was before Fergus left for Accra. He returned safely after an absence of ten days. The time didn't pass too slowly, though this is an odd place to find oneself encamped on one's own with two small children. His indigestion had been better while he was away, but we soon fixed that by means of my developing a sudden fever and the worst poisoned bite ever, the day he got back. The usual story, I didn't see what bit me and had not even felt the bite. It came up slowly and by Monday evening I could not put foot to ground so was reduced to hopping. If put up it was quite bearable, but instant agony when put down again and circulation returned. Two injections in my rear have not made any great difference, so I suspect nature is just going to work a slow recovery – it is still elephantine and purple, but bearable. Fever as usual responded to anti-malarial.

Peter Rabbit and the photographs came last week – both much appreciated. The local barber is on the veranda doing Fergus's hair and delighted with his picture. It now looks as if we shall leave here about the end of July: Fergus's itinerary is as follows: 7 August to Brazzaville for 'de-briefing', back to Accra 12 August to collect us if we travel together which begins to look unlikely again as he may have to go to Geneva *en route*,and I don't particularly want to take the children – just too complicated. From Geneva he proposes to take a fortnight's unpaid leave in NI leaving on 7 September or thereabouts for Boston. A kind letter from the McMullans invites us *all* to stay any time we are in Washington.

Four of the European zoos have refused the antelope, and only one remains to reply: perhaps this is just as well because last Sunday morning he appeared with what seemed a badly injured eye. Something or somebody must have hit him, or perhaps it was a genuine accident. The veterinary people have treated it, and it has cleared up well, but the eye remains slightly cloudy which has spoiled his perfect beauty. It is beginning to look as if after all we may be forced to 'dash' him to the President or risk releasing him in the game reserve at Damongo. If they take him far enough into the reserve he might join up with a herd of his own kind. On the other hand they might well reject him as being too humanized.

Must go now and start the evening round of preparations for feeds, baths etc. which is considerable in spite of having help. Both infants gave me only two really bad nights while Fergus was away, but have made up for it since his return. Mary now wakes at 10 or 11 and despite being given a drink whines on for hours at a low level just enough to prevent me dropping off. After she finally goes off, Katharine wakes and remains restless for ages wanting drinks and consequently pots. Mary has also taken to rising at 5 a.m. during the last few days. You know *nothing!*

Monday 12 July 1965

I expect you are sticking close to home today on the Glorious Twelfth – always meant to ask you if summer trippers make a nuisance of themselves on the way down to the shore. This will be a very rushed note because the post goes out tonight and I have just realized that I should tell you not to send any more letters to Wa as we intend to leave on 28th for Tamale from where we will all fly to Accra. Fergus has sold the car in Tamale for £350 which is not bad considering it is six years old, but then imported cars – when obtainable – are prohibitive. In Accra Fergus hopes to get the use of a Government car during our short stay.

Our journey will no doubt be one of endurance, further complicated by a cable today from Hanover Zoo saying they will take the antelope. He is far too big for a bottle, but gets it as an inducement to stay around the compound and return at nights. We have already begun packing and are lucky in that we can use the rest house crockery etc. for the last few days when all our own stuff will be in cases. Healths continue variable; indeed during the last five months seldom a week has passed without one of us being *hors de combat*. Both children have had a heavy cold imported by their dear little friends: cold not too bad, but accompanying hacking cough has had the usual effect on Mary's sensitive throat, so we have been clearing up sick with monotonous regularity. Three days ago I developed it along with high fever which, if repeated as often as I have had it, debilitates. Abdulai is hatching it today, but Fergus remains clear so far. Must rush now as I have to hoof down to the PO with this, Fergus having taken the car down to tennis with Katharine. Our invaluable baby minder will take care of Mary while I escape.

This seems to have been the last letter from Wa. I am surprised how many things were not mentioned which remain clear in memory. The trips down to the pork butcher who operated under a large mango tree in the village – killing was once a week only and the head a much sought after delicacy to be seized and swung off in a sloshing bucket. Sometimes we would foregather after tennis at the Love All Canteen for cool drinks. At that time some of our African friends were becoming almost paranoid: I recall one of them darting from the rusty metal table to check if there was someone on the other side of the fence listening to our conversation.

A grand farewell party was held to mark our departure, for which a very special stew was prepared containing virtually all meats and fishes locally obtainable. There was chicken, pork, catfish from the Black Volta which always tasted muddy, giant land snail – a particularly rubbery delicacy, and goat, the hairy ear of which protruded from the vast bowl, and was offered to me as an exceptional delicacy: I am sure it was very rude by local custom, but I demurred saying I thought it should go to my husband. There were meals at Tamale where the women of the house slaved in the back regions, never sitting down to table even if the host was their husband and a professional man; naturally I felt most uncomfortable being the sole female at table. I learned the sticky nature of fu-fu which is a white, sticky belly filler made from cassava. Much mirth is engendered by watching a guest unaccustomed to local food attempting to help himself: the secret being first to glaze a spoon with oily stew before plunging it into the communal dish of fu-fu which remains a leaden weight in the stomach for hours. I had also learned to decapitate snakes when necessary. Our veranda had to be checked before the children were allowed out to play because from time to time there were unwelcome intruders: never thankfully of any great size, but I did not enjoy having to employ a machete to kill a snake, particularly as many were subsequently identified as harmless.

In the end the kob was left at Damongo game reserve: it was not enjoying the road trip in its specially made crate, and we thought its chances of survival were probably better there than in the south. Whatever the destination, there was a risk that it might find its way into someone's cooking pot – sadly we shall never know if it adapted to the wild.

I went home to Ireland with the two children while Fergus went through sundry de-briefing sessions and discussions at Geneva. Shortly after reaching NI we all turned bright yellow, and were diagnosed as having hepatitis B. I was the recipient of much advice from people already embarked upon the MPH degree course at Harvard about foods to be avoided at all cost: coffee, eggs and alcohol in particular were off the menu; I had consumed all three on a regular basis, but did not confess.

After spending the best part of a year in Boston we returned to NI to prepare for the next African assignment which began early in 1967 and was based at Mwanza on the southern shore of Lake Victoria in Tanzania; by that time there were three children.

APPENDIX I

*ESSAYS BY FIELD ASSISTANTS AT KINTAMPO
AND LETTERS FROM FRIENDS AND
ACQUAINTANCES 1960–2001*

THE LEVEL OF English – as mentioned in the main text – of the employees at the Medical Field Units Headquarters in Kintampo varied from aspiring School Certificate to that of basic Primary School. Many had been educated by the White Fathers in Mission schools in the Gold Coast; their handwriting was neat, legible, and not always conventional copper-plate. The Kofi brothers, for instance, had entirely different styles. Francis, the elder, used pure copperplate, while Daniel wrote in an upright style verging on florid.

When my husband Fergus was appointed WHO counterpart to the Director of the Ghana Medical Field Units, the Headquarters of which was situated at Kintampo, he was allocated a number of field and laboratory assistants. Francis, who belonged to the Ewe tribe of south-east Ghana, was Chief Field Assistant and Daniel, who was not strictly a brother in the sense of sharing the same mother but more in the tribal sense which prevails throughout West Africa, was a trainee laboratory assistant. The latter learned to be a competent typist and became valued in the team for his skills in draughtsmanship, preparing many maps and diagrams for the project reports.

I see now that I asked far too much of them in terms of weekly output and comprehension: for instance in April 1961 I asked them to analyse a speech by Julius Nyerere, leader of the Tanganyika African National Union and Chief Minister leading the African side at the constitutional talks with Britain's Colonial Secretary, Mr Ian McLeod, and to provide alternative words for those I had under-lined in the text. That would have been difficult for a sixth-former in the UK. Here is the speech.

I think we may commit the same silly mistakes that have been committed by the other nations of the world. First, we are in danger of becoming the most Balkanised continent of the world. Unless we are careful, we are going to find ourselves, after the present wave of nationalism which is temporarily binding Africa together, entering a period of eighteenth century nationalism. The mistakes which have been committed in Europe are obvious. If we don't avoid them, we shall get into trouble; and what is more, we shall lose the opportunity of helping the progress of history. We are not, for instance, an armed continent. We come to independence when the world is frightened and talking about disarmament and all that. Now, one thing Africa could do, which could be very helpful, is to refuse to arm; and there would be very good reasons for such a refusal. If we arm in Tanganyika, no one would believe me if I said we were arming in order to defend Tanganyika from possible aggression by Britain or America or India or China or the USSR, because I could never defend our country against these world powers. So why should we arm? We could only be arming against Kenya or Nyasaland or Uganda. It is madness for Africa at this stage to arm against Africans. One contribution I think we could make to the present history of the world, is to refuse to arm – and really set an example to the other continents of the world.

It was a well-intentioned attempt to extend their limited vocabulary. I remember too embarking on the subject of countable versus uncountable nouns, not to mention correct use of the apostrophe. An essay entitled 'A Street Scene' was also requested: I am not certain who the author of the one which follows was, but suspect it was Francis Kofi.

A STREET SCENE

The news of the death of Abdul Amid Ababa spread rapidly in the municipality of Accra, Ghana's capital, on 3 December last year. The front pages of the local newspapers reported the incident of the rich Syrian who stayed in Accra for many years. His statesmanship and contributions to building of race-courses, schools and churches throughout Ghana made him famous and also dear to the people. His body was to be cremated on the Awudome

Crematorium and the great man's funeral procession was one of the impressive street scenes of our time. Before ten in the morning hundreds of sympathizers gathered near his home, the Avenidad Lodge, at Adabraka. The Cabinet Ministers including several prominent people from the neighbouring states, French Togo and Ivory Coast were there. These foreigners flew into the country by charted planes in order to witness the cremation of the Syrian, a friend to the poor and the rich. Church and political dignitaries bore the bier from his house to the street where a state charriot was waiting to carry the corpse. The crowd was dense and it was not easy for those who were carrying the remains of Abdul to reach the street quickly. Mr Padmore who took part nearly fainted because of suffocation and youth had to change him.

After placing the dead on the cart, Hamid, the Asian Priest, blessed it and the procession began. The priest dressed in a black robe with white waist band made of white cloth to match the copious turband of many folds, led the crowd. He held a cross and an incense burner which dangled while he stepped thoughtfully along the pavement. The horses, two in number, followed with their load and the vast sea of people moved quietly behind. Odd Fellows, who dressed in black, carrying open swords, were prominent in the crows. The blouses of the women, the variegated head gears which they wore and the black and red apparels of the men drew much attention. The strong scent of Eastern incense wafted in the air. Those who did not take part in the procession rushed from both sides of the street and stared with open mouths. Several others climbed on tops of trees, terraces, lamp-posts, roofs and vehicles just to look at the remains of the philanthropist. The procession was about half a mile long.

When the funeral procession reached the Independent Monument, the bier was gently lowered and a detachment of soldiers of the Ghana Army paid their last homage to the departed great man, Abdul Amid Ababa. President Nkrumah made a short speech in which he pointed out why the nation should lament for the great loss. At the entrance of the Crematorium many among the crowd drew back, and the remaining people, mostly men, went in. The corpse which was carefully wrapped in white linen, bedecked with flowers, sprinkled with incense, rosewater and perfume, was placed on a pile of faggots. The Asian priest who looked pale and depressed lit the great pile of woods. While the fire started burning, the surrounding mourners threw their flowers into the fire. The priest, on his part, sat on the ground looking into the sky where the smoke of the great blazing fire ascended. His lips moved silently and he raised his hands towards heavens. It is hard to forget a scene of this kind from the street to a pile of blazing faggots.

The two essays which follow are by either Francis or Daniel – because they are competently typed I suspect the latter. There were underlying strains in this brotherly relationship, veiled hints implying a degree of mental instability, and inadequate apprecia- tion of Francis's efforts. Of the two Daniel was the more reserved and sensitive. I have allowed the original errors of spelling and punctuation to remain.

MY TRIBE AND SOME OF ITS CUSTOMS

Both my parents are Ewe, a tribe which now occupies the south- eastern portion of Ghana and also the south and the central parts of the Republic of Togoland. It is a popular belief that the Ewe, long ago, stayed at Oyo, a place in southern Nigeria and from there they came and settled at their present places. During the great trek, the tribe suffered many hardships from hunger, poverty, wild animals, enemies through whom they passed and, above all, from their own tyrant rulers. As a result of their long suffering, the Ewe became hardy, powerful, resourceful and, in short, civilized before the introduction of the Western civilization into West Africa. Thus my tribe had their own way of worship, of curing deseases and their own customs most of which are unwritten, but handed over from one generation to another. Among these ancient customs is the 'Libation'. The Ewe believe that there is life after death and that all their ancestral ghosts live invisibly among them. According to this doctrine, they believe also beyond all doubts, that ghosts eat and drink as human beings do. The departed do not only drink and eat but they have supernatural power to bless and avert evils or curses. In order to invoke the spirit of the dead, libation is per- formed.

The invoker says his wishes aloud and pours a liquor, prefer- ably a strong drink, on the ground in little bits. In the olden days, only the palm wine was used but nowadays all imported spirits are allowed by the elders of the tribe for the performance of this important ritual.

Libation is performed at all occation when an Ewe wishes to undertake a perilous journey or has escaped from a great danger. It is also witnessed during all tribal celebrations.

One of the ancient customs which still exists among my tribe is rendering a witch powerless. My tribe believe in witchcraftcy. The Ewe look down opon the practice as they contend that witches live on nothing but on human blood.

When a person is suspected to be a witch, she is brought before an ordeal which usually proves if the allegation is true or not. A person who is proved to be a witch brings a disgrace to herself and all the people in her family. She is brought to the shade of a big tree, usually planted in the centre of the village. There, in the public, the suspect is shaved and his head washed with a potion made of several herbs, red clay and urine. The accused is forced to take some of the mixture too. After the washing and drinking ceremony, the witch often confesses all her evil deeds. The last event of this custom is to slaughter a sheep and pour its blood on the feet of the witch with a belief that she has been cleansed from her evil practices and that the power in her becomes inert. Her family pay a large sum of money to the chief and his elders in fine.

Many other customs still exist among the Ewe and most of them are exotic and blood curling. Those which involve human sacrifices are abolished by the law.

MY BROTHERS AND SISTERS

Our family is a very large one – I have only one brother and six sisters and among these people only two of my sisters are older than I. Thus I am the third by birth among my parent's children, and Rudus, my only brother, who is now twenty-five is the youngest of us all.

The days of our childhood were happy ones and I often feel certain that those pleasant times which rolled away will never come to me again. Our parents were prosperous farmers in the woody plains in the Volta Region of Ghana. We were born and bred in a farm-yard which stood on a well-drained land, the healthiest place in the vast clan's family land.

There in the woods about ten miles from Peki, the biggest and important town in the district, stood my father's compound house, a kind of a Roman villa; but having a brown stucco, a typical characteristic of a west African building.

I would be three years or four when my elder sisters were already of age: they had completed their elementary school education in the Peki Mission School. In the evenings they used to assemble the household children together and teach us nursery hyms and also how to read and write.

The happiest day I had when I was young was the day on which our elder sister was married. Our relatives from the neighbouring villages and towns visited us and my father had our fattest turkey killed for the marriage feast.

I could not stay long with my parents in the farm-yard and so three of my sisters and also Rufus, were born when I was in the Mission boarding school. Although we could no longer stay together as we were sent to different schools and colleges, we arranged to meet in the farm-yard to spend the Christmas with our parents. Now as all my sisters are married and Rufus too is now a prosperous transport owner, our parents alone remain in the farm-yard. The old servant, Jacob, who cared for us when we were young, is still faithful to them.

The only family disaster we had was the death of the sister who followed me by birth thus at present we are seven who are still strongly bound by family ties.

In order to rivive our childhood love, to make our children know one another and to make our old parents feel proud of us and happy, all my sisters and the only brother come from different parts of the country with their families, once in every three years for a feast in the farm-yard. We meet and feast under the same orange tree that stands in the middle of the house. [*This would indicate a perimeter wall with buildings, trees, and the whole referred to as the house.*] Any time we gather for such a reunion in the house where we were born and bred I recollect my childhood events which flush thrugh my mind and pass off as moving pictures.

Francis continued to work with the Medical Field Units, although with less enthusiasm after Dr Scott retired and a Ghanaian was appointed to the Directorship. With the help of a reference from Fergus he achieved his ultimate goal of an appointment with the WHO Guinea Worm Eradication Project in south-east Ghana. Francis must now be in his mid seventies, but continues to drive a taxi in New York in order to help with his extensive family commitments in Ghana.

Aglionby House,
Adisadel College,
CAPE COAST
16 September 1960

My Dear Dr and Mrs MacCullogue,

I have arrived safely at Cape Coast and at school. I am settled now
for hard work. I thank you very much for giving me the *Observer*
as an example of a good British newspaper. I liked it very much
indeed. Honestly! It was easy to read and understand. I did not
have to make constant reference to my dictionary as I read it. It
contained more news and stories and less advertisement, comparatively. My dad found it very interesting as I did and he is going
to be subscriber when he gets to Kumasi. I will recommend it to
our school library board. Already we do have the *Sunday Times*
and the *New York Times*.

Doctor, when I first saw the photograph of Archbishop
Makarios, I thought it was you in robes. So I wondered if you have
been a priest some time ago. Until I read what was written below,
I did not know it was the Archbishop.

I was very pleased when I saw that our new school tennis lawn
is completed. We will start playing soon. I will be playing many
games this term. I will play hockey, cricket and lawn tennis. I will
not devote all my time to these because you know "All play and
no work makes Tom a mere boy". I am as fit as a fiddle and I hope
you are likewise. Mrs MacCullogue, I think your foot a bit better
now. God bless you. Bye.

I remain your friend,
E. Charles Smart-Abbey

St Paul's Primary School,
NAVRONGO
1 February 1961

Dear Mother,

I am very glad to write you this letter to ask you about your health
please Mother I thank you very very much for my shoes I also

thank your husband for the fountain pen and Domenose [domi-
noes] and the money Mr Doctor kindly thank my friend named
Daniel for me. Please sir thank the boys who always came to catch
tennis balls too. Reply the letter.

By Yamba Adda

St Paul's Primary School,
NAVRONGO 19 July 1961

Dear Mother,

I am very glad to write you this letter to ask you about yur health
are you all well or not please mother tell my father [Adda] that the
rain as fell and we have planted some crops and mother I heard
that you will be going home at the end of this month and when
you are going home please mother tell Doctor that he shuld send
me a Dictionary, a big note book and some readers and his racket
too and he shuld send me the colour pencils too and his Drawing
book too and please mother if you will not go home please mother
send me a letter to come during holidays and they will let us off
from 3 August to 13 September and mother there is nobody to play
dominose with me in Navrongo.

From Benedict Yamba Adda

[Yamba was probably no more than eight years old at this time, if
the photographs I have of him taken in 1962 are taken into
account. The handwriting would put to shame most of today's
British primary schoolchildren.]

PO Box 16,
KETA
15 December 1961

Dear Doctor and Mrs McCullough,

There is no fear that you are not coming back to Ghana any more.

There are fresh rumours from clerks in our main office that Head Office, Ministry of Health has telegrammed the Medical Officer in charge at Wa asking whether accommodation has been reserved for you and wife as it was possible that the Bilharziasis project would begin very soon. By this piece of interesting news I am much happy that you are surely coming back in course of about three weeks.

Thanks for your nice letter with my two copies of photographs received just as I was going to board Government transport to Keta on leave and in a very enjoyable mood I am at present writing to you from Keta. To my surprise my parents and sisters have already heard of your benevolent work you had done to Francis and myself during your happy stay in Ghana. They were very sorry that they did not know you personally, but they hope to know you better when you returned to Ghana.

I am happy to inform you that Francis was promoted to Field Assistant Grade I with effect from 14 November 1961. He received congratulations from many friends abroad; and on this information we the staff also had some drinks to mark the date of confirmation.

Mr Buckman was not able to fix me up. I believe their recruiting system has been changed and it might therefore not be possible for him alone to recruit new persons. But at any rate I shall send to him a letter today in order to know his mind about any other possible arrangement to make.

I could not join Wa Tennis Club owing to the fact that their monthly dues and entrance fees are heavy enough for a person like me to afford. But to maintain my skilfulness at tennis I often have strokes with my brother Francis on a private pitch prepared by ourselves. I can assuredly say I am steadily improving.

I am looking forward for your quick return to Ghana I hope by now you receive information about where to resume work. And I can assure you that that Country will be GHANA.

With best wishes for Christmas and the New Year,

Yours sincerely,

Daniel Kofi

P. O. Box 5,
KINTAMPO
23 March 1962

Dear Sir,

I am in receipt of your letter with many thanks.

I was transferred temporally to Gambaga and so your letter came during my absence. I arrived at Kintampo on 20 March. I was very delighted with the contents.

I have also distributed the photographs accordingly, as directed. The owners are all quite well. I also received your parcel addressed to me yesterday. All the employees in the Ministry were astonished. I thank you very much and this has proved of your sincere love to me.

May God bless you in all your ways. I know you have replaced my late father for the kind love you have shown me. I am quite well and I hope you are too. Extend my sincere greetings and thanks to your wife as well.

I am your step son Kwaku Nsoah x his mark

[*This may have been written by the village scribe because of the x his mark?*]

PO Box 16. KETA
7 June 1962

My dear Doctor and Madam,

I am pleased to inform you that I safely arrived home yesterday and met my parents and other members of our family fit and happy. The journey from Wa to Keta was quite smooth and enjoyable.

I arrived in Kumasi just when Kingsway Stores had received new Maxply and Slazenger rackets. I was so happy and thought I could wait and buy mine at Accra because there was no guts for stringing the rackets. But to my bitter disappointment there was no Maxply racket in Accra. There were only five Slazengers in

Kingsway and none at all in UTC I nearly went mad then the salesman seeing my grief informed me that a staff of the UAR Embassy had bought one which he had in fact not paid for and that I should visit the store at 4 p.m. If by that time he failed to pay as he had promised he would give it out to me. I became worried and luckily I discovered that the man is an Ewe and I spoke to him and at last he gave it to me. However he promised to arrange for the transfer of some of the rackets from Kumasi to Accra when I told him that Kumasi had plenty. If our members at Wa who have no rackets really want to get them, they must hurry up quickly to Kumasi and clear the Maxply there. It is cheaper than the Slazengers. Maxply frame costs 75/6 while Slazenger costs 98/6. Kumasi stringing is, guts £2 10s. and nylon £2 5s. Accra stringing is guts £2 5s. and nylon 30/- Kumasi was short of guts and Accra was also short of nylon strings. Now the situation is as follows: Maxply rackets with guts is £6 5s. 6d., with nylon £6 0s. 6d. Slazengers with guts £7 8s. 6d., with nylon £7 3s. 6d. At Accra Maxply is £6 0s. 6d. and £5 5s. 6d. respectively, and Slazengers £7 3s. 6d. and £6 8s. 6d. respectively.

I saw Mr Chris Brindt and convey your greetings to him. He happily returns his to you. I hope by now your boxes have arrived at Wa. Have you moved to your Wa house now?

Frontier measures on Ghana and Togoland border at Aflas have been tightened and it is not likely that I will visit Lome.

Wishing you all the best, sincerely Francis Kofi

PO Box 567, ACCRA
12 April 1962

My Wholehearted Mum and Dad,

Your letter dated 29th September 1961 reached your son on the 7th day of October, 1961. Your material advice within, automatically redobbled my enthusiasm. That alone, expresed to me that, though I am black my parents who are white in N. Ireland are thinking and praying in the name of Our Heavenly Father for my best position in future.

Now! Father and Mother, kindly accept my apology for failing to send an immediate reply on receipt. The main reason was that your son misplaced the letters. And, I am quite confident that this is to your understanding. Thank you very much.

Towards the maltreatment, which has withdrawn your return to Ghana, kindly let me know your position in health plus the present appointment. Whereever you are, if your Son is aware of it, that will enable him to pay you a visit in a very fine Christmas one day.

My parents, I will be twenty-six years old on the 25th day of May, 1962 therefore thus your information in Ghana about your son. Attached to my appointment, I am now hunting for. But as the Government is without a National Fire Brigade I am up to now unemployed. With this too, kindly help me to gain through your advice an employment in immediate reply.

I have renewed my passport. The new one will expire on 9th December, 1966. Your son was amazed on the day that he went for the collection. It is valid for all countries (If it will not disturb you, I would throw away my profession, and join you as your servant.) But this is a matter of explanation.

Mum and Dad I am quite confident that, in the name of Our Heavenly Father, your future appointment will be better than that of the Government of Ghana. I am extending to both of you my warm greetings. And with a profound joy for your sincere reply.

Yours affectionately, Emmanuel Abougoye

KINTAMPO, 9 December 1962

Dear Mrs McCullough,

It pleases me very much to drop you these few lines to thank you ever so much and wish you good luck and happy days during your stay at home. Although I thought we would stay together a bit longer but due to your Conception which is taking you back home. I wish you the best luck for ever and may Almighty God bless you to bring forth well. I hope you will bring forth a male child and I shall be very grateful if you would be kind enough to inform me the date of your new born baby, and I shall name him Navro. [after Navrongo, his home village near Bolgatanga].

Do not bother very much indeed for God knows and sees everything. I wish you the best luck and safety journey till you return.

I shall do all I can to look after everything in the house and

Master as well till you return. I wish you safe journey and extend my best regards to all you family for me. Goodbye Madam till we meet Again.

Yours faithfully,
Francis Adda

At home, KETA, 7 July 1964

Dear Doctor,

You are reading from Daniel. I safely arrived at home on the 6th instant. I supposed it might interest you to know something about my trip to Keta.

I started from Wa on the 4th instant, last Saturday on an Ambulance by way of Tamale to Kumasi at 8.15 pm. I noticed the following day, Sunday that I was very tired to continue my journey so I decided to break the journey until the next day.

In Kumasi after a few hours rest I visited the Sports Stadium at 2.30 pm to witness a match between Ashanti Kotoko and Real Republicans. The Real Republicans beat Ashanti Kotoko by 4 goals to 3. After the match I called at Seth's house to greet him and to deliver messages I conveyed from Wa to him. Seth gave me supper and we later went to Picture house to see an interesting film entitled *The Saturday Island*. It is a romantic and adventurous film. On Monday the 6th inst. I continued my journey from Kumasi at 8 am and arrived in Accra at Mid-day. From Accra at 2 pm by Tema I arrived at Keta a few minutes passed 10 pm. I am now among my beloved parents and sisters who are very pleased to see me. Actually, the sort of hospitality and reception I received can be more seen and witnessed than described.

This letter is just to inform you of my safe arrival home. I am not yet out to see changes so far in progress. I hope we shall have a chat on that when I am back.

I believe everything goes well with Madam, Katharine and Mary. Please extend my compliments to them and inform them of my coming on 22nd instant.

Yours sincerely, Daniel Kofi

The following letter was written to my mother:

Rural Health Services, DENU, 5 May 1966

I am happy to inform you that your three photographs have safely reached me and I thank you sincerely for the trouble you have taken in making it possible. It is so very kind of you. The photographs have made me and my family so happy, especially the children; because they have afforded us the opportunity of seeing myself in a colour photo for the first time and comparing myself with others. I must be grateful to Dr and Mrs McCullough for their kindness and friendship.

Ghana, my dear country, is truely free now. When the years of correction and reconstruction are over, we hope, it will become a land of milk and honey. I wish the McCulloughs had come back to Ghana now to enjoy at least the freedom of liberty and speech and mutual trust that surround us now in pacification for the little they had suffered with us.

Let us hope you will be a member of a UK/NI Trade Mission to Ghana one day to see us in prosperity.

Will you kindly remember us to Auntie Dorothy.

With greetings and good wishes to you, thank you once more,

Yours sincerely,
Francis Kofi

District Commissioner's Office,
PO Box 16, WA
24 October 1963

Dear Madam,

UNITED NATIONS DAY

1. I am happy to unfurl to you my high appreciation of the spirit in which the appeal was readily responded to.

2. The Committee places on record its gratefulness for the magnificent books you so generously presented out of which good selections have been made for the awards referred to in my letter under reference. The rest of the books are being kept for future awards.

3. May this gesture lead to higher things in the struggle for the salvation of the unfortunate class of mankind.

Yours faithfully,

William? Henkel, District Commissioner

[*I remember Mr Henkel's courteous help when we arrived at Wa and that he was much respected in the district as being the son of a German colonial officer.*]

This letter is from George Cansdale to whom I had written for advice on animal care:

Dear Mrs McCullough,

Thank you for your very interesting letter of 19 February. I will first answer your specific queries.

(a) I think that reasonable cleanliness is advisable, but that hospital standards are quite unnecessary.

(b) Without knowing the composition of the milk which each kind of animal produces, there is no possible way of knowing whether the milk offered is anything near correct. There is likely to be wide variation in fat content and also in the solids other than fat in the various milks.

(c) We know very little about the growth rate of pangolins, but the one which you received was some weeks old at least. One was actually born in my house when I lived in Oda; unfortunately I did not actually measure it before letting the mother take it away into the forest, but its head and body measurements must have been about 4 inches.

(d) I think it is very rare for an animal to damage its tongue by biting it, but it is not impossible. However, it is true that mouth ulceration is often the sign of diet deficiency and I have known it in several animals.

(e) Cassava leaves are an excellent food for many animals. The tubers of some varieties are poisonous, but this seems to be rare in Ghana.

Perhaps I could now make some general comments about the three cases which you describe. Pangolins are virtually impossible to keep in captivity, as one would expect from such a highly specialized feeder. The anatomy is quite extraordinary, with the roots of the tongue running the entire length of the body and the physiology is likely to be equally odd. My guess is that the one you had was already taking some solid food when brought in. The fact that it accepted milk does not mean much, for adults often lap milk at first, though they soon become restless and eventually go off all foods in most cases. I think that for this animal and its close relations, all food should probably be diluted with a good deal of roughage such as bran or some finely chopped up vegetable fibre.

You did well to keep yours for three months. I had many through my hands, most of which were released in the forest after a few days' observation; the only two that I really got established were lost through sheer bad luck. One of these escaped from its box on board ship and spent some hours in a cold part of the animal room, where it got a chill from which it never recovered.

Your second case mystifies me, for my experience with genets at that size was quite different. I believe that you might have succeeded in getting its confidence if you had persisted. The other two animals which you mention live in the forest, so presumably this was also caught there. From your description I think it was more likely a palm civet, which makes a charming pet, and not a genet. The forest genet is very spotted at all stages, even when as small as the one you describe.

I know the Royal Antelope very well and it is a heart-breaking animal to keep as a youngster in West Africa. Of many attempts I reared only one, and got it safely to London thanks largely to my wife's hard work. This one also never learned to suck from a bottle, but it took milk from a spoon and soon began taking broken corn and chopped green stuff. Ours lived indoors where it got on well enough with some of the other small creatures. It seemed to feel more secure in the darker atmosphere of the house, and I think they should not be put in an outside run until fully grown; even then they need a great deal of cover, never willingly coming into the open. The duikers, as a group, are very much easier to cope with.

Please do not hesitate to contact me again if you feel there are other points where I can help you. You will probably be going back by sea, sailing from Liverpool. I was going to suggest that if you were flying back you might care to phone me as you go through London, but I see that you are going back in April, and I am afraid that I shall be in the Middle East all that month. With every good wish for a very interesting tour.

Sincerely, George Cansdale

During my absence in N. Ireland for the purpose of 'bringing forth' Fergus made the acquaintance of James Pope-Hennessy who was at the time touring Ghana while collecting information for his forthcoming book Sins of the Fathers. *They formed an instant bond, and when I met James for the first time shortly after the birth, I also found him congenial and easy to talk to. Meetings, however, tended to come to an abrupt end with the appearance of his current 'amour', a member of the Household Cavalry, whose demands for instant gratification, such as a visit to the local cinema or a quick meal, took priority.*

9 Ladbroke Grove, W11
Monday 26 November 1963

My dear Fergus,

You have been most fearfully on my conscience – I cd have written you forty-five letters in the time that I have worried at not having written one. But now everything impels me to write – the final thrust being a beautiful Ashanti whom I met in my off-licence on Sunday night – he lives almost next door, and comes from that town below the Escarpment north of the Pra. 'How did you know I was from Ghana?' he enquired – I replied: 'Well at any rate you don't look like a *Nigerian*' – this wily answer went down well.

Anyhow I have been longing to write to you, but got restrained by work and also by indolence. I wish to God you were here at the end of January, when the BBC Television are producing a 50 minute 'documentary' of my new book (which I'll send you of course). I am working on the script, and have a young Australian composer doing the music and it is all great fun but very exhausting. Why *you* would like it is because, with Wa in mind, I have *insisted* on a vulture sequence, to vulture-music. We have some simply splendid stills of Victorian cemeteries on the Gold Coast, and then we dissolved to what seems to be a 'still' of vultures –

but is it? Oh, no, no. Suddenly they take off and swoop down on some carrion on the ground. We also have Chinese executions, Chinese heads on spikes (Hong-Kong), the sounds of whipping from Glendairy Gaol, Barbados, and other cosy-ish items. You *will* agree that I was right about the vultures?

You should give up painting and take to writing, in *my* view; for your letters are first-rate, and so curious and original. How is Katharine Ruth Siobhan facing up to Wa? And does your man, whose name escapes me – the cook I mean – like her? PLEASE write and tell me *all* Wa news, I can see every inch of the place in my mind's eye and often think about it.

I have re-made friends with Paul Danquah, whom I knew years ago – he is the son of Dr D and a cockney to whom he was or wasn't married when he was here as a student. Paul is a barrister, but also acted the coloured part in the film of *A Taste of Honey* if you ever saw that. He is being my Elmina voice in the programme; tomorrow we are going to an entertainment called 'SOS Africa' in aid of anti-apartheid. I gave the off-licence Ashanti my telephone number but he hasn't rung up, or has when I was out, otherwise I'd drag him there too. I am looking for a secretary and was offered one Kojo Mensa, who was a young press aide at Flagstaff House in his day and was then expelled from New York for communist sympathies. He is very, very, *very* black, with a high hysterical screech when he mentions the Osageyfo. His eyes are that special kind of orange (the whites I mean are orange) which I connect with certain Ghanaian personalities and which I always fancy means addiction to some drug? That chief near the Volta Project, with whom I lunched and had the narrow squeak over the Queen Mother's attendants who were about to be offered to me had just the same look. So I politely refused Kojo Mensa.

Incidentally, I am just signing a contract for a three-year work to be published in six countries simultaneously on the History of the Slave Trade. This means a return to Ghana in 1964, I hope and pray. Can I call in at Wa?

We have been trying to get William Obuibisa (Elmina, remember; keeper of the monuments and a very cheery youth) to disgorge photos of Elmina from the sea. *I* wrote to him; the BBC producer wrote to him; I asked Paul Danquah *how* one could get an answer – 'Just give him a ring,' he said, 'I give my Dad a ring once a week.' So I did. And down the telephone here on my desk came marvellous Ghanaian laughter and the sound of the sun on the walls of Elmina. Finally he *has* sent them – but neither to me nor to my producer, but to the Director-General of the BBC, London with carbon copies of his letter to be sent to me, to the Keeper of the Archives, Accra, to the Minister for Internal Affairs, Accra, etc. etc. 'Further to my three-minute radio-telephonic conversation with Mr James Pope-Hennessy in London on the 3rd ult.' – that kind of thing. It is rather heaven, not so? And *so* typical.

I must leave you, though I have much more to say. Give my love to Elizabeth, whom I *enormously liked* – she, I suppose, must have thought me mad. I have stopped smoking entirely, so that my hands are as steady as steady can be.

Can you contrive to obtain a vulture feather? This because Paul Bonner, my producer, and I do *not* agree about the colour of West African vultures. He wants them black, *I* think they are grey. Which of us is right?

I do apologise for this very long gap for which there is *no* excuse. But don't strike me off yr list because of it.

Your v. affectionate James

Epidemiology Division,
Ministry of Health,
PO Box 2848,
ACCRA, Ghana
1 July 1983

Dear Doctor and Madam,

Many thanks for your letter of 25 May 1983 intimating me on the efforts you are making to find brother Daniel a job with WHO. I greatly appreciate everything you have been doing for our Kofi family. I hope God will bless and crown your efforts with success, for in these difficult times when he is virtually jobless and life in Ghana so unbearable, Daniel needs that job. I will then be greatly relieved of the worries and anxiety I suffer over him.

However, there is a light of hope for Ghana because our present government is honest and streamlining things efficiently which has already attracted international confidence and assistance for the country. I hope it will not be long when things will start changing for the better. In my opinion this is the best Government Ghana has ever had and I wish they had appeared on the Ghana scene much earlier. Even though the Govt. is doing its very best, the situation is already very bad. There is acute food shortage in Ghana as a result of recent wholesale farm burns and destruction caused by bush fires and last years drought in addition to mismanagement of past governments. There is so much suffering and near starvation now in Ghana and I am scarred for life. My immediate problem is how to survive with my family till the situation improves. I am no longer proud of my large family which I managed to look after so happily in the past years with my limited resources. It is a miracle that we are still surviving. Would you believe it that the cost of 2 Kg. maize which cost 10.00 cedis during your last recent visit to Ghana is now costing 300.00 cedis? Everything else has gone up by the same rate. My take home pay is only 650.00 cedis a month. It is a great pity that our dear country should suffer like this. Farmers who have reserve food to sell are the best and affluent people in the society now. It is too late for me to start any serious farming now because I can only do so outside Accra. I may have to transfer or retire to the rural areas of good farming regions to do that and this is not possible now. My salary can not buy enough food for my family and there is no way I can supplement my income. The women, my wives try to help but it is not enough because commercial activities are restricted. The government is however bringing in some food items at control price but they are not reaching every family adequately. The rains have been kind this year and we hope to have bumper harvest to supplement Govt. effort to ease the situation. We trust God will help us survive. A few weeks before Dr David Scott died he told me the words of comfort and encouragement you gave him during your last visit to Ghana. They are Words of Wisdom.

God Grant Me the Serenity
To Accept the Things I cannot Change,
The Courage to Change those I can,
And the Wisdom to know the Difference

He cherished them and was so grateful to you. The Ghana Medical School and Ministry of Health gave him a grand and fitting burial. Eulogies and Tributes were paid to him by many organizations e.g. Ghana Medical School, Ghana University, The British High Commission, WHO, Alumina of Cambridge University and finally the Epidemiology Division for the Medical Field Units. He was laid in state at the GMS Auditorium. In fact Dr Scott got what he wanted – to die and be buried in Ghana. I do not think you received the funeral programmes and papers that I sent to you per Professor Ofosu-Armah who came to Geneva immediately after the funeral.

Thank God I have managed to consolidate my position as the Acting Chief Technical Officer for nearly four years now. I have my weaknesses and make mistakes here and there. On the whole, I think I am generally accepted by both juniors and Seniors. The DMS Dr Abaagye-Attah jokingly calls me The Director of Epidemiology. So I think I am in the good books of the Big Men.

Brother Daniel has no permanent address now. You are safe to use my address above for him. I also have my application with WHO Regional Office Brazzaville for the job of Field Development Officer. Is there any way you could help? It is a long term plan anyway. All of us, the kids and their mothers, send our warmest good wishes.

Best regards, Sincerely, Francis Kofi.

Brooklyn, NEW YORK,
7 May 1997

My dear Elizabeth,

I thank you for your letter of 2 March 1997 and the beautiful pictures of some of the second generation McCulloughs. Let me congratulate you and Fergus for maintaining a loving and united family. I have also worked so hard to keep my family united and conscious of reaching out to one another. I can say we are a happy family.

I tried to act promptly on your request for the old photographs of you and us which you need to make your book more qualitative and complete. I have at long last managed to have photocopies of the kind of those old photographs I glued in an old album to make sure they are not removed. I will be mailing these photo-copied sheets, which look good to me, to see what good use you can put them to for your purposes.

I personally love photographs for historical and developmental purposes. I have managed to keep a very impressive collection of photographs up to date which will form my family museum in my houses in Accra and New York.

My sons Jerry and Fergus are taking good care of their mother in

Ghana in my absence. I transfer money over regularly to attend to their needs. Right now we are licensing our company FJF Ghana Ltd in Ghana to operate full Telecommunications systems in conjunction with an American International Telecommunications Co. based in Florida. I may be going to Ghana myself in the month to see the licensing of the company through. I am excited very much for having this opportunity to be involved in my country's telecommunications revolution and high technology.

I have no regrets for adventuring to the USA I have accomplished a lot by coming here. At this point it is no longer necessary to bring any of my children over here to live and work. What I see here tells me Ghana has better quality of life culturally, socially, educationally and spiritually. I will ensure economic freedom for them in Ghana to keep them safe from the Drug menasse that prevails here. We are a very happy and united family.

Our Best Regards and Love to you. Francis Kofi

Brooklyn, NEW YORK
8 August 1997

My dear Elizabeth,

This is the final package of the old and new photographs of the Kofi/McCullough life-long alliance I promised to send to you. It is to give you an idea of the kinds and quality of photographs I have in my possession. I think they are historical documents for posterity considering the humble beginning and origin of the Kofi family of Keta in the Gold Coast/Ghana. We are thankful to God for our blessings and accomplishments.

Brother Daniel is alive and struggling in Ghana. We are not so close as we used to be. He stopped listening to me for no reason. I leave him alone as he flops and driffs away from me. I have, however, decided to give him one more chance to involve him in a big way in Ghana to show him I still love him as my only brother. I am joining with an International Telecommunications company in the USA to revolutionize the Telecommunications Systems in Ghana/Africa. I will be going to Ghana to get my company in Ghana licensed to operate Telecommunications Systems. My sons Jerry and Fergus are Directors already and when I go I will find a use for their uncle Daniel to prove himself and earn good money.

I want to wake him up from the long slumber.

I will keep in touch. It is no secret what God can do. Best regards to you and your family.

Francis Kofi

Brooklyn, NEW YORK
30 November 1998

Dear Elizabeth,

I hope everything is fine with you and your children and grand-children. 1998 has been a busy year for me and I thought I was going to move over back to Ghana to live there for the rest of my life. Apparently, Gods plan for me is different. The reality is that I am more deeply entrenched here in the USA. I am now a citizen of the USA and have a good full-time job as a Dialysis Technician in the biggest Hospital Center in the USA. I have filed for some of my children to come over to live. We will be enjoying dual-citizenship as Ghanaians and Americans. I feel so good with myself. Fergus, my son is doing very well in Ghana. He has built a gorgeous house for his family about 10 miles away from Accra on Cape Coast road. Christine has been a very good mother and family-head in my absence. All the children have grown up into responsible and respected citizens in Ghana. God has blessed us.

I hope you and your family are also doing fine. How is the New Book coming along? Our best wishes and Love to you all.

Francis Kofi

Brooklyn, NEW YORK
4 August 1997

At long last the myth about the photos you so badly needed is broken. Believe it or not I have just returned from a two week vacation to Ghana to solve this problem once and for all. It has been nerve wrecking for me that it has taken so long. I hope it is not too late for the book. It was a real good feeling for me to be with my children, grand-children and their mothers. We are a great family by any standards. I am so proud and happy to be the father of this large and lovely family and thankful to God for the love and the blessings we have in our family. I wish you luck and congratulate you on the books you are writing.

Francis Kofi

Brooklyn, NEW YORK
4 May 2001

My dear Madam (the name we called you in days of old)

Just as I thought my life and my familys were so complete and full of joy and great satisfaction on all fronts after a wonderful 4 week vacation in Ghana, my joy and happiness I brought with me from Ghana got shattered on Novermber 28, 2000 exactly three days after I had returned to New York to meet my wife Esther radiant and so pretty with joy just for having me back home.

Then after the hugging and kissing she cut in and said 'Francis I am sorry I am just waiting for you to come. I am bereaved. My brothers wife who was sick in Greenville died and burial is today November 25 Saturday and the family are waiting for me. I have cooked and there is plenty of food to last you a week. I will be back on Tuesday, November 28.' I was sorry to hear this and I rushed to the Bank and got her some money to be more comfortable. She safely got to Greenville and called me and said everything was fine and that she would surely be back in New York on Tuesday, November 28 and I was happy and started preparing for her return with the things I brought from Ghana for her.

On checking my waiting MAIL I noticed and grabbed that familiar hand-addressed envelope and suddenly felt that family closeness and love that bound our two families together all these years. I was so sorry that you were sick but was glad also that you were getting over it quickly. I resolved to reply you quickly and encourage you in that situation. The thought of your letter bringing an end to the long break that came about in our long standing family correspondence enhanced the great joy and happiness I brought from Ghana, and I thanked God for it. I even thought of sending to you some pictures of the family and me in Ghana.

Then as if a Hydrogen Bomb was dropped on me a call came through on Tuesday morning just as I was getting dressed for work that my wife Esther died on the Grey Hound Bus mid-way on her return from Greenville, South Carolina to New York. Cause of death – Cardiac Arrest. It was a tragedy like a bad dream, but real. I was compelled to pay for her body to be conveyed back to Greenville about 300 miles away to her family already gathered for the previous funeral. I joined them the next day and we organized a fitting and impressive funeral and burial for her. It was the Grace of God that I passed through all that financially and emotionally.

Then as if that was not enough I suddenly developed a Thrombosed Haemorrhoid on 2 January, 2001 after resuming work. The pain from this was unbearable and prolonged. The surgery was postponed for two months till I finally forced and transferred to another Hospital and got it done on February 16. I am going back to work on May 6, 2001. I have been on disability for over four months now. I hope to take it easy to the end of the year when I think I will mature for pension. At the most by the end of the Year 2002 I should definitely retire and go back to Ghana. By then some of my children will have joined me and settled comfortably as citizens without a problem.

God gave me some wonderful people to come to my aide. They are more than family and my condition is even socially, physically and spiritually better now I am transformed.

Thanks be to God Alleluya, Amen. Best Wishes and Love to all of you, Children and Grandkids, Sincerely Francis K.

I wrote to Francis shortly after the World Trade Centre attack, but have not had a reply and fear that Francis may be dead.

Writing this as I correct the final proofs, a recent letter from his son confirms that he is alive and well, but has changed his address.

Appendix II

From The Guardian, Friday 22 March 1963

The Bright Side of Ghana – Enthusiasm for education
by James Pope-Hennessy

I was sitting one evening recently outside my room on the ramparts of Fort San Jago, the miniature hill-top fortress which the Dutch constructed as an outpost of their great castle of Elmina on the Gold Coast.

Opposite me, beyond the narrow lagoon, rose the whitewashed walls and turrets of the castle itself, but originally built by the Portuguese in 1482, and much enlarged after the Dutch Conquest of 1637. Eastwards the sandy coast, helped by coconut trees and dotted with the long surf-boats of the fishermen, curved away to an horizon on which the bulk of Cape Coast Castle could be dimly seen in the setting sun.

Below and back of Fort San Jago huddled the town of Elmina, small and endearing, with a market place and some old tumbledown houses dating back to the era of the Dutch. Behind the town were marshy salt pools, where egrets and herons stepped elegantly in the black water. As I watched I was wondering why reality so invariably differs from expectation.

In spite of much reading of the last-century books and papers on the Gold Coast forts and castles – Elmina, Cape Coast Sekondi, Shama, Groot Brandenberg, Axim and the rest – and in spite of the study of maps and photographs, I was no way prepared for the romantic and evocative beauty of these coastal strongholds, their white curtain walls and sweeping stairways of small yellow bricks, their archways and lookout towers and wrought-iron work. Even less was I prepared for the full-blooded, stimulating impact which a first visit to Ghana cannot fail to make upon a stranger.

Gay and confident

During a four and a half weeks' tour of the country as the guest of the Kwame Nkrumah University of Science and Technology, Kumasi, I had been both delighted and impressed. I had not expected such splendid and varied scenery, so genuinely warm and imaginative a welcome. Nothing I had read had revealed to me such major facts as the modern Ghanians' burning thirst for education or their great pride in progress which has not uprooted their traditions or conflicted with their tribal tenets.

Apart from vaguely thinking of Ghana as a country where the Queen has visited, and where political prisoners are said to be arbitrarily arrested and as arbitrarily released, I fancy that the majority of the public in this country has no very clear conception of what Ghana is like or means today. Partly inherited from that indolent old period when nineteenth-century Britons who happened not to be in the Manchester cotton trade or the colonial office did not bother their heads about 'our West African possessions' at all, this uncertainty must also be attributed to the very imperfect self-image which modern Ghana, by its radio and its newspapers, projects upon the outside world.

Carping news commentaries on the radio from Accra, for instance, with their monotonous repetition of the words 'imperialism', 'colonialism', and 'neo-colonialism', give the misleading impression that the people of Ghana – eager, inquisitive, go-ahead, sophisticated, racially tolerant – are a parochial breed of xenophobes. Nothing could be less true.

Proud and excited

Naturally there is great pride and excitement at the strides which Ghana, as a free nation, has made. Not only are there the great and expanding universities at Kumasi and at Legon, but a new one is at present under construction at Cape Coast. People speak with zest of the Volta dam project, and of the harbours at Takoradi and at Tema.

Nowhere does one meet with a wish to denigrate our contribution to Ghana's progress while it was still a British Crown Colony, nor to deny the help being given now by Europeans, Americans and Russians. Even the fact that I went to Ghana as the grandson of a nineteenth-century Governor of the West African Settlements aroused nothing but friendly interest and a desire to help me in researches and show me the places which I wished to see.

The only adverse comment came from a member of one of the glum little teams of Soviet geologists to be met with in many remote parts of Ghana today. He told me, speaking with authority, that the people of Ghana are interested only in their future and not in their past, a doctrinaire statement which my own experience did nothing to confirm. The wish to preserve the best of their past, with its firm and elaborate family system and moral taboos, is one of the most remarkable features of this remarkable African State.

Coming straight from the ice-bound January London into the heat and the happy, strident colours of Accra was enough in itself to induce a receptive and sympathetic mood. Accra, a large and noisy city with fine modern buildings and an apparently insoluble traffic problem, retains in its residential quarters the placid air of a nineteenth-century colonial town; there are veranda'd villas standing back in the large red-earth gardens in which bougainvillaeas, frangipani, and even straggly English roses grow.

But it is not until you leave the city behind you and head northwards along the road to Kumasi that the extreme visual beauty of Southern Ghana becomes apparent. The huge trees in the shadowy forests of Ashanti, the great lavish clusters of bamboos, the untidy wild bananas by the stream-beds, the villages in which tall Ashanti youths wearing togas of flaming colour stand about at evening in groups – these sights can never pall.

The campus of the Kwame Nkrumah University near Kumasi, an area some five miles square, hacked out of secondary jungle growth and now populated by spacious bungalows set well apart on the green lawns, lies within earshot of the forest. At night the tree-bear howls, and drums throb in the neighbouring villages. The university halls themselves and the administrative buildings are aesthetically pleasing and of practical design. The university's development, inspired by its distinguished Vice-Chancellor, Dr Robert Baffour, has been rapid; its ultimate aim is to educate some five thousand students at a time.

In the city of Kumasi, seat of the Asantehene and of the regional administration, an admirably planned Cultural Centre, devoted to Ashanti history and Art, belie the assertion of my Soviet acquaintance that Ghanians do not care to think about their past.

Educational drive

The educational drive symbolized by Kumasi's university as well as by the city's many schools is not confined to the more advanced regions of the country, those, that is to say, with a more coherent tribal tradition and a longer history of European contacts. At Tamale, capital of the Northern Region, and at Bolgatanga, capital of the dusty and impoverished Upper Region, new State-built schools are supplementing the extensive pioneer work of the White Fathers and, to a lesser degree, of the Methodists.

Close to some primitive mud village, with its circular red huts, you will often see a neat and airy little schoolhouse which looks as though it has just alighted from Scandinavia. After four o'clock the roads are thronged with children returning from school, slates and schoolbook balanced on their heads, or clutched in a satchel in the hand. Primary education is free and, where it can be enforced, compulsory. But the general urge to learn is intense.

The other night at Cape Coast, admittedly a highly Europeanized area, the police were struggling to defend the gates of the town hall against enthusiastic crowds of students trying to get into an already sold out performance of *Twelfth Night* by the Nottingham Players, while my own driver told me that he and his wife were planning to see *Macbeth* when the company came to Kumasi. English remains the *lingua franca* of Ghana.

Opinions formed in so short a visit to this great African country must be superficial. Yet you cannot be in Ghana a week without being beguiled by its gaiety and impressed by its earnestness.

1. The m.v. *Apapa* approaching Freetown

2. Axim street scene.

3. Vultures near Axim

4. Axim castle – old slaving station

5. Descent to Lake Bosumtwi crater – on honeymoon November 1960

6. Pangloss

7. Wood ibis at Daboya west of Tamale

8. Notice board in Kumasi

NOTICE
NATIVE Dr ADELABU
NIGERIAN CHIEF -
HERBALIST. HE CURES ALL
DISEASES e.g. INSANE PEOPLE.
BARREN WOMEN SLEEPING
SICKNESS ILL THUNDER
FITS IMPOTENCY ETC.
WE SELL DIFFERENT KINDS
OF INCENSE e.g. LUCK-
INCENSE & WATCH—
CRAFTS INCENSE
CONSULT
CHIEF HERBALIST
ADELABU HEALING
HOME HOUSE NO N.T.13
NEW TAFO KUMASI
REGISTERED IN GHANA

9. Boiling fresh water mussels on the White Volta near Daboya

10. House at Kintampo

11. Fire near house at Kintampo with cattle egrets waiting for flying insects – Boxing Day 1960

12. Neighbour at Kintampo who had the foot abscess

13. Round house at Dorimon with author and Simbu's dog

14. View of dam from round house at Dorimon

15. Mosque at Dorimon

16. Neighbours at Dorimon

17. Dorimon market

18. Fergus, the author and Katharine — April 1963

19. House at Wa

20. Fergus and Adda's son Yamba with the 'dominose'

21. Kasena house with ladder to roof, grain store and chicken holes

22. Dagoma compound in model village built for Royal visit in 1959

23. Fergus with Francis and Daniel Kofi

24. 'Chop' seller at our back door – Wa, August 1964

25. Abdulai, Mousa, Mary and 'chop' seller

26. The author and Katharine – January 1964

27. Fergus and the kob

28. Katharine and the kob – June 1965

29. Mousa Moshi and Katharine – January 1964

30. Katharine and friends – December 1965